UNEARTHING SEEDS OF FIRE

Sowing Freedom

To those who gave us seed to hold and sow
Debts past and present
Too many to name or know

To those who plow with us now
Some known
Others never heard of anyhow

To those who are of us, are cherished
for being and becoming themselves,
and never tire:
Charis, Thorsten,
Mary Thom, Sam,

who quicken our love of man and freedom,
who strengthen our will to sow and plow,
And our hope to reap freedom's joy—
Unearthing seeds of fire.

—Frank Adams

Acknowledgments

THAT THOSE WHO have helped with this book remain friends after having to weary out error testifies to the endless spirit of humanity in each: Myles Horton, of course—witness, source, reviewer, and first critic—and my wife Margaret, who understood when the idea for this book got hold of me. I am especially in debt to Joyce Dukes, former librarian at Highlander, and Jane Roth and Karen J. Baumann, who catalogued Highlander's records for the State Historical Society of Wisconsin; to Hope Blackwell, who shared in the book's start; to Ken Kennedy, a writer who had learned at Highlander; to Jane Kelly, my editor. All were willing to question obliqueness. Inspiration for the title derived from the poems of John Beecher.

Contents

Introduction

THIS BOOK is a result of my efforts to understand an idea in education that I first heard of in 1959, when I was newspapering.

My fellow workers in Local 219, American Newspaper Guild, AFL-CIO, had elected me secretary of the local. We were a fragile challenge to the management of Norfolk Newspapers, Inc., owners of three daily newspapers, a radio station, and a television channel in Tidewater Virginia. Their fortunes seemed to expand as our local's diminished. That I, a cub reporter, could have been elected a shop steward one year and secretary the next demonstrated the local's lack of leadership. I barely knew the philosophical difference between Sam Gompers and Big Bill Haywood. But there I was—one of several guildsmen designated to negotiate with the bosses for a new contract, perhaps one that would contain a strike clause, a provision we had never had.

As much out of desperation as inspiration, I wrote to a friend who was an international representative for the guild, asking where locals like ours could learn how to negotiate contracts, to build a union in hostile circumstances, and to develop leadership at the shop-steward level.

His response, though of no practical help, sparked my interest in Highlander and, in a way, led to this book. There was a school in Tennessee, he said, the Highlander Folk School, which worked with unions to provide the sort of education I was seeking. Many of the South's union locals had used it. He said that when the school refused to repudiate the allegedly communist-dominated unions, which had been expelled from the union movement a decade earlier, most unions had stopped sending shop stewards there. He added that the top leadership in the AFL-CIO frowned on unions that continued to use Highlander for training.

Having been an adolescent during the Joseph McCarthy years, I knew something about the techniques of Red-baiting used in the 1950's. I had been in Northeastern North Carolina when Dr. Frank Graham, former president of the University, was viciously Red-baited and denied, by the resulting hysteria, a seat in the U.S. Senate. I thought the red scare was used for ornery meanness and undemocratic purposes. If this Highlander Folk School was a union school that, when faced with Red-baiting, wouldn't let the unions tell it what to do, then, I got to asking myself, what kind of school was it? Who ran it? What did they do?

Before I found my answers, the civil rights movement burst on the South. Most newspapermen in Norfolk were busy covering white Virginia's reaction to the Supreme Court's decision of 1954 that prohibited racial segregation in public schools. "Massive resistance" was Virginia's official response. It meant propping up Jim Crow laws in every way possible and closing public schools in Prince Edward County, Front Royal, and Norfolk. Segregated "academies" opened and received tax dollars.

Before white Virginians understood what had happened on February 1, 1960, in Greensboro, North Carolina, hundreds of blacks—mostly young—were at dime store counters in Norfolk, Hampton, Newport News, and even Petersburg and Richmond demanding an end to segregation in public places. I was covering a sit-in at a lunch counter in Portsmouth one warm day in late April when I was to hear of Highlander again, and of another unusual school, Goddard College in Vermont.

One of the demonstration leaders had recently returned from Raleigh, North Carolina, where several hundred sit-in participants from across the South had gathered to hear Dr. Martin Luther King and others. There had been talk of plans, the young demonstrator reported, to form an all-student organization to keep the sit-ins going. He also mentioned a song which a man "from a place called Highlander" had sung, "We Shall Overcome." The young black was teaching the song that day, and the Portsmouth demonstrators were lining it back to him. Among the demonstrators there was only one white person. He, I learned, went to Goddard College. He told me about the college. It had never used grades, given tests, or required particular courses. Students learned by doing. The white student was studying sociology and was in Portsmouth learning about groups in conflict by being in a real conflict.

As the civil rights movement continued to swirl across the South and spread North, I grew more and more disillusioned about newspapering. Hardly a day passed that I, as a police reporter, didn't see the human and civil rights of blacks and poor people being violated. Word of these violations seldom appeared in print. Yet when some white official uttered new defiance of the black struggle, it would be front-page news.

We weren't getting anywhere with the newspaper union's struggle against management. Fellow workers seemed to be fired on whims; wages were low for men, lower for women; we still had no contractual right to strike. Gradually I began to think that the people who determined how and where reports on the black movement would be played in the newspaper were the same people who kept the wages low and the hours as long as the law would allow and denied employees the right to strike.

I began to get restless. I had gotten into newspapering for reasons rooted in idealism. After high school, I had entered the University of North Carolina, hoping to learn how to write. It hadn't taken long to find out that the University intended for me to study what it wanted, not what I wanted. I left and volunteered for the draft. After two years in the army, an experience that distorted my judgment to the point of doubting the soundness of my original decision to leave the University, I returned for another dose of learning that had nothing to do with my goals.

Again I left school and started driving a truck, hauling fruit and vegetables out of the South to the huge northern markets, until I heard of a job with the *St. Petersburg* (Florida) *Times.*

Here, I thought, was my chance to start to write and be a useful citizen. Innocently, I thought that if you could expose an evil, you'd help to end an evil. I didn't realize that there were some evils which were not to be exposed; or, more importantly, that there were some evils which, if exposed, were altered just enough to appear changed, when, in fact, nothing had happened. I fell from innocence in St. Petersburg and Norfolk.

I was thinking about driving a truck again when Goddard College provided another option. The *New York Times* reported that Goddard had started an external degree program "for adults twenty-six years or older who, for one good reason or another, left college." I was accepted into the program in 1964. A full-time night job with the newspaper and a part-time day job with the Norfolk Public Health Department enabled me to pay tuition. I was off and learning as never before in my life—and enjoying it for the first time.

Before the year was out, Goddard needed a director of information. I was hired and moved to Vermont with my wife and two children.

At Goddard, which had many ties with Highlander, and many similarities, I came to learn some things about learning and why people will learn. Through experiences with teachers there like Royce Pitkin and George Beecher, through reading authors like Theodore Brameld and Carl Rogers, and through reflection on my own experiences, I was learning things that were necessary to me.

Before leaving Goddard in 1967 to return to the South, I had joined the faculty to teach journalism and to help start an urban studies program. Besides the Bachelor of Arts degree at Goddard, I had earned a master's degree in the Arts of Teaching at

Antioch-Putney Graduate School, which had campuses in Putney, Vermont, and Yellow Springs, Ohio. These academic and teaching experiences provided a theoretical and practical background sufficient to lead me to believe, perhaps brashly, that I could begin to answer the questions about Highlander I had first asked in 1959.

This book is biased. I believe that education should foster individual growth and social change and nourish the fundamental value of complete personal liberty while encouraging thoughtful citizenship in community. I believe that education must be born of the creative tension between how life is lived and how life might be lived in a free society. Such education is suited for the young and for the older.

Highlander, as clearly as any school I know of in the United States, reflects my own educational philosophy. While I have been writing this book, I have been working for Highlander trying to learn how to "do" this philosophic notion. Deliberately, for to have done otherwise would have distorted the idea of Highlander, I have kept out of this book any attempt to define Highlander's pedagogic characteristics—structure, teaching methods, curriculum, discipline, philosophy, goals, and the like. Yet these academic variables are included, embedded in the narrative, as they are naturally rooted among the people from whom Highlander grew.

This book is based on biased sources: Myles Horton, who got the idea of Highlander and learned over the years how to put it to use; the school's own records, tape recordings, and newspaper clippings; and people who also learned at Highlander. All royalties will be used to continue Highlander.

Frank Adams

Gatesville, North Carolina
1973

1

. . . an answer that can only come from the people . . .

OZONE, TENNESSEE, would seem an unlikely place to stumble upon an idea that could hold a man's imagination for life. In the summer of 1927, Myles Horton, a rising senior at a small Tennessee college, came to Ozone to organize vacation Bible schools. His experiences there shaped ideas and questions about education that would eventually become Highlander Folk School—and his way of life.

Ozone is on the edge of the Cumberland Plateau, a natural barrier between eastern and middle Tennessee. Even by the late 1960's, only 350 persons were listed by census-takers as Ozone's population. Fall Creek eases down the plateau behind Ozone, flows under what is nowadays called Route 70, and drops suddenly off a ledge into a rocky pool several hundred feet below. When Horton first came there, even the beauty of the falls couldn't do much to raise the community's spirits. Greed had exhausted the area's resources of timber and coal. A used and tired people could either finish up what work was left or get out. Most people in Ozone, and indeed in much of mountainous Tennessee, were poor. Times were hard. Horton heard people wonder with grim humor how much harder times would get—with no idea the Great Depression was still to come.

The Presbyterian Church had sent Horton, the summer before his final year at Cumberland University, to the east Tennessee mountains to head the vacation Bible school program. To him the work was neither exciting nor challenging. The more he came to know the people of the four counties assigned to him and to understand their problems, the more he sensed that memory verses, hymns, and games didn't have much to do with the daily problems faced by either the children or their hard-pressed parents. "I couldn't put this in words," he said years later, "but such education failed to connect with their lives."[1]

Life and ways had changed fast in places like Ozone while the land's bounty lasted. As the coal mines inched further and further inside the mountains and corporations slashed timber from thousands of acres of virgin forests, people who had once been farmers, eking out livings on tiny hillside clearings, or who had been small-time loggers, were caught up in the "new" ways of making money. Neighborly customs and a barter economy were modified. People got to needing cash to live. But the mines began playing out. The hillsides were stripped bare. Times changed again.

Some of those laid off from the mines or the lumbering camps, believing recruiting agents' stories, would leave home hoping for jobs in the few textile mills beginning to spring up in the mountains. Frequently, work in the mills was not to be found—or was found to be disagreeable by men used to the outdoors. People would return home embittered. Horton watched countless friends he had made that summer leave their families with high expectations, only to come back forlorn in a few weeks. For the men who stayed home, there was the certainty they would see their children go hungry, cold, and poorly taught, while they would be powerless to find paying work to end the misery. To make their burden worse, a handful of withered old-timers talked endlessly of the days when all a man needed was a good eye and a squirrel rifle to provide his family with fresh meat. Such was the tragedy of Ozone, and much of the South, in 1927.

As Horton traveled from one community to another starting

vacation Bible schools and talking with people, he became convinced that the church's conventional education program was not meeting their needs. Nor could he learn of any school, public or private, where teaching was directly related to mountain people and their common problems. Near Ozone one day, he decided to experiment. He had no real plan, but he started by asking parents of children attending Bible schools to come to the church at night to talk about their problems.

To his amazement, they came. Some walked through the dusk for several miles down the hollows, knowing they would have to go home in the dark. The things they talked about were basic. How could jobs be found? How does a person test a well for typhoid? Could the once-beautiful hillsides ever grow trees again? At first, they shared what they knew with each other. Horton's inability to answer most of their questions didn't bother them. Soon, however, they started asking him to find someone who did have the answers. The county agent was helpful. So was a man who knew how to test wells.

Horton called his meetings community meetings. They quickly became so crowded that his supervisors in the Presbyterian Church suspected him of misrepresenting attendance figures. They told him that nobody had ever gotten that many people to a night meeting in the mountains.[2] Once neighbor began meeting with neighbor, they learned that many answers to their questions were available right there in Ozone. They didn't need experts. They just needed to start talking to each other. For a people not much given to speech, however, that was hard at first.

To make talking easier, Horton would get someone to start the meetings with a singing game or a retelling of one of the beloved mountain stories passed orally from generation to generation. Eventually, warmed by story and song, the people would talk long into the night, sharing with and explaining to each other. Then they'd walk back home, back to the hollows, to try out what they'd learned.

By summer's end the people around Ozone were urging Horton to stay on and not to return to college. One of the few prosperous residents in Ozone, having heard of the community meetings, asked Horton to supper one night. She offered her home as a permanent meeting place—if Horton would agree to stay. Cumberland University became at once unimportant and important. Horton was evolving an idea which he couldn't describe in words. He had learned that the people knew the answers to their own problems. He had learned that the teacher's job was to get them talking about those problems, to raise and sharpen questions, and to trust people to come up with the answers. Yet, he could not wholly trust the people or this way of learning. This was not what he had heard in school all his life. One more year in college, he reasoned, might bring him the answers he felt he still needed. To the potential donor of a meeting place he explained that he needed time to think. At the community meeting, he promised to return "when I have something to offer."[3] That fall Horton was back in college.

Myles Horton came by his faith in education naturally. His parents, Perry and Elsie Falls Horton, placed great store on learning. They had both been teachers, though they had little more than grammar school educations. In the early 1900's, anyone who took summer courses in training institutes could qualify to teach in the lower grades. The Hortons believed in, and reared their children to trust in, the American idea that, through education, the individual gets ahead.

When Perry Horton left teaching to take a higher-paying job as county court clerk in Savannah, Tennessee, his children were already imbued with the conviction that nothing could or should stand in the way of their educations. Subsequent changes in job and residence only confirmed this belief in his four children: Myles, the eldest, born July 5, 1905; his brothers, Delmas and Dan, born in 1907 and 1910; and their sister, Elsie Pearl, born in 1915.

In 1918, Perry Horton was defeated at the polls in his bid to continue as county clerk. The family moved to Humboldt, Tennessee, where the elder Horton had a hard time making a living by selling insurance. Still, all the children went to school. Even when they moved out from Humboldt to the nearby Fork Deer River, where the family started sharecropping and became used to doing without material things, the children continued school. In fact, before every move, Perry Horton wrote the district school superintendent to ask about his policies and practices. Schools for the children, not their father's job, was always a determining factor in where the Hortons lived.

The family was religious, and, like most small-town Southern families, much of their social life centered around the church, in this case, the Cumberland Presbyterian. Not a revivalist church, it was subdued in comparison with many Southern mountain congregations. Neither the church nor Horton's family looked at society critically. Nonetheless, both manifested a superficial concern for those who were poorer than themselves: the blacks who lived across the tracks, segregated by place and task; the poor whites, also segregated, up in the hills and in cotton mill villages, out of sight. The Hortons gave what they could of their own scant supplies of food and clothing in times of need or emergency. This was the extent of a church member's responsibility.

The Horton family displayed that independent forthrightness characteristic of the frontier tradition. Perhaps this was a result of their paternal forebear, Joshua Horton, who, with a party of settlers, established in 1769 a colony on the banks of the Watauga River. They thought they were settling in Virginia. Two years later, they discovered they were actually in North Carolina. When the state of North Carolina refused to give them protection from the Indians their settlement was encroaching upon, the pioneers decided to organize a government of their own, making them among the first white men born on North American soil to form a free and independent state. The resultant Watauga Articles were drawn up in 1772.

In Horton's immediate family, independence of spirit took the form of voting Republican in the predominantly Democratic South. Perry Horton was adamant in his disavowal of unions. They intruded on a man's independence. In fact, until he later got to know some union people at Highlander and came to understand the importance of collective action, he used to say he would take a job as a strikebreaker.

These were some of the family roots from which young Horton was nourished when he entered Cumberland University at Lebanon, Tennessee, in 1924. A literature major, required to read widely in the English classics from Chaucer to the Romantic poets, he came, momentarily at least, to believe the view later expressed by historian C. Vann Woodward that "there was nothing issuing from his native region in the way of arts and letters that was worth notice."[4] Like others before him, and after, Horton was being educated away from his culture and led to underestimate his heritage. In this sense, his experience at Cumberland was Southern traditional.

Outside the classroom, Horton was unconsciously learning from social conflict. His first such experience took place within a few days of his arrival at Cumberland. As was their custom and self-declared privilege, the fraternity men announced their plan to haze the freshmen; they told Horton he had to join a fraternity. Balking at such high-handed treatment, he organized the other freshmen against hazing. The freshmen were not hazed, and Horton himself never joined a fraternity.

Again by chance, in 1925 more yeast was added to Horton's rising social consciousness. John Thomas Scopes went on trial in Dayton, Tennessee, charged with teaching high school students about evolution. For months, although Horton was unaware of it, intellectuals and religious fundamentalists across the nation had been waiting for the storm that would break in Rhea County and shake a nation. Horton knew of William Jennings Bryan. Bryan was familiar to his culture. But the trial was under way before Horton ever heard of Scopes, became aware of the law he had supposedly violated, or heard of his lawyer, Clarence Darrow. During summer vacation, Horton was earning tuition money in the Humboldt box factory at the rate of 25 cents an hour. Most of his information about the trial came from daily accounts in the Memphis *Commercial Appeal.* When he tried to discuss the trial with his co-workers or kinsmen, they turned away. To a man, he learned, they supported the prosecution. Horton was all for Scopes. He admired Darrow's courtroom performance. His incredulous elders refused to believe that a young man of religious background could accept Scopes' "heresy." Horton finally had to stop talking about the trial. Nonetheless, as he continued to read about the proceedings and to consider their significance, he realized that he had taken a firm step away from the mores of his own society.

Horton was pushed farther from custom by three experiences stemming from his membership in the Cumberland Young Men's Christian Association. In 1927, as president of the campus chapter, he went to Nashville, a big city to his eyes, for a state YMCA conference. There, for the first time, he talked with foreign-born people and, equally strange for a young Southerner, exchanged ideas with blacks as equals. That, however, was inside the YMCA conference building. Away from the Vanderbilt University campus, Horton became conscious of segregation for the first time. He tried to take an attractive

Chinese girl to supper. No restaurant would let them in. Later, when he sought to know a black student better, he found they couldn't enter the public library together. He learned firsthand of racial injustice, and concluded that no one should have his rights denied for such a reason.

Horton ran afoul of the established order at Cumberland and in Lebanon through his YMCA membership. Lebanon's most influential citizen at the time and one of Tennessee's leading businessmen, John Emmett Edgerton, a woolen manufacturer, spoke before the Cumberland student body shortly after Horton returned from the YMCA conference. A past president of the National Association of Manufacturers, Edgerton sought to promote the employers' drive against unions by linking open shops to the chauvinism that followed World War I. In a speech made during his NAM presidency, Edgerton had said, "I can't conceive of any principle that is more purely American, that comes nearer representing the very essence of all those traditions and institutions that are dearest to us, than the open shop principle."[5] To the Cumberland students he made much the same claim. Workers, he told them, were wrong to think they could decide things for themselves. He said that industrialists should determine what was good for the working man. Horton's understanding of the union movement was slight, but Edgerton's speech shocked him. Could employers claim the right to make social decisions for people whose lives they already controlled economically? No, Horton decided. By denouncing unions, Edgerton had given Horton his first real interest in them.

Soon afterward, acting on an idealistic impulse, Horton went to Edgerton's Lebanon mill to talk with the workers. Explaining what their boss had said, he argued that they were human beings who should exercise their inalienable rights. Horton recalls that his appeal was spirited, but naive. It fell on uninterested, perhaps even fearful, ears. Horton himself was confused and disappointed that the workers didn't rise in rebellion after hearing his remarks. He returned to the campus downcast, only to be greeted by university authorities with orders to stay away from Edgerton's mill. Word had traveled fast. Undaunted, Horton returned to the mill, but still to no avail. This time, university authorities threatened him with expulsion. Horton didn't change the mill hands' situation, but he did learn how power can be wielded.

Horton graduated from Cumberland in 1928 and took a job as student YMCA secretary for the state of Tennessee. But Ozone was still on his mind. As he traveled for the YMCA, he visited high schools and colleges in search of one that might offer an education that matched the needs of people in Ozone. He found none. He did make some valuable discoveries in books by William James and John Dewey. As countless success-minded Americans have done, Horton learned from pragmatist James that, as Horton put it later, "you can change things by your own actions."[6] Dewey spoke more directly to his interests: "As long as the isolation of knowledge and practice holds sway, this division of aims and dissipation of energy, of which the state of education is typical, will persist."[7] Still underlined in Horton's aged copy of Dewey's *Reconstruction in Philosophy* is this passage: "If ideas, meaning, conception, notions, theories, systems are instrumental to an active reorganization of the given environment they are reliable, sound, valid, good, true."[8] This became the basis upon which Horton would assess his work.

Horton may have been growing in his personal understanding of the underpinnings of liberal educational philosophy, but his work for the YMCA was out of kilter with time, place, and custom. Everywhere he went as secretary, the meetings he organized were interracial. This caused ripples in colleges, arched some eyebrows in high schools, and raised angry hackles in public places. Horton had an innocent's faith that the YMCA's statement of purpose obligated him to undertake such work: "The Young Men's Christian Association is a worldwide fellowship of men and boys united by common loyalty to Jesus Christ for the purpose of developing Christian personality and building a Christian society."[9] Complaints about Horton's activity reached his employers with increasing volume and velocity. They were as pleased to have him resign as he was to leave.

At Ozone Horton had begun to bridge the chasm between "knowledge" and "practice"; he had glimpsed learning arise from the questions of concerned citizens; but, having insufficient faith in himself and in the people, and having been taught all his life by other methods, he couldn't return to the work he had started. His experiences with the YMCA revealed to him the gulf between Christian theory and application, and this would possibly have hardened into cynicism had it not been for a Congregationalist minister in Cumberland County, the Reverend Abram Nightingale of Crossville.

Horton had frequently visited Mr. Nightingale while crisscrossing the state. The minister knew about the young man's conflicts between self and society. He had introduced Horton to many new ideas and a lot of books, including Dr. Harry F. Ward's *Our Economic Morality*. When Horton left YMCA work, Mr. Nightingale urged him to go to Union Theological Seminary in New York and study with Dr. Ward. He went as far as to secure an application for Horton and, when it was submitted, sent a long letter of recommendation. "The men at Union won't give you any answers to your problems," Horton recalls Mr. Nightingale telling him, "but you need background. You just don't know enough."[10]

2

. . . to teach a capacity to learn . . .

NEW YORK CITY proved to be eventful beyond Horton's wildest speculation. A few days after his arrival, the stock market crashed. Bankers committed suicide. Huge corporations went bankrupt. New York's unemployed were forming bread and soup lines. And Horton became a student of probably the most socially-activist academic men in America.

Abbott Kaplan, an urbane northerner, years later, described his friend from Tennessee: "This little hillbilly fellow, and that was what Myles was, wandered up to New York to Union Theological Seminary to get the Word of the Lord. Instead, he ran into Reinhold Niebuhr, who was speaking with almost as much authority as the Lord, and apparently had a greater social conscience."[1]

Niebuhr was just starting his teaching career when Horton arrived. For some, his teaching and writing against any over-simplification of the social gospel was bitingly clear. For Horton, his class lectures seemed formidable. Once, during a break in one of Niebuhr's seminars on Christian ethics, which would form the basis for his book, *Moral Man and Immoral Society*, Horton informed him that he was dropping the course. "I told him I didn't have the theological background to understand his arguments," Horton recalls having said. "Two priests and a Ph.D. from Columbia who were in the seminar overheard our conversation and said they didn't fully understand him either. I was feeling better when I heard them. I didn't drop the course. I just worked harder."[2]

In that course, Niebuhr attacked the uncritical idealism of

social gospel advocates and liberal theologians. He lashed out at the notion of inevitable progress, then current in theological circles. He used Marxism to criticize liberal social Christianity, declaring himself a socialist, or Christian Marxist.

Horton was drawn to the man as much because of his defense of working people as because of his theology. Niebuhr was caustic about capitalism. He called it an expression of a dying civilization and declared business oligarchies were "chief examples of social stupidity."[3] He opposed the New Deal at the time, saying it was only a prop to continue capitalism. He admired the Soviet Union. All of this was new to Horton, but he liked what he heard.

In addition to his teaching, Niebuhr headed a group called the Fellowship of Socialist Christians. They argued for fundamental change in both American politics and theology. They called for an alliance of progressive churchmen with the labor movement to accomplish "the ideal fraternal organization of society."[4] Niebuhr and Socialist Party leader Norman Thomas founded *The World Tomorrow*, a journal dedicated to socialism as "the ultimate and logical outcome of the labor movement" and "a social order based on the religion of Jesus."[5]

While Columbia was a heady world for Horton, it was Niebuhr's personal friendship with the young man that counted finally. He encouraged Horton's dream—the idea of a school in the mountains for mountain people. Niebuhr thought Horton could best accomplish this goal by becoming a minister, but he didn't withdraw his support in the face of Horton's obstinate refusal to accept his advice. Niebuhr listened. He introduced Horton to others who would listen. And he agreed to help in whatever way he could if Horton actually got the project going. Horton wrote to Niebuhr years later, "it was your inspiration and encouragement which provided the reservoir of strength and commitment that still keeps me going."[6]

Trying to understand Niebuhr's theological lectures doubled Horton's study time at Union. He was also using the Columbia University Library across the street, reading about early Christian Socialists, radical Christianity, the English Fabians, Thorstein Veblen, and Karl Marx. They all made sense to him as he tried to shape what he had come to call the Ozone Project. Perhaps more than any one writer, Vernon Louis Parrington, the historian who had won a Pulitzer Prize for his three-volume *Main Currents in American Thought*, helped Horton to gain an understanding of the nature of society. Parrington's use of literature to demonstrate the effect of social and economic ideas gave the English major from Cumberland a theoretical framework from which to view the world.

Although John Dewey was teaching at Columbia in 1929, Horton was less influenced by the man than by his writings. Since the late 1880's, Dewey had maintained that civil and political democracy were meaningless without equivalent economic and industrial democracy. Much of what Dewey was thinking and saying at the time supported Horton's understanding of Tennessee reality. One of the first public descriptions of the purpose of Highlander Folk School was a thinly-veiled crib from Dewey's *Democracy and Education*: "It is the aim of . . . education to take part in correcting unfair privilege and unfair deprivation, not to perpetuate them . . . it must take account of the needs of the existing community life; it must select with the intention of improving the life we live in common."[7]

Other scholars whom Horton came to know and value for their interest in, and influence on, the Ozone Project were George S. Counts, Eduard C. Lindeman, and Joseph K. Hart. Counts maintained that schools should be honestly partisan, teaching children "a vision of what America might become in the industrial age." He believed that society should be a coordinated, socialized economy directed to the interests of all people, not just the profit of a few. Counts' lectures became the basis for a series of articles which has had lasting impact on American education: "Education—for What?" which appeared in *The New Republic*.[8]

Lindeman and Hart were perhaps most directly influential on Horton's Ozone Project. They had both written books on adult education and were among the first Americans to argue that adult education be recognized as a potent agent for social change. Hart, in fact, despaired of accomplishing fundamental social change through the education of children. He argued that adults had to learn how to live a new social and economic order before they could teach it. "America is prosperous—beyond the dreams of that Denmark of the early nineteenth century which nurtured the germ of . . . folk schools. We need no such education for the sake of economic productivity—we have not yet learned to use intelligently the wealth we have at present."[9]

Lindeman, a Dane himself, had examined the role of adult education in both Denmark and the British trade union movement. He was of the opinion that "adult education will become an agency of progress if its short-lived goal of self-improvement can be made compatible with a long-term experimental but resolute policy of changing the social order."[10] He asked, "How can education supply directive energy for collective enterprise? The most concise answer is threefold: (a) by revealing the nature of the social process; (b) by transforming the battle of interests from warfare into creative conflict; (c) by developing a method for social functions which will make the collective life an educational experience."[11]

Until this point in Horton's education, he had never encountered professors who did not confine their teaching to academic subject matter. "My hopes for the Ozone Project soared," he recalls.[12] As he had done in Tennessee, Horton started looking about New York City for examples of the sort of education that was forming in his mind.

He visited Brookwood Labor College, first directed by A. J. Muste, a former Dutch Reformed minister and a leading advocate of labor unions and pacifism. Modeled after Ruskin College, the labor education institution in Great Britain, Brookwood offered a congenial faculty and student body. One student, Elizabeth Hawes, would later join Horton in Tennessee. Brookwood was too academically oriented for Horton, and it placed too great an emphasis on urban problems to be of much use for Appalachians, he felt.[13]

The settlement houses he visited provided an air of vitality, informality, and a vibrant relationship between staff and community. These were qualities he hoped to duplicate at Ozone, but with less emphasis on urban ills.

Most of the institutions Horton visited offered only what he came to call "national education," an education not adaptable to a particular people or region, especially not to a region with the peculiarities of the Southern mountains. As Horton saw it, everyone in the United States had to learn the same subjects in the same sequence or fall woefully behind "the national average." In his judgment, most of what passed for education did not grow out of the needs of the people who were being educated. Often education worked actively to the disadvantage of poor adults. Curricula were imposed on people, both children and adults, with little sympathy for their individual or age differences or personal needs.[14]

Horton studied utopian communities in the hope of discovering how people who started such places had learned what they needed to know. Again he was disappointed. Most of the utopian groups had turned inward, he found, consuming the energies of their members with internal squabbles. Education, Horton thought, should help people work in harmony to fulfill common needs, not lead small groups of individuals to better themselves at the expense of others. Moreover, the utopian communities had been exercises in living apart from society. Horton wanted to find educational ventures that would challenge society as people found it.

If he had reached an impasse in finding educational models in the New York City area, Horton did achieve several personal gains. He met and came to form strong friendships with James Dombrowski, a quiet but intense Southern intellectual, and tall, handsome John Thompson, whose outgoing Southern heartiness masked his brilliant mind. Both were students at Union. They felt, as did their teacher Niebuhr, that one role for intellectuals was to put their intelligences to work to leaven out society. Both men would later join Horton in the mountains.

At Union, as he had while serving as a YMCA secretary, Horton accepted his associates as equals. His social relationships had been limited mostly to whites. In New York City, where blacks lived with fewer overt legal and social restraints than in Tennessee, Horton encountered many blacks who weren't students. He could recognize them as individuals, but they remained unknown to him as persons. He felt uneasy. For overcoming this reaction, a probable result of his Southern background, Horton credits the writings of the black poets. Their yearnings he could identify with: freedom, pride in self and race, determination to be part of America. With only slight modification, he could see his hopes for the people of Ozone mirrored in the black poets' hopes. Horton read Gene Toomer, Countee Cullen, Claude McKay. He became acquainted with Charles Bertram Johnson, Arna Bontemps, Dr. E. Franklin Frazier, and Dr. W. E. B. DuBois. For years afterward he carried in his wallet a copy of Langston Hughes' "I Too":

I, too, sing America.

I am the darker brother
They send me to eat in the kitchen
When company comes.
But I laugh,
And eat well,
And grow strong.

To-morrow
I'll sit at the table
When company comes
Nobody'll dare
Say to me,
"Eat in the kitchen"
Then,

Besides, they'll see how beautiful I am
And be ashamed.

I, too, am American.[15]

To the extent to which they paralleled his interests, Horton also read sociological surveys and theory. Gradually he broadened his understanding of the nature of academic disciplines without adopting a discipline himself. He left Union for the academic year 1930–31 and went to Chicago to study with Dr. Robert E. Park, the famed sociologist. Through Park, Horton came to understand and accept the theory of crisis, conflict, and mass movements as mechanisms for social change,[16] and these elements were to become fundamental to his concept of education.

Also, he read Dr. Lester Ward's *Dynamic Sociology*, a controversial book at the time, and began to see himself as a "dynamic sociologist." Ward argued that education is action, and that social progress is possible only through "dynamic action."[17] Ward affirmed what Horton knew to be true in Ozone—that poor people have both the will and the appetite to learn, but lack only the means. Dr. Park's position on the potential which differing age groups, especially adults, have for collective social action, coupled with Dr. Ward's thesis that poor adults need only the opportunity to learn in order to do so, provided academic underpinnings for Horton's notions. He was still embedded in scholastics.

Nevertheless, Horton continued learning outside the classroom. He frequently visited Jane Addams, founder of Chicago's famed Hull House. She often tested Horton's fancied "radicalism." Her faith in American democracy was strong. Horton recalls that she would quote Abraham Lincoln, saying he made clear that democracy was the "most valuable contribution America has made to the moral life of the world"—in spite of the mistakes, shortcomings, and excesses of people.[18] Horton, the budding socialist, had no ready reply. His own faith in people was deep, but he wasn't as hopeful as she was that democracy would ever fully mature in the United States.

Miss Addams' vision of the democratic decision-making process was right out of Horton's rural past. Although she had worked for most of her professional life in the midst of an industrial city and had, in fact, grown up with the rise of industrialization in America, she once told Horton, "To arrive at democratic decisions, you need to have a bunch of ordinary people sitting around the stove in a country house or store and contributing their own experiences and beliefs to the discussion of the subject at hand. Then you take a poll of the majority opinion of those present, regardless of who they are, and that is a democratic decision."[19]

In retrospect, some might argue that she was naive to think that America, even in those days before advanced technology and megalopolitan development, could return to such ideal ways. But her opinion, coming from an internationally-known reformer and directed to Horton's own limited experience, bolstered his confidence in "moral man." For years, until experience taught him otherwise, he, too, felt that morality existed within the American democratic framework.

He didn't realize it at the time, but of more practical relevance to his Ozone Project was Miss Addams' talk about the harassment that she and others at Hull House had experienced. Their unpopular views on war (opposed to it), women's rights (for them), and other causes had attracted threats and intimidation. To know that she had not let the attacks "get under her skin" or impede her mission at Hull House later proved valuable to Horton. Equally instructive was the fact that Miss Addams maintained the same attitude toward accolade as toward attack. Horton remembers being at Hull House when she and Dr. Alice Hamilton, who had inaugurated the idea of industrial medicine, returned from a dinner in honor of Miss Addams. Dr. Hamilton asked her what she was going to do with the medal she had received. "Hock it," Miss Addams replied. "It's worth about fifty dollars, and there are lots of things I can use the money for."[20] She was, Horton says, the most innovative activist he met. "She put her intelligence to use as well as anyone."[21]

Miss Addams' greatest contribution to Horton was, in the end, her willingness to listen to his ideas. She declared one day that he was really trying to start a rural settlement house. Her conclusion was a fairly accurate description of Horton's dream of the Ozone Project up to that point.

Horton's attempt to "get some background" was given another push by a Danish-born Lutheran minister. The Reverend Aage Moller, who had opened his church to University of Chicago students for folk dances, heard of young Horton and his idea. Moller had been a teacher in a folk high school himself and encouraged Horton to visit Denmark and the folk schools. Horton had read about the folk school movement and its contribution to the growth of a nation in which "there was neither rich nor poor."[22] He had never dreamed of going there. There just wasn't that kind of money available.

Denmark was a ruined nation when the folk schools emerged. Prussia had defeated the Danes for the second time in 1864. The nation was nearly bankrupt. Many Danes were forsaking their native ways, and even their language, to learn German and German customs. For centuries, Danish village life had been rooted in the soil, but by 1864, the church and the schools were calling old traditions pagan. A poet, preacher, and scholar of Scandinavian mythology, Bishop N. S. F. Grundtvig, after nearly a decade of pondering the confusion and misery around him, fashioned a theoretical program for what he called schools of learning. They would be free of traditional forms and methods. They would direct education toward fostering the integrity and natural intelligence of village and farm people. They would revive native cultural traditions.[23]

In 1844, Grundtvig tried to found such a school, but it failed. The school, used only as a means of preserving the Danish language, was not as broad in scope as its founder's dream. In 1851, a shoemaker, Kristen Kold, tried, along with one other teacher and fifteen students, to bring life to Grundtvig's original idea. Kold's school, near the village of Ryslinge on the island of Fyn, was closely connected with the daily lives of the students. No books were used, only the spoken word, and much singing. Kold championed the cause of the peasants in their struggles against landlords, the church, and the nobility. Learning flourished there, and, in the next thirteen years, twenty-six more folk schools opened. By 1925, when Joseph K. Hart visited Denmark, over 300,000 young Danes had found what they wanted to learn in the folk schools—and had learned. The schools were free of government control. There were no grades, ranks, tests, or diplomas. Lectures were limited to Danish history, mythology, religion, and language. Teachers were often young idealists, sensitive to injustices existing in their native land and hopeful for the future. Each folk school had an "emotionally charged," clearly-stated purpose.[24]

Anyone eighteen or older could attend. Those who came supported the schools in any way possible: by work at the school, food from their farms, or money, if they had it. They stayed as long as they were able. Music and poetry were used by teachers to stir the students. Lectures for residential students were often repeated in the evening for older people who came from the countryside.

Horton knew these facts about the folk school movement in Denmark from his reading. But the descriptions failed to explain fully to him the great vitality of the schools. Though the methods approximated his own first tentative efforts in Ozone, he remained skeptical.

Moller felt that Horton would never understand until he visited the schools himself. The temptation to go to Denmark was tempered with practical considerations. His family depended on him for some financial support. Professor Park had offered him an assistantship, which would have allowed him to complete work on a doctorate in sociology. The American Missionary Association had offered him the principalship of a church-supported school in Tennessee. Horton's young radical friends pleaded with him not to leave: 1931 was to be the year for dramatic social change in America, and he should remain to become a part of history, to help shape the future.

Only Niebuhr backed the idea of his proposed trip. He still believed that Horton could accomplish his goals through a rural church, but he wrote: "You say that the people of the mountains integrate their social and religious life around a personality, and I imagine it wouldn't take long for them to find out just what kind of religion is on tap in your particular church. But on the whole you will have a freer hand if you organize a folk school. I think a visit to Denmark for study would be splendid."[25]

Niebuhr's encouragement was all that Horton needed. By the end of the summer of 1931, he had earned enough money for his passage. Once he reached Denmark, he made a living by doing manual labor and by giving occasional lectures on the United States. Horton immediately began to investigate Denmark in depth. He studied the language and the social and political movements that had resulted in a society free of conspicuous poverty or riches. He examined the strong trade union movement and the farmers' cooperatives that were spread throughout the country. Only in the folk schools was he disappointed. Most seemed without vitality, looking backward to enemies long since vanquished, fighting ghosts of their grandparents' battles. There were, however, exceptions.

At a workers' folk high school at Esbjerg run by Paul Hansen, who later became a member of Parliament, Horton found students learning about the basic problems faced by Danish working people and farmers, as well as the international problems faced by the country. Participation was encouraged at all levels; no issue was too small to be discussed.

Horton later wrote to Hansen: "The successful adaptation of the high school idea to the needs of a labor school suggests many possibilities for work of a similar nature in other countries. It was instructive to learn that the most desirable features of the older type of folk schools could be retained. In the transition, you have not lost the emotional warmth made possible by intimate personal contact, nor have you discarded the idea that each school should have a purpose or mission."[26]

When Horton had learned enough Danish, he interviewed many of the older folk school directors. These conversations helped him to see more clearly the distinctive qualities of the early schools, and were among the most rewarding moments of his stay in Denmark. The talks helped him understand why even skeptical foreign critics have found the schools pivotal in the nation's extraordinary economic recovery.

Horton found that many of the directors were unconventional educators. They were men on fire to correct injustice, to awaken the peasants to the misery restricting their lives. The schools, each with a distinct purpose, sought to evoke among students, as one director told him, "a picture of reality not as we have met it in our surroundings, but as we ourselves would have formed it if we could—a picture of reality as it *ought* to be."[27] Toward that end, the schools made wide use of poetry and song. A revolutionary spark seemed inherent in these ways of communicating. Horton found that the early schools, while not underestimating the students' need for factual information or the ability to reason with clarity and sharpness, were nonetheless chiefly eductive. They sought to develop feelings and will more than memory and logic.

Joseph K. Hart has described a further essential characteristic of the schools which Horton had also found in his conversations with the older directors: "A folk school in America, as in Denmark, would probably center about a personality of some real teacher; a man who is capable of learning, and who can teach, not so much by his teaching, as by his capacity to learn. America's great lack, at present, is the lack of men of this sort. We have plenty of men and women who can teach what they know; we have very few who can teach their own capacity to learn."[28]

Horton, since the day he came to understand fully the truth of Hart's conclusion, has been struggling to increase his capacity to learn from hard-pressed people. In Denmark, Horton began to trust himself. He saw more clearly the role he could play in a changing society. He became convinced that the people, no matter how poor or untutored, would know what they needed to learn, if he could only learn to listen to them and to translate what he heard into an educational program.

Free of doubts and sure of the validity of his educational idea, Horton was at the end of his long search for "background." He knew what he must do: get behind the common judgments of the poor, help them learn to act and speak for themselves, help them gain control over decisions affecting their daily lives. The answers to the problems of the poor, in Ozone and elsewhere, must emerge from the poor themselves, he concluded. The sooner the poor were trusted to develop and express their own ideas—their own creative ideas—the sooner America would begin to achieve the kind of social structure that could end poverty and racial prejudice, set aside exploitation and the reasons for war. Although this idea was a simple one, Horton had been a long time in coming to it. Rather than learning to make decisions for the poor, as he sought to do in the beginning, he now knew that he should help people make their own decisions. Once that approach to education had evolved, it stuck—and became the idea behind Highlander. He wrote in Copenhagen on Christmas night, 1931:

"I can't sleep but there are dreams. What you must do is go back . . . get a simple place . . . move in . . . you're there . . . the situation is there . . . you start with this and let it grow . . . it will build its own structure and take its own form. You can go to school all your life and you'll never figure it out because you're trying to get an answer that can only come from the people in the life situation."[29]

3

. . . coming here, getting information, going back and teaching it . . .

FRIENDSHIPS and coincidences led Myles Horton from Copenhagen to Grundy County, Tennessee, where he soon would begin a school of freedom.

He left Denmark in January, 1932, and returned to New York and his friend Niebuhr. Together, they outlined plans for the school. Niebuhr wrote the first fund-raising letter describing, for want of a better name, the Southern Mountain School.[1] He introduced Horton to Sherwood Eddy, then secretary of the International YMCA, who gave the school its first contribution—$100. Others who gave help and lent their names were Norman Thomas, Professor Arthur L. Swifts, and George S. Counts.

With some money in his pocket, and more hoped for, Horton's next tasks were to find a location and teachers. His Union classmates, John Thompson and James Dombrowski, agreed to join Horton after they finished their graduate studies. Thompson, a lean Tennessean, was completing his studies for the ministry with the same intellectual zest that had earned for him, in one year, a Phi Beta Kappa key and a diploma from Beloit College. Dombrowski, son of a Tampa, Florida, jeweler, was exercising his intellectual skills by writing *The Early Days of Christian Socialism in America*, first as his doctoral thesis, then as a book.[2] Like Horton, they wanted to change the life of their native South.

Having secured commitments from his friends, Horton headed south to talk with Dr. Will Alexander, director of the Commission on Interracial Cooperation in Atlanta. He told

Horton of Don West, a Georgia native who had studied theology at Vanderbilt University with Dr. Alva Taylor. According to Dr. Will, West had also been to Denmark and was thinking of starting a folk school. Horton could find him at a church conference at the Blue Ridge Assembly in North Carolina, Dr. Will said.

Horton hitchhiked to North Carolina to talk with West. Indeed, West had been serious about starting a folk school to counter the South's social ills, but he was currently under contract to teach school in Kentucky. Horton was persuasive. West decided to break his contract, and the two left the Assembly—at first in West's aging automobile, then, when it broke down, hitchhiking, in search of a place to begin a school.

They ended up at the Crossville home of Horton's first sponsor, Mr. Nightingale. He knew of a place they might inquire about, a house northwest of Chattanooga on Monteagle Mountain, which belonged to Dr. Lillian Johnson. Mr. Nightingale filled them in on Dr. Johnson's unusual background. She was the daughter of a wealthy Memphis banking and mercantile family. She had a doctorate in history from Cornell University, had been the president of Western State College in Oxford, Ohio, and was a leading Southern suffragette and a member of the Women's Christian Temperance Union. She had traveled to Italy to study the cooperative movement and had returned to the South determined to help spread the cooperative idea.[3] She had bought land in Summerfield, a Grundy County community between Monteagle, a fancy summer vacation community, and Tracy City, a less-than-prosperous coal mining community.

She had built a sturdy, two-story house with a high, peaked roof and clapboard siding, stained brown. By any standard it was Summerfield's finest home, with two indoor bathrooms, one upstairs and one down. A vine-shaded porch level with the lawn stretched the width of the house. Her living room had been a place for the play-party games of neighborhood children, as well as a lecture hall where people from outside shared ideas with her neighbors. Farmers had come to talk about stock-breeding methods and new agricultural techniques.

She had remodeled a schoolhouse and had persuaded two young, university-trained women, May Justus and Vera McCampbell, both from mountain communities, to come to teach. Since 1930, according to Mr. Nightingale, Dr. Johnson had been talking about retiring and giving her home to someone who would carry on her work.

Horton and West set off for Grundy County.

Dr. Johnson welcomed them and listened as they unfolded their dream of a community school. At first, she was shocked, Horton recalls. Her approach to education and social service was structured and well-planned from top to bottom. The idea of a community residential school without courses or a planned curriculum, where intelligence would be nourished without a diploma to certify its validity, was wholly new to her. But she had always welcomed new ideas and, in the end, gave the two enthusiastic young men a year's probationary lease for the house, beginning in the fall.

Buoyantly Horton and West moved in on November 1, 1932.[4] They started immediately to make the house into a residential center. The spacious attic was turned into a dormitory. The living room became a place for classes, meetings, square dancing, and dining. Extra beds were added in the three bedrooms on the second floor. They mailed out requests for books to start a library and took $50.00 from their meager treasury to publish a collection of West's poems, *Between the Plow Handles.* They sold poetry and mistletoe, which they gathered, in order to buy groceries. Cash receipts from June, 1932, when Niebuhr sent out the first appeal for funds, through February, 1933, totaled $1,327.30, according to scrupulous records.[5]

They decided on the school's name. As was fitting, the name reflected the people, the place, and the school's purpose. In the 1930's, Highland was the popular name for Appalachia. A Highlander was an Appalachian. To Horton, and other intellectuals of the day, folk was a word that had both an anthropological and a political meaning. Highlander Folk School was begun.

As they sought out students, they also learned about the region and began to define their purpose. They had no intention of teaching from books. The life, work, culture, and history of Grundy County, the Cumberlands, and the South were to provide teaching materials.

The people of Grundy County were poor. Horton and West didn't need a government census survey to know that fact. Coal-mining and timber-cutting provided most of the jobs—when, and if, jobs were available. Three years after Highlander opened, a state government study confirmed their initial impressions and certified Grundy among the eleven poorest counties in the United States.[6]

Grundy's woes in 1932 could be traced, in large part, to the historical peculiarities of the South itself and to the Compromise of 1876, which resulted in the election of Rutherford B. Hayes as President of the United States. Until then the South had remained essentially agrarian, with a rigid caste system. The Compromise of 1876, engineered by defeated Confederate generals and opportunistic Southern industrialists, allied with Northern bankers, brought railroads and industry into the South to take advantage of widespread unemployment. Low wages could be assured by pitting the races against each other and by the widespread practice of leasing convicts to private industry.

In the late 1800's, countless Grundy County men walked the hills looking for work in the coal mines. Free men watched helplessly, as each day nearly 400 convicts from a huge stockade in Tracy City were marched into the mines to dig coal at virtually no cost to Tennessee Coal and Iron Company, parent of today's giant U.S. Steel. Throughout Appalachia the situation was similar, and it was rankling mountain miners. When a mine opened and convicts were not immediately available, free men were hired for low wages. If free miners tried to strike, there was usually a good supply of men who would work and promise not to strike; or, if not, convicts could be leased.

On August 14, 1892, Grundy miners, fed up with the situation, and organized by the covert Knights of Labor, rebelled against convict-leasing by the state. They marched on the stockade in Tracy City, captured it, put 390 convicts on a freight train, ordered the engineers to head for Nashville, then burned the stockade to the ground.

Word of the revolt spread quickly. The next day 1,500 more convicts were freed from stockades at Inman, Oliver Springs, and Coal Creek; all were at mines owned by Tennessee Coal and Iron. Armed miners and the state militia fought for months in Eastern Tennessee. But, by the summer of 1893, even with public opinion on the miners' side, the combined forces of the state and the coal companies had gradually retaken the mines and reactivated them, still using convict labor.[7] Nonetheless, the revolt that started in Tracy City was the beginning of the end of convict-leasing in Tennessee. In 1899, the legislature outlawed the practice. As late as 1970, Grundy men still took pride in their rebellion and talked of it in country stores.

Here, then, in a place where life had been a struggle for subsistence, Horton and West found themselves trying to start a school that would be directly related to community life. Their New Year's greetings in 1932 offer a glimpse into their work:

> Our four regular boarding students from neighboring states have become an accepted part of the local community, and each is in charge of some phase of community activity. Dorothy (John Thompson's sister) has her girls' club meeting every Wednesday afternoon.

Soon Elsie's (Elsie West, Don's sister) dramatic club will be producing plays to help with the regular Saturday evening community meeting. (Walker) Martin, whose father was a coal miner, is carrying on a vigorous crusade for a new social order. He has regular weekly meetings in outlying communities. One of these is a mining camp twenty-five miles away. Martin's interest in this work is so great that he walked most of the way out and all the way back in order to attend his last meetings before Christmas. Dee (Ferris), our thirty-five-year-old student, left school recently when he got a few days' work on the road. He took with him a lot of books and literature. Dee was formerly a member of a plasterer's union. Now, as he swings his pick three days a week working on the road, he is urging on his fellow workers the necessity of a labor organization with a social vision.

Four regular classes are held each week, with an average attendance of twenty to twenty-five. These classes are: psychology, cultural geography, revolutionary literature, and a course in the study of our present social and economic problems. In addition to those classes, there is a seminar on how social change is brought about. Much of our class discussion is based on information gained by investigation of actual labor situations in the Southern industrial area. Such firsthand information is obtained by both students and teachers. The people of our own surrounding communities are eagerly reading all the books we have and are asking for more. We are fortunate in having the support of our community, many of whom help cut wood and divide their meager food supply with us.

After Christmas we are planning a special two-week course for fifteen additional boarding students. Some of these students will come from the strike area round Wilder, Tennessee.[8]

Highlander was barely into its infancy when circumstances summoned it to manhood at Wilder, a bleak valley town over a hundred miles north of Grundy County. Horton, who had been alert for places in the South where contention was rising, had heard of a mining company at Wilder that had locked out striking miners. He went up in November to see what was happening.

Wilder was a company town; coal profits were its reason for

being. The town's only store was owned by Fentress Coal and Coke Company, as were its few unpainted shacks. Miners were paid in scrip good only at the company store, which charged higher prices than independent stores in the area. The company made weekly deductions for rent on the shacks, for a bathhouse which didn't exist, and for a doctor who was infrequently available. No matter how hard or long the men worked in the mines, they couldn't break even, much less get ahead. As their debts piled up, and food at home dwindled, their indignation and desperation mounted. Finally, they struck.

Almost immediately, the company shut off the electricity and took the doors off the houses. It was winter and bitterly cold. A rotting, unused trestle was blown up, and Horton figured the explosion was a pretext by which the company could call on the governor to send in National Guard cavalry troops to protect private property.[9] Horton estimated that it cost the state more to guard the mines for the three months the troops stayed in Wilder than the company had paid in taxes over twenty years.

To get the mines going and to break the strike, the company circulated handbills and ran ads in mountain newspapers offering wages higher than they had previously paid the strikers, full protection, room and board, and a "woman at night," Horton recalls.[10] The response was good, as could have been expected.

The Red Cross, supposedly responding to the emergency created by growing hunger in the community, handed out food and flour to the strikebreakers, but not to the strikers and their families, who were literally starving. The county chairman of the Red Cross was the wife of the mine superintendent.[11]

Having learned as much as he could about conditions in Wilder, and having arranged for students and teachers from Highlander to support the strikers, Horton returned to the school and commenced writing letters to newspapers across the state appealing for food and clothing for the strikers. John

Thompson, who had joined Highlander by this time, later wrote, "I will never forget the long line of gaunt, haggard, brave people who lined up to receive the scant rations we handed out to last them a week. Each family got a pound of dried beans, a half-pound of coffee, two tins of canned milk (if they had a baby), half a pound of sugar. These rations saved many lives, but meanwhile many babies had died of starvation."[12]

The strike was led by Barney Graham, a tough mountain man. Nothing the company did seemed to break the strikers' morale, in part because of Graham. Constant harassment and insults from the National Guard, a young and cocky troop with its first taste of authority, seemed only to deepen the strikers' resolve to win. The company let it be known that if Horton and Thompson didn't stop bringing food into Wilder, they wouldn't get out alive.[13] There was an attempt to bomb Highlander, the first of many such attacks. The students and teachers stood guard night and day for two weeks.

Horton persuaded Norman Thomas to come to Wilder to speak at a mass meeting of the 700 strikers and their supporters on March 5, 1933. Thomas's words were stirring, but a song written by one of the strikers, Uncle Ed Davis, was the hit of the afternoon. The cheering crowd insisted that it be sung a second time. "It was their song; it was their life," Thompson wrote.[14]

THE WILDER BLUES

Mr. Shivers said if we'd block our coal
He'd run four days a week
And there's no reason we shouldn't run six,
We're loadin' it so darn cheap.
It's the worst old blues I ever had.

Chorus: I've got the blues,
I've shore-God got 'em bad.
I've got the blues,

The worst I've ever had!
It must be the blues
Of the Davidson-Wilder scabs.

He discharged Horace Hood
And told him he had no job;
Then he wouldn't let Thomas Shepherd couple
Because he couldn't take the other fellow's job.
It's the worst old blues I ever had.

Mr. Shivers he's an Alabama man,
He came to Tennessee;
He put on two of his yeller-dog cuts,
But he failed to put on three.
It's the worst old blues I ever had.

Mr. Shivers told Mr. Boyer,
He said, "I know just what we'll do!
We'll get the names of the union men
And fire the whole durn crew."
It's the worst old blues I ever had.

We paid no attention to his firing,
And went on just the same;
And organized the holler
In L. L. Shivers' name.
It's the worst old blues I ever had.

I'd rather be a yeller-dog scab
In a union man's backyard,
Than to tote a gun for L. L. Shivers,
And to be a National Guard.
It's the worst old blues I ever had.[15]

Horton was arrested in Wilder and charged by a National Guard officer with "coming here and getting information and going back and teaching it." This was his first arrest. He was marched off at bayonet point to the state police headquarters, where he was held for eight hours before being released. Charges against him were dropped, police said, for lack of evidence. He went back to Highlander and began writing letters to newspaper editors about the incident.[16]

The strike leader, Barney Graham, was shot in the back as he went to fetch a doctor for his ailing wife one Sunday evening about sunset. Ironically, he fell in front of the company store. Witnesses later testified his killers bashed in his head and stood guard over his body, refusing to let anyone take it away until about 10:00 P.M.[17] Another song was written, "The Ballad of Barney Graham," by his grieving twelve-year-old daughter.[18] A thousand mourners attended his funeral. Other union men's homes were shot into; some were dynamited. One scab was shot and killed; another wounded. Six union men were arrested and jailed for five months without bail.

Finally, the company began to evict strikers from their rented homes. This, coupled with the loss of Graham's defiant leadership, broke the strike. Over 200 men and their families were out of food, jobs, and homes. Horton persuaded Dr. Arthur Morgan, the innovative head of the fledgling Tennessee Valley Authority, to hire as many strikers as possible to work on TVA projects.[19] This was the start of a long relationship between Highlander and TVA that foundered only in the 1960's, when the TVA turned to strip-mining coal for its generating plants and mountain people began to protest the practice. Many TVA staffers taught at Highlander, helped raise funds to keep the school going, served on the board of directors, and, in general, backed an institution frequently even less popular locally than TVA.

The Wilder strike had a powerful impact on Horton and on Highlander. The miners had proved that they would not tolerate slave wages. They had struck and stayed out and endured hunger, cold, even violence. Horton and his friends had gone to Wilder to spark the workers' latent revolutionary spirit, but it was already burning before they arrived. Uncle Ed Davis and Barney Graham were better able to fan the fires of rebellion than the oratory of Norman Thomas—or Highlander's exhortations. Horton himself learned that, if teaching had any real place in bringing about social change in the South, he would have to teach within the experiences of people like Davis and Graham. He would have to learn, not how to convert, but how to bring forth. If Highlander were to be educational, not pedagogical, it had to be rooted in the life of the people.

The lessons of Wilder were not obscure, only difficult to practice. For example, shortly after the strike was broken, Horton was discussing economics in class. He asked the handful of students present to explain the theory of surplus value, almost parodying his own schooling. An unemployed nurse from Gruetli, Tennessee, Willie Lehr, who'd brought a basket of onions, bacon, and canned fruit to Highlander to pay her tuition, told him: "When I was working at the hosiery mill in Chattanooga, we were told that we would have to take a wage cut or the mill would go out of business. Of course, we took the cut. About ten weeks later, I read in the paper that the daughter of the mill owner was sailing for Europe to spend the winter. I suppose it was the surplus value we had produced that paid her way."[20]

Horton's own strongly felt ideologies threatened to obstruct his ability to let education grow from the students' needs. Shortly before Dombrowski was to leave New York City for the Cumberlands, Horton wrote him as follows:

> If I understood our purpose correctly, we will all be working at the same job but will be using different approaches. Our task is to make class-conscious workers who envision their roles in society, and to furnish motivation as well as technicians for the achievement of this goal.
>
> In other words, we must try to give the students an understanding of the world in which we live (a class-divided society) and an idea of the kind of world we would like to have. We have found that a very effective way to help students to understand the present social order is to throw them into conflict situations where the real nature

of our society is projected in all its ugliness. To be effective, such exposure must be preceded, accompanied by, and followed by efforts to help the observer appreciate and digest what he has seen. This keeps education from getting unrealistic. While this process is going on, students need to be given an inkling of the new society. Perhaps this can be done best by having a type of life that approaches as nearly as possible the desired state. This is where our communal living at the school comes into the picture as an important educational factor. The tie-in with the conflict situations and participation in community life keeps our school from being a detached colony or utopian venture. But our efforts to live out our ideals makes possible the development of a bit of proletarian culture as an essential part of our program of workers' education.[21]

Highlander, and Horton's thinking, did stand apart from much of what was called workers' education in the 1930's. Highlander was not teaching reading, or some work skill, or how to get along with society as it was. Like the Danish folk schools, Highlander could, and did, teach basic knowledge and skills, but nothing was taught at Highlander that would help workers become accustomed to exploitation. That the school was growing in understanding of this educational problem is illustrated by one of Horton's anecdotes. "Shortly after the Wilder strike—after we'd gotten the strikers jobs with TVA—some of the people around Summerfield asked us to organize an employment agency. At first, it seemed like a pretty good idea. It came from the people. If it worked, it would be of help. But we refused, and told them our goal was to help workers unite with other workers for common strength and not to help some individuals rise above others."[22] An employment agency probably would have added to the betterment of a few, but the community's collective strength probably would have diminished. By refusing the request, Highlander demonstrated its philosophy of mutual aid among people, and confronted the problem of individual interests.

Horton and the others had hardly assimilated the lessons of Wilder when the Grundy County bugwood cutters struck.

Bugwood, knotty crooks of trees which can be found in any cut-over forest, is unfit for sawing into lumber, but it was harvested for use in distilling wood alcohol. In the summer of 1933, Tennessee Products Corporation paid seventy-five cents a day to bugwood cutters. One of them, Henry Thomas, who had made good money logging before the Depression, said years later, "I got to figuring that my pay amounted to two-and-a-half cents a meal for the members of my family. So I went around to the other woodcutters and said to them, 'It takes a sharp axe, a strong back, and a weak mind to cut bugwood at seventy-five cents a day. Let's strike!' "[23] They did.

Again, Highlander's staff and students were in the midst of a conflict, this time in their own community. At first, the woodcutters tried, but failed, to organize an affiliate of the American Federation of Labor. The big union wasn't interested in small locals. With Highlander's cooperation, the woodcutters formed the Cumberland Mountain Workers' and Unemployed League. Within a week after the charter was written, a majority of the woodcutters had agreed with the stated purpose: "to be loyal to one another and to the purposes of the organization, which are: (1) to prevent the wholesale destruction of our forests; (2) to better the condition of the community by raising wages."[24]

Men, women, and children picketed Grundy forests for miles around. No bugwood was cut. Horton recalls that one group of strikers was challenged by a company representative, who told them, "It's against the law to strike. You will all be in jail before the weekend." The strikers told him that Section 7-A of the National Industrial Recovery Act guaranteed workers the right to collective bargaining—a fact, Horton proudly notes, they learned at Highlander.[25]

The strike didn't last long. Wages weren't raised. But no

bugwood was cut that summer. Will L. Brown, secretary of the League, concluded, "We really don't want to cut down the trees at all, but on the other hand there isn't any work to do. It looks strange to me that the government would be paying the CCC boys a dollar a day for planting trees at the other end of the county while we are cutting them down here for seventy-five cents."[26]

Real gains were intangible. Henry Thomas, nearly thirty years later and almost blind, summed up Highlander's role for a visitor on the porch of his Summerfield cabin: "People were in pretty bad shape. But at Highlander we learned how to handle our daily problems, to do by organizing, by showing our power and our strength. The most important thing the people ever learned from Highlander was what we learned then—how we could help ourselves."[27]

The bugwood strike sparked community interest in Highlander. A cooperative nursery school was started. Mothers took turns caring for the children and teaching them. Whole families came to learn the history and organization of cooperatives. Some experimented with a cooperative garden and canning operation. Poor land and a dry summer produced a poor crop. The project failed. But the participants planned to try again, with better preparation. An official of the Federal Emergency Relief Act was brought to the school to explain how to apply for federal grants to start farm co-ops. With the help of one of TVA's experts on cooperatives, the local people made detailed plans. They filled out the complicated formal request themselves. In March, 1935, FERA made a grant of $7,000 to the Highlander Folk Cooperative. The people were elated.

A few days later, however, they learned the money had been held up at the regional FERA office in Nashville. John Edgerton, the antiunion woolen manufacturer whose workers Horton had exhorted a decade before, had heard of Highlander's involvement with both the Wilder and the bugwood strikes. He demanded that the grant be withdrawn, saying that it would be used for "the teaching of anti-American doctrines."[28] Famed revivalist Billy Sunday was in Tennessee at the time and, during a special sermon in Chattanooga, he denounced the grant, protesting the use of taxpayers' money by "a communistic institution."[29] Edgerton and Sunday won. The grant was rescinded. Pleas from organized labor, ministers, teachers, and other Tennessee liberals fell on deaf federal ears.

People in Grundy learned in spite of their defeat. They learned who, in fact, governed Tennessee. They realized that their major support had come from organized labor and that Edgerton's attacks had focused on labor unions. They became convinced that their hopes for social change lay with the labor movement. No one from Highlander had to tell them these things.

Edgerton's opposition to the FERA grant was not his last attack on the school. In 1934, some Highlander economics students suggested that Horton invite Edgerton to present the views of the Tennessee Manufacturers Association on labor unions. Edgerton's reply was a curt no. He didn't stop there. The next day, June 28, 1934, he posted a letter to all TMA members on the organization's letterhead, a part of which is as follows:

> Yesterday, I received a letter from Mr. Myles Horton, one of the promoters of the so-called HIGHLANDER FOLK SCHOOL at Monteagle, Tennessee, inviting me to have a representative of the Tennessee Manufacturers Association to appear before the student body and present our views. . . . Assisting Mr. Horton in operating the school is a M. Dombrowski, who is armed with Russian posters collected during a recent visit, Miss Hawes, organizer for the Amalgamated Clothing Workers in East Tennessee, and two or three others.

. . . the students are trained as labor organizers and that Mr. Dombrowski "who has traveled in Russia," will tell all about his impression of the Soviet and its accomplishments.
. . . I declined the invitation in courteous, but vigorous terms. This enterprise of destruction requires no comment from me. It is about the boldest and most insulting thing to the Anglo-Saxon South that has yet been done.[30]

This was the first deliberate attempt to Red-bait Highlander. Others followed. Usually, if possible, Highlander ignored the charges and went on with its work.

By 1936, the staff had developed three educational programs, each based on their students' needs. A residential program lasted six weeks and was held when enough students could be assembled. The residential program was for union members who showed promise of becoming organizers or local leaders. Usually they were elected to come by vote of their locals. Most of them came from textile and mine unions and from the few farmworkers' organizations of that time. College graduates interested in workers' education also attended.

What the school called its extension program was really a way for students to learn, by experience, the nature of social conflict. Highlander students assisted strikers, provided manpower during union-organizing drives, and did routine chores like running the mimeograph machine. Frequently, study groups would be held on picket lines, where labor songs and group-singing techniques could be taught and then be used immediately. Through the extension program, Highlander was able to recruit new students and to keep in contact with former students as they worked "for the new social order."[31] Extension students usually remained in the program for one year, roaming over the South wherever conflict was occurring.

The third element in the school's program centered around community life in Summerfield, Tracy City, and Monteagle. An outdoor stage was built. Young and old took part in dramatics. As many as twenty young adults and children were enrolled at a time to study piano with Rupert Hampton, who had studied organ at Union Seminary. Ralph Tefferteller, a Tennessean, played the fiddle, organized folk dances, and called square dances—despite admonishments from some devout Grundy church people that "dancin' was sinnin'!"

The three programs merged frequently. There were always arrivals and departures at the school. There's a long, unsigned, undated letter in Highlander's files which, because it was written by a student, tells much about the atmosphere.

As the sun peeks over a mountain ridge high up in the Cumberlands, you see students in twos and threes coming from the cabins near the main building of the school, and within a few minutes a group of young men and women are gathered around the huge fireplace in the living room, ready for a hearty breakfast.

Thus starts the day at Highlander Folk School. Now at 7:30 there is quite a scramble about washing dishes. "Well, we won that time but we'll catch it at noon." At 8:30 the "Bell," which means Labor History class by Jim Dombrowski, where we have a discussion on the split between the AFL and the CIO. At 9:20 we have Economics conducted by Bill Buttrick, and at 10:15 Dramatics. We are practicing our mass chant, "Tom Mooney Lives Again," which we are going to give at the Textile Workers' Organizing Committee (TWOC) convention next week in Chattanooga. Now a short walk to the gate and back, just for a breath of fresh air.

At 12:30 dinner is served. Now that we have had dinner we will wash dishes and do our cleaning. At 2:30 we have Union Problems, taught by Myles Horton. Today we had Edna Lamb, John Pate, and Bill Flanagan answer questions on Union Problems. At 4:30 everybody is out for volley ball. Boy! What a game. Darkness has arrived and there goes the supper bell, and after this game everyone is hungry.

Now, after eating for thirty minutes, Zilphia [then Johnson, but later Myles Horton's wife] passes out the song books and it's likely we will start with "Arise You Workers" and finish with "Whirlwinds of Danger." Well, it's dishes again but we don't mind them this time. When we have finished, we will have our speaker of the evening, Tommy Burns of the Rubber Workers, who, by the way, is a *very* interesting speaker.

Now at 10:30 things are getting quiet as the students slowly wander off to their rooms for a good night's rest. Ho! Hum! Guess I'll turn in too. Goodnight.[32]

Deeper insight into how a Highlander class operated was provided by Willie Lehr.

It was in this class that we actually thrashed out and tried to get answers to the immediate serious problems that confront us all in our local unions. Everyone had the right to stand up and ask any question that might concern the organization of workers. Myles would then throw the floor open for discussion.

For example, John Pate from the North Carolina TWOC would tell Telesforo Oviedo from the Texas Pecan Workers Union what he would do in case of a speed-up. If perchance Oviedo was not satisfied with John's answer, he might ask Cecil Holmes from the Alabama Rubber Workers just how they recently fought the tremendous technological development and consequent unemployment in his industry. You see, we never took one man's opinion or experience on a subject. Instead, we worked under the theory that it's much more likely that thirty people will be right and the one individual wrong."[33]

Whatever the students learned they were encouraged to practice. A class on labor journalism held in 1934 published five issues of a militantly pro-labor mimeographed newssheet called *The Fighting Eaglet*. Strike news was carried in a column called "On the Firin' Line." Cartoons deflated big business. There was news of events at the school. There was poetry. The students hoped that the paper would spark local unions to produce their own mimeographed newspapers. A school report on the summer school activities for the year noted, "Bundles of the *Eaglet* were sent weekly to the local hosiery union at Harriman, the textile unions in Lennois City, a Socialist local at Wheat, the farmers' organization of Sherwood, the United Mine Workers locals at Wilder and Davidson, and to the Norris Dam."[34]

Practicing what was learned in the extension program was not without its perils. Usually the students would live in the homes of strikers. Often, these were the homes that were shot into. Teaching songs on a picket line could be dangerous. Marching in a demonstration at Daisy, Tennessee, nearly cost the life of Wellesley College graduate Hilda Hulbert, Highlander's librarian, who was learning about the work of women who wanted to organize trade unions. She wrote in her diary what happened when a George Washington Day strikers' parade exploded into violence outside the struck mill: "I'm sitting here in a chair by the fire in the home of a Daisy union worker about half a block from the mill. I have been here since 2, when they brought me back from the hospital." She wrote that when the marchers reached the mill gates, shots blasted from "the mill windows . . . I heard Myles saying, 'Don't shoot. A woman's been shot!' . . . They say they kept shooting, but I didn't hear it after I got mine." She and three strikers were wounded that day. She was struck in the leg.[35]

Even the seemingly less dramatic community program could produce sparks. Don West and Horton were barred from county school buildings by the chairman of the Grundy Board of Education. West had been holding a series of well-attended meetings in county schools to discuss "Conditions in America Today" or "America as She Might Be." The school board chairman considered the talks "political teachings."[36]

The banishment from the public school buildings took place only a month after the young men had moved into Dr. Johnson's home. The Wilder and bugwood strikes quickly followed. By late in the summer of 1933, the staff was nervously wondering if Dr. Johnson would let them continue to lease her house. Preparing for the worst, Dombrowski and several other staffers had set up another base at nearby Allardt in a tiny house given to them by friends. In April, West had left Highlander for Georgia, where he hoped to start another folk school and build a chain of workers' cooperative libraries. Dr. Johnson agreed to let Horton and the remaining staffers stay on at her home, but it wasn't until 1935 that she wrote to Dombrowski from Memphis saying she would deed the house and 200 acres of land to the school. "I have made these last years a sort of test of your experiment," she wrote. "Don't worry about the property because none of my family would contend any wish of mine and they know that I want it all for the good of the community."[37]

Her faith in the Highlander idea grew steadily. Two years before her death in Bradenton, Florida, where, in retirement and at the age of ninety, she was working to improve race relations, she wrote to Horton: "What Highlander did for me was to accustom me to association with people of a class and a race I had not known before, except as they served me. The industrial workers, and the Negro became personalities in their own rights. I saw beneath externalities, and came to have a better understanding of their problems. This new attitude has been a great help for me in the work here of organizing our interracial work for a recreation program for Negro youth."[38]

Even the firm assurance of a home didn't solve Highlander's internal problems. To live out their ideals, as Horton had said in his letter to Dombrowski earlier, staff and students did all the cooking and cleaning. They maintained the house and built several additional cabins. A garden became a financial mainstay but required hours of work. A good bit of the time was spent in staff meetings, often to iron out interpersonal frictions. Every staff member had a host of responsibilities. Rupert Hampton, for instance, taught piano, kept the school's books, washed clothes, and split the stovewood. Everyone lived and worked without pay. Petty annoyances often became major sources of trouble, especially when opposing views were held by outspoken young dreamers. Dorothy Thompson, John's sister, expressed her beliefs in a short paper probably written in August, 1934. "I feel very strongly that people working with the labor movement and for a new social order should set almost perfect standards for themselves personally."[39] Notes made by Elizabeth Hawes about the same time reflect a less stern attitude. "We may give lip service to our revolutionary ideal, yet even fail to make a start, in which case it were better not attempted."[40]

There seems to have been no time in Highlander's history when the school was free of internal debates. What seems to have kept friction from splitting the school, turning it into a tiny utopian village, or halting its educational work was work itself. After forty years, Horton observed, "Struggling with the real problems growing out of conflict situations and our participation in community life kept the school from becoming a detached colony."[41]

In many respects, Highlander's experiences over the years provide substantial evidence to support Joseph Hart's theory of what folk schools in America would have to be. In 1926, he wrote:

> It was my task, to point out to students that education did not, and does not begin in schools, and that it never can be fully got inside schools; that it was, and is, a matter of the vital interrelationships and participations of persons and groups *in communities*; that the nature of the circumscribing community might have more to do with the ultimate outcome of education—at least for all but the very few—than had any specific item of learning; and that, therefore, if *teaching* was to have any real share in *education*, it must learn, somehow, to work inside the experiences of those being taught, and not forever hang around on the periphery of experience, piously hoping that something might happen inside."[42]

The neighbors Highlander was living and working with weren't preoccupied with building a new social order. They wanted food and jobs. The staff learned this the hard way. Once, according to Horton, they persuaded a handful of Summerfield neighbors to start a potato-growing cooperative. A garden plot was prepared. Seed potatoes were ordered. As soon as they arrived, the potato-growers ate them. Delayed gratification was, and remains, a well-fed, middle-class notion. It has little to do with the reality of poverty. Slowly, this and a host of similar experiences—which each new staff member had to experience individually—caused Horton, and others, to realize that poor people have demands and needs too immediate for them to discuss ideas and theories of what might someday come to pass—if hunger hasn't claimed them in the meantime.

Education at Highlander had to be problem-centered, and the problem had to be the people's, not Highlander's. In this respect, as far as institutions can be, Highlander had to be sensitive and flexible. Each staff member had to learn a new and different tempo of interpersonal relationships.

Horton soon learned that poor people were usually quiet around strangers, or people they considered "well-spoken," meaning educated. When asked a question, some might take half an hour before answering. They'd be puzzling what the question meant, what words to use in reply, even why the other person had asked that question. Only as the staff came to understand the people and their ways of life, did they learn how to hear what the people wanted to learn or find within themselves enough security to move away from traditional academic methods. Once they stopped trying to teach the way they had been taught, mutual learning could begin.

When Horton and others arrived at this point—the rejection of some of their own middle class traditions—there was a temptation to go all the way and reject their own individuality. "To think that sharing their poverty, living in their cabins, picking at bed ticks and lice while going hungry is somehow to be as one with the poor is false logic," Horton asserts.[43] He and others have tried this—and failed. For one thing, most people, poor or rich, quickly detect sham. For another, Horton could not be they, nor could they be he. But they could and did learn from each other, each respecting the individual character of the other. "Insofar as I have learned to listen to people and to honor and respect them as individuals, I have been a good teacher," Horton declares. "When I have failed to do this my teaching has failed."[44]

In short, the staff at Highlander had to learn how to project a vision of their ideal world practically, not by lecturing on Denmark or the Soviet Union. They had to talk about how to make unions work for people, how people could gain a voice in economic affairs through cooperatives, how people could gain control of government.

Dolph Vaughn, a blacklisted coal miner, taught Highlander the still-valid educational method of peer group learning. Vaughn came to Highlander as a Grundy WPA worker about 1935 to learn how to organize unions. Actually, he was better able to tell other WPA workers in the classes how to organize than was the Highlander staff, Horton recalls. Through Vaughn, workers learned about work cards, the WPA forms needed before a job could be secured, and how those cards could be used to build a union. Vaughn had never been a newspaperman and wasn't much with big words, but until he took an interest in the labor journalism class, few students would even try to write their own news releases or mimeograph a paper. "Formally educated staff members have never been as effective in teaching as the people, once they saw themselves as teachers," Horton declares.[45]

It was through a coalition of WPA locals, other Grundy

unions, and a political organization which sprang from them, that Highlander gained another enduring experience.

When the WPA first started in Grundy County, grievances about the way it was being run abounded. Anyone who angered a foreman or supervisor was laid off. Foremen and supervisors were usually chosen because of previous loyalty to the coal companies. Safety regulations were ignored. Talk of unions wasn't tolerated. With unemployment at eighty per cent of the county's population, WPA jobs meant $19.20 a month, and that meant food.[46]

Through friends in Washington, Highlander obtained a complete set of WPA work regulations and all related administrative orders. The staff learned, and taught the disgruntled workers, that what was ordained in Washington was not being practiced in Grundy.

Elaborate safety rules were set down in WPA regulations, and there was no law against unions. Most importantly, however, the workers learned that they were getting paid "unskilled" wages for work classified by the WPA as skilled. Every worker in Grundy, except the foremen, had been classified unskilled. The WPA regulations were being violated in letter and in spirit.

Just as word of violations was circulating among county workers through classes at Highlander, the Tennessee Taxpayers Association released a study of Grundy's county government, declaring it corrupt.[47] WPA workers quickly organized six locals in six parts of the county. Dolph Vaughn was elected business agent. The locals affiliated with the International Hod Carriers and the Builders and Common Laborers Union of America. Within weeks, one local had won the right to elect timekeepers and supervisors and to rotate all higher paying jobs among all the workers. Skilled laborers had begun to be paid for skilled work jobs.[48]

Prospects for further concessions seemed promising. Suddenly, the WPA regional office in Nashville struck back. Grievance committees, formed to take to the state administrator the complaints that couldn't be resolved locally, were given a runaround in Nashville. Most complaints, if processed at all, took weeks to be heard formally. Projects that were working non-union men in Grundy received preferential treatment. Union men were being laid off without cause. Foremen openly began to make fun of the unions' inability to protect their members or to solve grievances. Horton wrote in the winter of 1937: "Knots of gloomy men watched the gains of more than a year of hard work and sacrifice slipping through their fingers. Word that the union was done for spread through the county. Membership dropped."[49]

For men who had supported the union it was a time of starving. They decided in March, 1937, to make a stand. They struck nine of the fifteen WPA projects in Grundy, demanding union recognition, assurances that grievances would be adjusted, replacement of the county administrator by a man "more honest and more human," and immediate reclassification of all county workers from unskilled to semiskilled.[50] They telegraphed President Roosevelt at Warm Springs, Georgia:

> A man died a few days ago of starvation. The doctor said after an examination that he had never seen a man with less in his stomach. Scores of families in these mountains are in similar condition. We are desperate men forgotten in these mountains. For weeks we have attempted by every peaceful means to show the WPA district administrator that conditions imposed upon us are intolerable. We are trying to deal with this situation without violence, but it is more difficult to restrain hungry men when they see WPA funds squandered illegally by officials.[51]

The next day in Nashville, Col. Harry S. Berry, the state administrator, told the press:

A communistic organization has for months been feeding muscovite hope to relief clients in Grundy County. . . . Those clients are receiving the same wages as clients in other counties of the state of similar classification, and their monthly earnings are fixed in Washington.

My advice to relief clients is summed up in the famous wartime cartoon, picturing the British soldier, Old Bill, entitled, "If you know a better 'ole, go to it."[52]

Berry notwithstanding, the strikers received assurance from Washington that their demands would be investigated. Federal WPA officials eventually settled the issue of job classification. Those men who had been able to keep their jobs won a raise. This, in turn, renewed interest in the unions. In Laager, where the strike started, all the men on the project were organized. The number of union locals functioning in Grundy grew to eleven. During the winter and spring of 1938, there was talk among the workers at union meetings at Highlander about turning to politics. On April 28, over 250 delegates from locals in Grundy and adjacent Marion County convened to figure out how to help candidates favoring unions win the upcoming August Democratic primary. A candidate who won the primary was virtually assured of election in November. WPA workers ratified a constitution calling for the creation of the Labor Political Conference. They agreed to invite all candidates to appear before locals to explain their platforms and express their views. They collected $20.00 in campaign funds to back a slate that union men could support.

Eventually, the union men decided on Roy B. Thomas for sheriff and J. L. Rollings for school superintendent. For road commissioners, the men who controlled county WPA funds, they came out for Charles Adams, Jim Fults, and Bob Crouch. The election was close, but the union-backed slate won. In theory, workers now had a direct voice in the schools, in the courthouse, and on the job.

But shortly after Thomas was handed the symbols of his office—pistol, badge, and keys to the jail—his annual salary was cut by the state of Tennessee from $800 to $400. The sheriff's customary allowance for gas was eliminated. He was given no money to hire deputies. The power company cut off the lights in those parts of the courthouse under his supervision. Union men responded by raising among themselves enough money to keep him in office.[53]

The road commissioners came under pressure also. While the federal WPA office stipulated that county road commissioners were to administer all county WPA funds, the newly elected Grundy commissioners hadn't even received their own salaries for two months. They attempted to replace supervisors and foremen appointed by previous commissioners, but their efforts were blocked by the Nashville office. Berry kept the old commissioners on the payroll, despite protests from WPA officials in Washington. He demanded that the union-backed commissioners resign and, when they refused, had new locks put on the equipment sheds, physically locking them out. He told *The* (Nashville) *Tennessean* he would terminate the WPA jobs in Grundy if the new commissioners didn't resign, adding, "The highway commission [has] attempted to build roads by the hammer and sickle rather than the pick and shovel."[54]

The commissioners refused to quit. WPA jobs were shut down. More than 700 men were thrown out of work. Ten days later, on February 10, 1939, about 500 jobless men, with their wives and children, moved into the county courthouse, vowing to stay until they were promised work.[55] Stay they did for ten days and nights. Committees were organized to cook what food could be found, to negotiate with WPA officials, and to put out a mimeographed newspaper each day on Highlander's machine. The Highlander staff held discussion groups daily on such topics as "What Are We Fighting For?"[56] The group elected its own deputy sheriffs to maintain order.

We the People, the mimeographed newspaper, reported in its first edition, "WPA office of Tracy City running full-time, day and night—twenty-four hour service—meals served—everyone having a good time. . . ."[57] In the evenings, there were fiddle playing and group singing. The favorite song was "We Shall Not Be Moved."

In retaliation, Berry set up WPA projects on state roads in the county to circumvent the commissioners' jurisdiction. In union strongholds like Summerfield and Laager, men from other counties were trucked in to replace local workers. In all, over 300 scabs went to work. The federal WPA stepped in at this point and negotiated a settlement. The *Chattanooga Times* reported on February 21:

> . . . occupation of the Grundy County WPA headquarters by unemployed workers ended at nightfall here following an all day conference between representatives of the WPA, the two labor unions involved and Nels Anderson, director of Labor Relations of the WPA, Washington.
>
> Anderson came to Tracy City after a series of complaints filed first with the state authorities and finally direct to Washington, concerning what leaders of the workers claimed were attempts to "break up the unions" by laying off union men.[58]

The workers won the right to work but lost their fight to have that work controlled by the road commissioners they had elected. A compromise ended what Horton believes to be one of the few times in the South when workers controlled the means of production. Syndicalism. The word was never mentioned during the bitter effort to build the union movement in Grundy, and the idea got only a brief test. "The demands of the workers were not unreasonable," Anderson later wrote Horton. "They asked for nothing except a chance to earn a living. . . . I never met anywhere people who were more wholesome in their attitude toward family, community, government. . . . It was probably not a satisfactory adjustment for the workers, but as good as could be arrived at under the circumstances."[59]

Horton concluded after this experience that any attempt through education to help powerless people gain control of a political unit as small as a county faced almost certain defeat. A county was no match for a state. Only if a broad social movement emerged, would people have a chance to change government fundamentally, he concluded. Since 1939 Highlander has put its energies into education tied to a growing social movement.

4

. . . goodbye, old bosses, we're going on strike . . .

ON JUNE 7, 1937, about 175 mill hands walked out of the Jennings Mill in North Lumberton, North Carolina. With deliberate care, they drove stakes around the entire cotton mill, then tied a rope from stake to stake until the mill was encircled. At the main entrance, they knotted the rope's ends to a tiny American flag. Having done all they knew how to do to form a picket line and having hung the American flag, most of the strikers retired to the shade trees beside the company store to see what would happen. A few went in search of Myles Horton.[1]

In April of that year, Horton had taken a leave of absence from Highlander Folk School to work for the Textile Workers' Organizing Committee. He was one of thirty persons recruited by the union to launch an organizing drive in the South. By 1937, Highlander's staff had a body of understanding gained from working with miners and community citizens. The impetus for leaving Highlander temporarily grew from Horton's desire to learn about organizing and about the lives of textile workers. The textile industry had become a major economic force in the South and was perhaps the single largest source of income for working people. If the nation's unions were going to open an organizing drive in the Southern textile industry, and if Highlander was to fulfill a useful educational role for Southern workers, then, the reasoning at Highlander concluded, the staff had to gain firsthand knowledge about the lives of these workers. Elizabeth Hawes left to work with the Amalgamated Clothing Workers. Horton and Dombrowski left for TWOC. Horton went as an organizer, not an educator. In Lumberton, he learned the differences and strengths of each role.

In May of that year, Horton had organized the first Southern local for TWOC at McColl, South Carolina. It had 1,200 members. He had been working on a second local in Bennettsville when TWOC officials in Atlanta told him to go to Lumberton, where workers were voluntarily signing up members and were being fired for doing so. Horton had been in Lumberton about three weeks prior to the spontaneous Jennings strike on June 7. He was working with Furman Strickland, a former cotton-mill worker, who was also with TWOC.

The small delegation of strikers, led by H. E. Lawson, a weaver, found Horton at the Hotel Lorraine, just off the tree-shaded square dominated by the Robeson County Courthouse, in the heart of Lumberton, the county seat. News of a workers' rising in North Lumberton had not reached downtown. A handful of idlers chatted peacefully on benches. The town's popular drugstore was doing a brisk business; the ladies of Lumberton were sipping Coca-Colas in the medicinal coolness. It was midmorning.

Horton and the strikers' delegates soon left the hotel for North Lumberton. Horton was rapidly reviewing in his mind all he had learned about the town and about Mansfield Mills, Inc., the owners of the struck Jennings Mill.

The only paved street in North Lumberton stopped at Jennings Mill. So did the single water line. There was no sewer. Bare, unpainted frame houses formed neat rows, all located some distance from Lumberton proper. The mill workers, or lintheads as they were called locally, could walk to Lumberton for groceries and supplies or maybe a cowboy movie on Saturday afternoons. Townspeople commonly expressed their belief, however, that millworkers were happier living among their own kind. North Lumberton had a counterpart in East Lumberton, where Mansfield Mill was located; Lumberton proper stood between the two.

Living around the three Lumbertons, here and there, were the blacks. A few of them found work in the mills at segregated, low-paying jobs. Many worked on nearby tobacco farms. For the most part, however, blacks worked as domestics in the big houses edging Lumberton's quiet streets.

Also living in the area were Lumbee Indians. Like blacks, Lumbees worked where and when they could at the discretion of whites. There were separate schools for whites, blacks, and Lumbees. Blacks and Lumbees went to the movies through separate side entrances which led to the balcony of the local theater; whites entered by the front door. Lumbees offered an opportunity for exploitation unique in North Carolina. If poor whites wouldn't take a particular job, employers could usually find blacks who would—and pay them less. In Lumberton, if blacks wouldn't take the unpleasant chores, Indians could be gotten. Such was their poverty.

Although not discriminated against racially, poor whites also were abused by economic exploitation. For example, shortly after Horton got to Lumberton, a company overseer was convicted of violating the Child Labor Act by permitting a fifteen-year-old girl to work the six P.M. to six A.M. shift. For ten nights of work, according to testimony, she was paid $28.05, less than twenty-five cents an hour. Lumberton's Recorder's Court fined the overseer $10.00. He was the young girl's father. But the crime was kept in the family, as was the punishment. His codefendents, O. C. Morehead, general superintendent of Mansfield Mills, and G. V. Pruitt, manager of the mill in which the girl had been victimized, were acquitted of all charges, as were other defendants.[2]

Horton learned that what made the case unusual in Lumberton, and what had caused it to make headlines, was the fact that it had come to trial at all. He and Strickland had been recording similar violations as evidence to prompt National Labor Relations Board hearings, which had been ordered for June 10, three days after the spontaneous shutdown of Jennings Mill.

North Lumberton had been tense since the company first discovered the voluntary organizing effort. A mob of over 200, including the mayor of East Lumberton, who was a mill employee, marched on the house of union leader C. H. Manning. His life was threatened. Later the same night, after the mob left, Manning's house was stoned and his young son felled by a chunk of concrete thrown through a window. In addition, Strickland's car was set upon by a crowd and every window broken as it sat parked outside the Hotel Lorraine. No arrests were made.[3]

But June 7 became the last day for some time that well-to-do Lumbertonians would be assured that lintheads, blacks, and Lumbees were happy-and-content, and in their places. Superintendent Morehead had ordered a stretch-out; that is, the workers were told to do more work in the same time. In this case, twice as much work as usual was demanded. One doffer was given thirty-two frames formerly doffed by two men. Spinners were told to go from ten to twenty sides. Card hands had their work doubled. Slubber hands were given a third slubber to twist and untwist.

Workers told Morehead that they couldn't handle the extra load. He said that they would or they would get out. They left.[4] In his role as organizer, Horton didn't have many options to suggest to the workers once they had set up their picket line. The strike, at that point, had to be consolidated and spread. Unity was the key. There was no use worrying about what consequences the walkout might have on the NLRB hearings. There didn't seem to be any question in the strikers' minds: they wanted union recognition.

Horton and Strickland had been working to persuade the

most prestigious and best-paid mill hands—the mechanics, weavers, and loom fixers—to join the union. Their symbolic value to the less privileged workers was great. These efforts paid off. By eight o'clock the night of June 7, twenty-three mechanics, weavers, and loom fixers closed down another mill belonging to Mansfield Mills, Inc., the Mansfield Mill, in East Lumberton. Within an hour, over 400 workers from Jennings joined them. They threw up a human picket line and set forth their demands: the stretch-out at Jennings must end immediately; those fired for union activity must be rehired; the union must be recognized.

The spirits of the strikers were high. There was singing on the picket line. Millworkers poured out grievances that had silently accumulated during the years they had worked for Mansfield Mills, Inc. They retold stories from other strikes they had been through. A few of them had been in Gastonia, North Carolina, in 1929, when the company and the state had suppressed a strike by combining forces. Ella Mae Wiggins had been shot and killed there, leaving five children, and becoming one of the South's early labor martyrs. One of the supervisors of that Gastonia mill had been O. G. Morehead, who was now the boss at Mansfield Mills.

That first night, most of the strikers stayed on the picket line all night. Sensing that there probably would be no confrontations and realizing that there would be busy days ahead, Horton went back to the hotel about midnight. Around three o'clock the next morning he was awakened by a commotion on the square. Some North Carolina highway patrolmen were assembled for predawn instructions before leaving for the struck mills. They were armed with machine guns. Horton overheard the patrol commander say, "We'll just have to break this thing up," before dismissing the troops for breakfast at the hotel.[5]

Horton dressed and hurried to the mill. Several hundred people were still there. Explaining the highway patrol's preparations, he urged them to go home and stay there. He asked strike leaders to send back a big American flag, their prettiest daughters, and some people who could play the guitar or banjo. When the highway patrol arrived in their silver-tinted coupés, they found not a mob, but a group singing union songs around a campfire. The American flag waved over the placid scene.[6]

The girls sidled up to the police cars and asked innocent questions: What were the patrolmen doing there? Who asked them to come? Were they going to help the strikers? Would they go on the picket line? Within an hour, the highway patrol had left.

The next day there was another massive picket line. Nearly every workingman stayed outside the mill, with his family. The highway patrol wasn't seen. The third day, most of the strikers went to the National Labor Relations Board hearings, but the highway patrol checked the mill and found more pretty girls and a few singing pickets.[7] This routine kept up until the highway patrol apparently got tired of responding to calls from the company that a mob had arrived, or from the sheriff that the situation was out of hand.

The strikers regarded the trick on the patrolmen as good fun. It served to increase unity and to swell membership. Nearly 70 per cent of them had signed cards requesting union representation.

The company reacted by getting Governor Clyde Hoey to keep the highway patrol at the mills indefinitely. They brought scabs from across state lines. Telegrams from company officials were sent to employees at other mills, offering good jobs and high wages.[8] The scabs went to work guarded by armed highway patrolmen on each shift.

None of the scabs were black. This was unusual in the thirties, but so was a visit Horton had received during the strike's first hours. A group of black workers at the Jennings Mill told him:

"Mr. Horton, you've got a lot to do. You just please keep away from our end of this thing and just let us take care of that."[9] Horton was puzzled. At first, he feared the blacks might have been hired as scabs. He wanted the union to serve all workers, but he didn't want trouble between the races. This would be a setback for the union. His suspicions were groundless. No black accepted a job during the strike, and none crossed the picket lines. They all stayed away from work. How they managed, Horton never learned. They never sent another delegation.

To retaliate against the use of scabs and give the highway patrol a headache, Horton hit upon a spoof that the strikers quickly approved. He used his hotel telephone, which he knew to be tapped, to send the patrol on fruitless nighttime rides. He would call union friends in McColl and ask them to bring in four or five truckloads of people to bar the scabs from the mills. As prearranged, his friends would say, "Yes, we'll bring them into East Lumberton on back roads at 3:00 A.M." About 2:30 A.M., each time the stunt was pulled, the highway patrol would roar off in their silver cars to chase phantom truckloads of workers.

The troops would return to the Hotel Lorraine at breakfast time, facing another long day of guarding the mills, to find Horton sipping coffee and reading the morning newspapers. The strikers found the routine hilarious, and kept the secret. But tricks don't win strikes. The scabs were coming to work in increasing numbers. Production began to climb, although not as fast as the company apparently wished.

On June 18, Horton was arrested for the second time in his life. Sheriff Mark Page said that seven strikers, urged on by Horton, had, two days before, stabbed H. B. Willoughby, a non-striker, as the afternoon shift changed. All eight were jailed briefly, and released on bonds of $100.00 for Horton and $25.00 for each of the others. At the Recorder's Court trial,

Horton denied aiding and abetting the fracas. Judge Leslie J. Huntley delayed a decision for one week after hearing evidence.[10] Three days after the trial, a nonstriker was arrested for hitting Horton as he talked with a newsman at the picket line.[11] On June 30, Judge Huntley convicted Horton of aiding and abetting in the stabbing. He was given a thirty-day jail term, which was suspended for one year on good behavior and payment of $15.00 and court costs. Two men, James Chandler and W. R. Lamb, were convicted of assault. The other defendants were acquitted.[12] All appealed to Superior Court, where the cases were thrown out months later.

In the meantime, the company asked for a court injunction prohibiting strikers from standing within fifty feet of the mills, barring Horton from being near the mills, and making him personally liable for any trouble that occurred there. Horton asked Osborne Lee, a Lumberton lawyer, who had represented TWOC in most of the union's cases, to contest the injunction. Horton wanted to enjoin the City of Lumberton, and Robeson County, and the State of North Carolina against any interference with the civil rights of the workers and himself. He based his argument on the right of peaceful assembly. Lee felt the case was legally too unique and refused it. Horton contacted W. H. Abernathy, the lawyer who had helped defend the Gastonia strikers. Reluctantly, Abernathy took the case.

On June 30, both the company and the union appeared before Judge N. A. Sinclair in Superior Court. He heard arguments for both injunctions. The courtroom was packed with strikers. Horton wanted each of them to testify, which would have taken weeks—just as Horton well knew. Judge Sinclair ordered that depositions be taken from four or five of the men, ruling that they could speak for all. Judge Sinclair did not take a deposition from Horton.

Judgment was as Horton hoped. Both parties were denied

injunctions. Judge Sinclair said, "Any injunction should never be issued except when relief can be furnished by no other means. It has not been made to appear that the law enforcement officers of the state have exhausted their power to preserve the peace in East Lumberton, and the court cannot assume that the state is so weak and helpless it cannot enforce its own laws without application to court of equity."[13]

Judge Sinclair's decision was a battle won for the union, but, clearly, it was losing the war. Scabs continued to run the looms. Morale was high, but the union's funds were running low. Time was on the company's side. Moreover, the strikers were worried about "their" looms and the damage which the inexperienced scabs might do.

Hatred and anxiety spilled over on July 6. Fifteen strikers broke from the picket line and raced into the Mansfield Mill behind the scabs.[14] Company guards had no time to lock the doors. When the scabs realized what had happened, they started coming out through windows and doors. From outside, Horton couldn't tell whether the scabs were being thrown out or were fleeing under their own steam. Inside, the unarmed strikers went from loom to loom yelling at the scabs to get away from "their" machines. In the melee, one strapping Indian belted a highway patrolman with such force that the man was somersaulted down a flight of stairs into the arms of other startled patrolmen.[15]

When the lint settled, twenty-five strikers had been arrested for trespassing. In the trial which followed, all charges were nol prossed.[16]

Lumberton hadn't seen the end of the turmoil initiated by Morehead's stretch-out order. On the morning of July 8, between 300 and 400 strikers showed up at the local welfare office, crowding it so thickly that the front porch caved in.[17]

The strikers had been reduced to a steady diet of beans. Welfare aid, to which strikers were entitled, was difficult to get. The county welfare director refused to accept the union's list for welfare certification. Each needy person had to come to her office in person to be certified, she told union leaders. Appeals to Washington had apparently fallen on deaf ears. The strikers decided to beat the director at her own game. They all showed up at once for certification.

Harassed welfare officials first called the police, who were powerless to move the crowd in or out of the building. They pleaded with the union president to disperse the crowd. He said he was there only to get certification for food for his family. No one budged.

The strikers won. That afternoon a welfare official from Raleigh, the state capital, arrived to negotiate with the union. Within hours, four truckloads of food were available for distribution. The next day a crew of Raleigh social workers came to help the Lumberton officials certify the strikers in groups of fifty. WPA food for fifty-four families arrived on July 12.[18]

To protect and extend the growing sense of solidarity, the union, still unrecognized by the company, began holding mass meetings every night except Sunday. It was the biggest show in town. Over 2,000 strikers, their families and friends, the curious, company officials, a few scabs, the highway patrol, who were keeping an eye on things, and the local police attended. Every night union leaders welcomed the press and thanked the lawmen for coming. Mill village youngsters played guitars and sang, mostly religious songs, but popular and union songs too. There was buck dancing. There was speaking: union men came up from McColl; CIO officials came down from Charlotte. But mostly, Horton, the organizer, talked about their circumstances: how long they had worked without raises, how bad their working conditions were, and why they had the right to union recognition—the last being the only basic legal issue at stake.

Some nights Horton gave short courses on labor history. He illustrated the principles of political action by pointing to the sheriff, saying that here was a good reason strikers should register to vote. They needed a man who would take their side, instead of the company's. He pointed to the highway patrolmen. Their presence in Lumberton by order of the governor demonstrated why the workers should elect a labor governor, he argued. He explained the Wage and Hour Law, currently before Congress, and discussed international labor problems.

Soon, however, strike leaders ran the speakings, a sign of their growing self-assurance. The nightly meetings and other union activities increased the resentment that had been growing in Lumberton. Company officials asked ministers to speak against the union and Horton. A young Episcopal minister, who had been to Highlander while a student at the University of the South in Sewanee, near Monteagle, told Horton of the request. But Horton wrote Dombrowski, "We have had practically no trouble with preachers here in Lumberton. Once during the strike the company got a Holiness preacher to preach about a hundred yards from where I had announced a union meeting. I sent all our people to hear him with instructions to pass the word around that there would be a union speaking immediately afterwards and to bring the crowd with them. We had one of the largest crowds we ever had before."[19]

A day or so later, Horton got the visit most Southern union organizers received in those days. About midafternoon, he heard a shout outside his hotel window. Just below was a carload of four men he had never seen before. They were armed, drinking, and, strangely, alone. The town square was empty. No cars moved along the street. The Lumberton police, who usually clustered around the courthouse, weren't to be seen.

"Damned Communist!" one of the men yelled. "We're going to get you!"

Horton figured his time had come. Suddenly, he remembered a long-barreled six-shooter which a Holiness preacher who worked in the mills had given him when he first came to town. Despite Horton's claim that he didn't know how to use a gun and would rather not have one for fear it might cause trouble, the preacher had insisted that he keep it. Horton raced to the dresser, got the pistol, and went back to the window, fearful he would shoot himself accidentally.

"Okay," he called to the men below, "I'm ready for you." He let the gun barrel glint in the window. "But it won't be as easy as you think. You've got to come in the hallway, you've got to come in the room, and I'm going to protect myself."

They laughed, one shouting back that protection wouldn't do much good. They got in their car and drove around the empty block. When they returned, one asked, "You want to write a letter or your last words and testimony?"

"Yeah, there's one thing I like to do more than anything, and that's to organize people so they can do things for themselves. I think it would be good for me to organize you fellows right now."

The four men nearly bent double laughing.

"No, it's not funny," Horton called, letting the pistol glint again. "Everybody needs organizing."

"This mill didn't need organizing," one shouted back. "This town doesn't need organizing. We don't want people like you. We are the last people who want to be organized."

"You are the people who need it most," Horton called back, thankful he'd gotten them to talking. "If you aren't organized, you are going to have a problem. One of the four of you is going to kill me. There's no question about it. But I'm going to kill at least one of you, maybe two. Now you've got to get organized so you can decide which one of you is going to be dead in a few minutes. You have to decide how this thing is going to be worked out."

Silence followed.

Horton hammered on: "You, beside the car. Do you want to die? Are you going to be dead in five minutes? Or you, next to him? Which one of you fellows is ready to die?"

No one answered.

"Now, I'll get two of you, and I might get three. One of you will get me. Now, if I can help you get organized so you can decide which is the one person that is sure to get me, and the other three who may get killed, and who's going to get killed first, then we can get on with this business."

The men wavered. They got in their car and left. Horton says that was the best organizing speech he ever made.[20]

But still the strike went on. The union seemed to be winning the right to represent workers but losing its solidarity and income. Some strikers, to put food on the table, had taken other jobs in Lumberton. Others had left to work in mills elsewhere. The scabs were running the mills at near capacity. Manpower was dwindling on the picket lines. Pressure was mounting, especially from the local businessmen, whose income had fallen off. As the days went on, some of the strikers came to feel that Horton and the local leaders should have been able to settle the strike sooner.

Ironically, the company provided the solution. Late in July, they advertised in the local newspaper for the strikers to come back to work. Although the ad was intended to make the strikers look bad before a second National Labor Relations Board hearing, which was in the planning stages, Horton urged them to go back to work. His position was accepted at a Sunday evening rally: they had to go back to work to keep the union strong; the organization of the union, and its perpetuation, would be their victory. Some said they'd been sold out; others cried. In the end, Horton's strategy prevailed.

The morning of August 2, union members entered the mill long before any scabs appeared.[21] When the scabs showed up, they demanded to go to work. Horton saw some of them thrown out of windows, but only a few. Most left by the front door. Within a week, all the scabs were gone. Then the union people started to carry out Horton's strategy. Sometimes they worked; sometimes they didn't. Looms operated by nonunion men broke down without apparent reason. Threads broke constantly on "some" workers, while others whizzed along. One harassed foreman asked union leaders what was wrong. They told him that 70 per cent of the employees belonged to the union, 30 per cent didn't. "We don't mind losing the strike," they said, "and we aren't going to do anything to hurt nonmembers. But our hearts aren't in it. We just don't have any enthusiasm for working with nonmembers."[22]

Soon, a quota chart appeared in the mill, with an honor roll for those who made the quotas set by the company. Within a few days, it became apparent that only union members made their quotas. Nonunion workers, no matter how expert or skilled, never made it. They couldn't get any cooperation. Before another week had passed, the foreman was back, asking what the union wanted. "A contract," the leaders replied bluntly. "We are going to stay right here. We're not going to strike and we're not going to leave the mill. But you don't get any production, unless we get a contract."

By the end of January, the union and the company had negotiated an agreement for a consent election, which was to be conducted by the National Labor Relations Board to determine if TWOC should represent the workers as their sole bargaining agent in matters pertaining to wages, hours, and working conditions.[23]

Horton left town before the election was held. He was confident that what had begun with a rope tied around a mill would end with ink on a dotted line.

The Lumberton strike was never immortalized in labor legend or song. Nonetheless, events there changed Horton's mind about education and, thus, changed Highlander.

The strike was a means to an end. For the workers, it was the way to get better pay and safer working conditions. To the extent that they united, they won concessions. To hold their gains, workers had to stay united, stay on the job, and stay in Lumberton. They would, therefore, have few opportunities to teach others how to win a strike. For Horton, the strike was a way to learn how to perfect organizations and to spark enthusiasm for working-class emancipation. Before Lumberton, he felt that, through organization and zeal, there was a possibility that a working-class social movement might emerge and transform society. After Lumberton, he knew that working on one strike at a time severely limited this possibility.

A social movement is more than one strike, and more than one or two determined leaders. A movement is many risings by many people who revolt at being treated like machines, as the Jennings Mill employees had rebelled at Morehead's stretch-out order.

As an organizer, Horton found he'd been forced to take a more direct part in the strike than he had wanted. This went against his grain, not because he minded a good fight, but because the more he did, the less the strikers did for themselves. Horton didn't want to run a union, or any other organization. He wanted people to learn how to run them, to control them, and to use them to carry out their own aims. He had been struggling with this problem when he asked the court to take depositions from all strikers. He had arranged to have so many strikers come to court for two reasons: to testify and to see courts in operation. He wanted the strikers to learn how to tell lawyers what they wanted directly, not through a spokesman.

Related to this was Horton's personal involvement in the union's decision-making process. The workers had decided to strike on their own. Horton, as an organizer, had sought to find ways to help them learn how to run their strike on their own. He had carefully set up committees charged with the responsibility for welfare, recreation, and the strike itself. But the people weren't practiced in making decisions. No matter how many times he told them that their union would be only as strong as their decisions made it, they had placed great store on his "expert" advice. He had rarely taken part in committee work. He had offered suggestions, pointed out alternatives, and furnished additional information. He had never pushed a committee. Nevertheless, he had carried more weight than the local leaders—by being the organizer, the authority.

For example, the strike committee was meeting at a time when many strikers felt the company would win. The committee was unable, after hours of talk, to agree on what steps to take next. Horton kept to himself. As the meeting wore on, the men turned to him for ideas. "My answer might be better than yours," he said, "or it might be worse. But it would just be one man's answer. If I make this decision, what will you do when I'm not here and you are faced with tough decisions?"[24]

The hour was late. The meeting had gone on and on. One man started crying. Suddenly, one of the strikers pulled a pistol on Horton. "You son of a bitch," he yelled, "you *are* going to tell us what to do!"

Horton was too startled to move. Other committee members grabbed the gun from the man and sat him down. Eventually, as tempers cooled, the committee reached a decision, learning, in the process, that they could.

The mass meetings bothered him, too, even though they

seemed to be a great success and were well attended. No organizer in those days, and few now, would fail to use the union-building potential of mass meetings. Group singing brings people out of the silences of their individuality, especially when they are hard-working people conditioned to "yessir" and "nosir" the boss day after day. Having most of the speaking done by people known and trusted—the weaver H. E. Lawson, or people like the strikers, the workers from McColl—ultimately spurred the union's growth to nearly 2,000 members. People talked about the speakings in their homes and looked forward to them. That was education, Horton concluded, mass education.

Precisely because it was mass education, Horton saw its limitations. Mass meetings could not be made up of people with a single common purpose. Not all the people who came to meetings had walked the picket line. Not everyone got to speak. The organizer could not select who would come once the flyers went out. An educator could.

If the only people invited to Highlander were those who were learning to define their interests and who were already committed to struggle against oppression, then, Horton reasoned, education at Highlander would be more effective.

Horton, at Lumberton, learned again how much conflict is present in the lives of poor people, and the value of conflict as a tool for education. The well-educated, the middle class, and particularly persons of good will, usually find a way to talk away conflict. Horton had done that at the window of the Hotel Lorraine. Conflict is a daily reality in the lives of powerless people. They are kept at work they don't like by the force of economic necessity. If they buck, they are fired. Saturday night brawls are interpreted as a way to let off steam, settle grudges, prove manhood. When well-intentioned people rule out conflict as a way for poor people collectively to solve problems, they ignore the facts of life. They limit the options of poor people and hinder the flowering of real self-determination, Horton concluded.

Horton has never taught people how to use violence, nor has any Highlander staff member. He still can't twirl a pistol. Highlander staff members have armed themselves, but only to protect their right to be at Highlander when others have attacked. The strike in Lumberton taught Highlander the necessity of basing education on an understanding of the nature of peoples' lives, instead of dictating what their lives should be. What Horton really learned in Lumberton was that he wanted to educate, not organize, and that education had to recognize the fundamental ways by which people live, and to change as those ways changed.

5

. . . a singing army . . .

HIGHLANDER JOINED the Southern union movement when it was "a singing army," as John L. Lewis, president of the United Mine Workers, described it in an introduction to a 1939 Highlander songbook.[1] His phrase sums up Highlander's work after Lumberton.

First enliven, then enlighten had been one of Kristen Kold's maxims as he helped the Danish folk high schools to flourish. The Highlander staff, especially two women, took Kold's maxim and translated it into a practical educational program that sent countless new leaders into the fight to build unions. Years later, a veteran of Southern union and civil rights struggles, Jim Pierce, executive director of the National Sharecroppers Fund, said, "I got the inspiration and the skills for what I've been able to do at Highlander away back in 1950."[2]

At Highlander music enlivened. Classes on specific union problems enlightened. Singing together and giving plays had equal importance at Highlander residential workshops with courses on contract negotiation, parliamentary law, public speaking, or union problems. Nearly one hundred labor plays were written by Highlander staff members or students between 1935 and 1952, and countless songs about working-class struggles were compiled. To count the number of weekend workshops, two-week institutes, two- and three-day conferences held at Highlander during these years by aluminum, garment, auto, mine, textile, rubber, pecan, farm, teamster, and other unions would be almost impossible. At Highlander, in contrast to other workers' education centers, these meetings were part of each union's ongoing work, not just brief educational respites. Highlander students were always in the thick of strikes, organizing educational and recreational activities. A Labor Chatauqua, founded at Highlander, toured the South for a short while.[3] Local union leaders saw the value of Highlander. They sent promising workers to the school and came frequently themselves as guest speakers or resource persons for particular classes. The hosiery workers from Tennessee, Georgia, and Alabama convened in 1938 and noted in a resolution "that education has already been carried on, particularly in the tri-state area, in cooperation with the Highlander Folk School and that it should be a vital part of the union, as much a part of the union activities as the holding of a meeting."[4]

Two staff members who played important roles in the development of Highlander's labor education program were Zilphia Mae Horton and Mary Lawrence.

Zilphia Mae Johnson, the daughter of an Arkansas coal mine owner, first came to Highlander to study at the suggestion of Claude Williams, then pastor of the Presbyterian church in Paris, Arkansas. Shortly after her arrival on March 6, 1935, she and Myles Horton were married. She directed most of the school's work with music and drama during the labor period. She organized group-singing sessions at workshops and taught union songs on picket lines. She wrote and collected labor songs and chants that were used throughout the nation.[5]

She had studied music at the College of the Ozarks and possessed a special quality of warmth which enabled her to relate to differing people. She could help people forget their personal problems and, at the same time, help them understand the problems of others. People who wouldn't usually sing with strangers would sing with her. There was a quality about her that inspired trust.

John Handcock, a member of the Tenant Farmers Union,

taught Zilphia a song he had sung with blacks called "No More Mourning":

> No more mourning, no more mourning,
> no more mourning after while,
> And before I'll be a slave, I'll be
> buried in my grave.
> Take my place with those who loved
> and fought before.[6]

With Zilphia's help, Handcock's song spread throughout the South.

Huddie Ledbetter, called Leadbelly, thick and stocky from years of hard work and prison in New Orleans, was a superb folk singer, who was the first to popularize the twelve-string guitar. He met and sang with Zilphia. In 1941, they gave a benefit in Washington, D.C., to raise money for Highlander. The song Zilphia encouraged Ledbetter to introduce that night, "Bourgeois Blues," became a classic:

> Me and my wife ran all over town,
> Everywhere we went the people
> would turn us down.
> Lawd, Lawd it's a bourgeois town,
> I got the bourgeois blues,
> I'm gonna spread the news all
> around.
>
> Me and Martha was standing
> upstairs,
> I heard the white landlord say "We don't
> want no nigger up there."
> Lawd, Lawd he's a bourgeois man.
>
> Land of the brave, home of the free,
> I tell you folks, listen to me.
> Don't try to buy no home in
> Washington, D.C.[7]

The songs Zilphia found most useful to Highlander's work, and the labor movement, were those sung by hard-pressed people fighting for a better life. She wrote about such a song:

> Down at Chattanooga some clothing workers had organized and asked for recognition. The company refused and they went out on strike. They asked us to come down from Monteagle to help them with handbills and keeping the strike going. It was decided to have a Washington's birthday parade since the workers felt they were striking for freedom—economic freedom.
>
> There was a minister in the parade. A band. Children and strikers. We were marching two by two behind the band and when we marched by the mill, they opened up on us with a machinegun. Several people were hit. The woman on my left [Highlander's librarian, Hilda Hulbert] was hit in the ankle.
>
> I looked around and the police had disappeared. There had been quite a few of them around, too. One was lying in a ditch. I said to him, "What are you doing there?" He said, "Well, lady, I've got a wife and three kids!" In about five minutes after the firing stopped, a few of us stood up at the mill gates and started singing "We Shall Not Be Moved." And in about ten minutes, people began to come out from behind the barns and little stores around there, and we stood and sang "We Shall Not Be Moved." That's what won them recognition. That's what a song means in many places. That song is almost a labor hymn.[8]

People often came to Zilphia for help in writing songs or improving parts that didn't seem to fit. She would sit down at the piano or take up an accordion, then, note by note, phrase by phrase, help them discover the tunes or words that were buried in themselves. During a strike in Harriman, Tennessee, a hosiery worker named Hershel Phillips, wrote "The Union Call." Zilphia helped him polish it a bit, and the song was widely used.

She immediately recognized the powerful quality of a song that two union members brought from Charleston, South Carolina. (Sadly, for the credit due them and for Highlander's history, there is no record of the names of those two strikers.) She and Pete Seeger, a folk singer who frequently visited Highlander, modified the words and tune slightly, and "We Shall Overcome" was created.

Zilphia has expressed her own feeling about music:

> Music is the language of and to life. Music has been too generally thought of as an art form for leisure time, performed and enjoyed by and for the chosen few. The people can be made aware that many of the songs about their everyday lives—songs about their work, hopes, their joys and sorrows—are songs of merit. This gives them a new sense of dignity and pride in their cultural heritage. Their lives can be enriched also by learning folk songs of other nationalities. The folk song grows out of reality. It is this stark reality and genuineness which gives the folk song vitality and strength . . . .[9]

Zilphia and Myles Horton lived simply when they were first married. Together, they built a one-room log cabin on Highlander property, a long walk through the woods from the main building. They carried water from a brook, where they also bathed, even in winter. A fireplace of native stone provided heat, and cutting wood furnished physical exercise for a couple who spent most of their lives at tasks of the mind. In 1936, Zilphia ended a letter to Myles, who was off at a conference, by telling him, "Oh, yes. John, Hoyle, and I are going squirrel hunting Monday morning. I shot a cigarette in the center the other day, sort of restored my self-respect."[10]

When their children came along, Thorsten in 1943 and Charis in 1945, the Hortons had to change their style of living. They moved from the woods to a larger cabin nearer the center. They had running water and a telephone. Like their first house, it was spare, but, because of the children, it grew. Eventually, Thorsten and Charis shared in planning the additions.

Like students at Highlander, the Horton children were encouraged to take part in and learn from the world around them. Books were not the only source of education, nor were adults. In the cooperative nursery Highlander formed, the Horton children learned from other children.

On the other hand, Highlander was not a family school. No children were permitted in workshops, conferences, or classes. Their presence distracted the adults and impeded the learning process. There was always a staff member in the kitchen or the office to keep an eye on the children. Elsie and Perry Horton had moved to Summerfield by then, and, when necessary, filled the traditional role of grandparents.

"We never pretended or played like we were children, or that we had interests limited to the interests of children," Horton says. "Zilphia enjoyed singing children's songs and both of us enjoyed playing some children's games. Things we didn't like, and couldn't do naturally with them, we didn't do."[11]

When Thorsten became interested in mountain lore and hunting, he sought out J. D. Marlowe and Henry Dyer, both famed as hunters in those parts. "He knew I didn't know anything about hunting," Horton says, "so he didn't waste his time asking me to teach him. He went to the experts."[12] When Thorsten wanted to learn to swim, however, he went to his father, whom he had seen teaching others.

Their lives were not idyllic. Charis suffered severe burns when her dress caught fire during a lawn party. A single candle engulfed her in flames. She ran to the room where Horton was running a workshop and fell screaming into his arms. He swept the fire off by running both hands down her body and wrapping her quickly in a rug. She was hospitalized with little hope of recovery, but, with the aid of extensive grafts, physical therapy, and perseverance, she eventually recuperated. Two years earlier, when she was four, Charis had been felled by polio, and doctors feared she would never walk again. Today, as a result of extended medical care and a strong will, she can walk, and without visible effect of the disease.

Thorsten couldn't seem to learn to read. He complained that "the words pull apart."[13] Despite test after test, no firm diagnosis was ever made, so no workable cure was ever prescribed. Although he eventually outgrew the disability, it kept him out of conventional schools much of his life.

Throughout their good times and bad at Highlander, the Hortons learned to share work and responsibilities, not for expediency, but on principle. At times the method caused problems. When Horton was subpoenaed in 1954 by the Eastland Committee to testify about his knowledge of the Red menace which the Mississippi senator saw sweeping the South, the Hortons conferred with their children about Myles' testimony. The position he planned to take, that he would testify only about his own beliefs and actions, could result in his going to jail for contempt of Congress, maybe for a year. Thorsten and Charis agreed that he had to uphold principle. With characteristic practicality, they even started planning projects to help him pass the time in jail and figuring out ways to keep in touch with him. As it turned out, the children's plans were unnecessary.

Two years after the Eastland hearings, in 1956, tragedy again struck the Horton family. On April 11, Zilphia died of uremic poisoning in Vanderbilt Hospital, Nashville, after a brief, painful illness. Had the operation been perfected, a kidney transplant might have saved her life. Horton's recollection of Zilphia's last days reflects the quality of their relationship:

> When we realized she wouldn't live, we spent the last few days alone. She was calm. We talked about the good times we had, and the problems, and the fun together. She regretted we could not do the many things we had planned together. She felt she had lived a useful life, and hoped she left behind some things which would con-

tinue to be useful. But, most of all, she talked about the children. She wished she could see them grow and develop as creative, happy people living for something worthwhile and enjoying life as we had done.

Her calmness at the end held me together, even when the doctor told me she was dead. Two hours later, the doctor came into the room again and told me gently I had cried enough. My sister had been waiting for me for a long time, he said. He gave me some sedatives, and I went home with Elsie Pearl. The next morning, I left her home in Murfreesboro for Monteagle. I took Thorsten and Charis down by the side of the lake and told them Zilphia had died. After a few sobs, they wanted to know what she had said about them. I told them, "Zilphia told me that she wanted Charis to be Charis, and Thorsten to be Thorsten, and Myles to be Myles." Those were her last words.[14]

Thorsten and his cousin, Butchie Garant, published a mimeographed newspaper on April 15, the day of Zilphia's funeral. The paper showed life continuing. Highlander's summer calendar was printed, showing a rural adults' school set for June, a furniture workers' school for the first of July, and three workshops on school desegregation for July and early August. They reported on the progress being made in developing a lake at the school. "J. D. (Marlowe) says his fish wall will be finished in about four more days. The lake will be filled up in two weeks if the weather is what it's been lately." They carried a poem by May Justus, entitled "A Song for Zilphia":

So many songs we wrote, my dear,
Some old now, some still new;
I wish that I might write one more,
One just for you.

The music that your music made for me
Was like a singing bird's:
How can I make a song for you
With only words?

But you who knew, still know, I think
The right note from the wrong;
Take this and make for friendship's sake
Your own sweet song![15]

Finally, the boys wrote an obituary.

Zilphia Horton died Thursday night around 9:30 P.M. Her funeral was held at four o'clock P.M. All her friends were there. Butch Garant and Thorsten W. Horton took pictures of the funeral. Thorsten W. Horton and Doc Paine picked wild flowers for the funeral. Everyone in the room saw her and cried. We all went to the graveyard and saw her put in her grave. The preacher gave a wonderful sermon for her. May Justus wrote a poem for her which is in this newspaper. Aubrey Williams gave a speech, both were unrehersted [sic]. The funeral was at Highlander Folk School where the walls were covered with wild flowers. The Horton family walked to their house from the graveyard and had supper."[16]

Anguish overcame Horton after the funeral: "I went into a tailspin and was unable to pull myself together. Thanks to Zilphia's sister and her mother, Mrs. Guy Johnson, and my sister and her family and Mom Horton, life for the kids went on."[17]

Saul Alinsky, the Chicago organizer, heard of his friend's despair. A year or so before, his own wife had drowned while rescuing their daughter. Alinsky, knowing what Horton was suffering, telephoned to insist that he come to Chicago to work on an application for funds that Highlander was planning to submit to a foundation. He also wanted Horton to complete a report on the use of an earlier grant from the same foundation. That document, he told Horton, was due in just ten days because of a rescheduling of the foundation's board of directors' meeting.

Horton went to Chicago and worked with Alinsky night and

day on both the grant application and the report. The deadline came closer and closer, yet everything that Horton wrote Alinsky rejected. It wasn't what the foundation would want, Alinsky kept saying. Highlander was desperately short of funds; Horton had to finish and finish well.

Finally, in the early hours of the day when the foundation was supposed to meet, Alinsky told Horton that what he had written was acceptable and would be in the hands of a secretary in time. He confessed that the meeting was still weeks away. The deadline had never been advanced, he said. But Horton had been moved away from grief by a man whose gentleness seemed masked by a flint-hard facade.

Mary Lawrence, like Zilphia Horton, helped set Highlander's patterns for educational work with unions. She took education to the workers rather than bringing workers to education. She was the daughter of a Reading, Pennsylvania, doctor. She came to Highlander in 1938 shortly after graduating from Duke University, where she had been a leader in YWCA activities. Through Highlander she got her first experience in the union movement, first as an office worker for a teamster's local in Louisville, Kentucky, then with the Workers' Education Committee of Louisville, then with a textile workers' local, where she helped to start a mimeographed newspaper. The teamster president's notion of education was to make speeches. Not many workers were interested in the education committee. Mary became convinced that education should be organized "only where there is a demand for classes and where you have succeeded in organizing a program for the whole membership." Any education should take place "with the growth of the union."[18]

In 1940, the aluminum workers' local in Alcoa, Tennessee, asked Highlander for help in stimulating interest in the union among new members. Mary Lawrence was given the job that summer. She persuaded the local executive committee to add a string band and skits on labor by a young drama group to the regular business agenda. She got a shop paper going. But little endured of her efforts. The paper folded when she left.

A less dedicated person might have become discouraged by these experiences. Mary learned from them and was sent to New Orleans, where CIO membership had boomed from 675 in 1939 to 15,000 two years later. At the suggestion of Matt Lynch, who had been a student at Highlander and was then on its executive council, Fred Pieper, the CIO regional director, had asked Highlander to help him start a program to develop leadership among new members.[19]

Mary Lawrence worked the program out. Soon after her arrival, she formed a representative, interracial committee of local leaders to arrange meetings and draft programs for the Industrial Union Council. This group identified as their first priority training for local officers in the skills necessary to keep the burgeoning unions together. Mary developed a curriculum to suit the needs of each local. After various kinds of courses were approved by the Industrial Union Council Education Committee, she took the suggestions to the executive committees of the individual locals. Once they had approved the proposed courses, as a final test of their usefulness, she would demonstrate them during meetings of the union locals. Through this procedure, she ascertained what members really wanted to learn—union history, grievance-processing, labor problems, parliamentary law, or publicity.

She also set up a month-long officers' training school. Real situations were used for teaching. If a local president had a speech to make, he and the entire class worked on the outline. If a president was weak or inexperienced at running meetings, he was asked to conduct a class on how to run meetings. Whatever they learned, they were expected to take back to their locals to use—and teach others.

For example, a sugar workers' local in Reserve, Louisiana, faced with upcoming contract negotiations, studied other contracts, taking clauses or ideas from them which suited their needs. They wrote the first contract proposal, and justified its demands for higher wages by making a cost of living survey. They got what they wanted.

Mary Lawrence used the union meeting itself—not classes—as the place for her work. Too many union members, she found, were leery of education. "The best education is carried on within the framework of the union structure itself," she wrote.[20] She attended hosiery workers' meetings and noted with the officers afterwards the mistakes in parliamentary procedure they had made. She taught furniture workers how to draw signs at the site of picket lines. She talked with shop stewards in the shops.

Promising union leaders were invited to Highlander for residential workshops. Mary wrote a weekly column for labor newspapers on the importance of education and helped found legislative committees in the locals so that members would be acquainted with political candidates and issues. She wrote a handbook, *How to Build Your Union*, which was widely used.

In 1947, she assessed her work in New Orleans in a paper entitled "A Study of the Methods and Results of Workers' Education in the South."[21] She found that of the twenty-four union members from New Orleans who went to Highlander between 1941 and 1942, eighteen continued to be active in union affairs. Seven of them were full-time organizers or business agents.

Mary organized similar programs in Atlanta, Louisville, and Knoxville. By 1944, she was running educational programs in Memphis for rubber, auto, steel, textile, and chemical unions. About 1,200 union members regularly participated. Later that year, she was named education director for the CIO in Tennessee.

Looking back in 1942 over ten years of workers' education, a Highlander report noted, "About ninety per cent of Highlander's alumni are international union officials, local union officials, or organizers in the South. Last year alone, the number of students trained in resident, community, or extension classes totaled 425."[22] On Thanksgiving weekend in 1945, over a hundred alumni held a reunion at Highlander. They represented more than twenty internationals in Georgia, Alabama, North and South Carolina, Louisiana, Tennessee, and Arkansas. After one resident term that same year, the president of an oil workers' local from El Dorado, Arkansas, wrote, "My union sent me to Highlander to get and bring back to it the knowledge and spirit of unionism which is not to be obtained elsewhere. If I am able to take back to them only a small part of the fire, enthusiasm, and militancy which has been instilled in me here, I will consider it a job well done."[23]

Just as it seemed that Highlander and the labor movement were permanently joined, there were hints that their unity was coming unglued. Mary Lawrence's leaving to take a job with the CIO was one indication. Another was the power struggle going on in the CIO for control of the organization. This fight diminished the organization's early militancy and vigor. The goal of working-class emancipation was being submerged beneath a bureaucratic struggle for power. By 1949, an organization which had thrived on upsetting the apple cart was fearful that its own bottom might overturn its top.

Horton speculates that the split between Highlander and the unions may have resulted because many of their shared goals had been accomplished. Union membership had increased across the South. Maintenance of membership clauses in contracts, plus the rules of the War Labor Board, added stability to that membership. Wages were up. Union integration was on the upswing.

But where, asked Highlander staffers, was the political consciousness of the workers? Not a single union local whose members were to make the atomic bomb at Oak Ridge, Tennessee—or elsewhere—uttered a word of protest against that terrible bomb. Pacifist members of the Workers Defense League planned a 1946 demonstration at Oak Ridge. They were forced to call it off when local CIO officials declared the demonstration "would do irreparable harm" to the organizing drive they were conducting among the atomic workers. The union told the league that, if they persisted, the union would be "forced to take drastic measures to denounce your program, which we would not like to do."[24]

Highlander staffers wondered why Walter Reuther's aides, who were planning his Southern campaign for re-election as the UAW president, invited only white local leaders to a strategy meeting at Highlander—and that only two years after the UAW's vanguard decision to send both black and white workers to Highlander for leadership development! The staff did not learn that no blacks had been invited until about an hour after the strategy session had convened. A black union leader arrived late, uninvited, but determined to attend. The Highlander staff decided to break into the UAW meeting with an ultimatum to integrate or leave before the next meal.[25]

The UAW conferees complied, but compounded their original hypocrisy in the next issue of the national UAW newspapers. On the front page was a photograph taken at the session with the uninvited black committeeman much in view.

To many on Highlander's staff and board of directors, though certainly not all, labor's reactionary impulse reached its zenith in 1949, when the CIO convened in Cleveland, Ohio. Its main order of business was to expel members of the Communist Party, any fascist organization or other totalitarian movement, and any person or organization who consistently aided other organizations to accomplish their own purposes rather than the objectives and policies set forth in the constitution of the CIO. To this end, the convention placed on trial ten affiliated unions, actually expelling two, the United Electrical, Radio, and Machine Workers and the Farm Equipment Workers, for alleged communism. The CIO also withdrew from the allegedly communist-dominated World Federation of Trade Unions.[26]

Horton felt that the union bureaucrats were using Red-baiting to preserve their status quo. He predicted that ten years would pass before a single top CIO leader left office. He was wrong. It was eleven.

Highlander itself felt the approaching purge some weeks before the Cleveland convention. The school was notified in July by Stanley H. Ruttenberg, the director of the CIO's Department of Education and Research, that the union would not hold its usual workers' institute at Highlander that year: "Rightly or wrongly they [several Southern Directors] have the opinion that at Highlander there exists some left wing 'Communist' influence."[27]

Actually, the CIO was miffed because Highlander had refused to sever its working relationship with the Mine, Mill, and Smelter Workers, one of the last militant unions in the South. Ruttenberg asked for an amended statement of policy from Highlander declaring that it was "opposed to all kinds of totalitarianism including communism, fascism, and nazism."[28] Without this declaration, or one of a similar nature, the CIO would withdraw both students and economic support from Highlander.

Highlander's board, at its annual meeting in November, did draw up a revised statement of purpose, but one that failed to satisfy the CIO:

> The purpose of the Highlander Folk School is to assist in creating leadership for democracy. Our services are available to labor, farm,

community, religious, and civic organizations working toward a democratic goal. The nature of the specific educational program will be determined by the needs of the students. Use of the services of the school by individual organizations will be in accordance with their own policies so long as those policies do not conflict with the purpose of the school.[29]

The CIO sent out a directive telling locals to stop using Highlander, but Highlander's association with the unions did not end at once. There were few enforcement powers in the CIO's constitution; thus its threat of nonsupport was difficult to carry out. In fact, two years after the bitter exchange between the union hierarchy and Highlander, Horton was asked by the United Packinghouse Workers, an affiliated union, to become its director of education. He did develop a shop stewards' program to teach union officials how to learn what the rank and file expected of their union, how to act on these wants, and how to teach other members the same thing. This program resulted in a written shop stewards' manual which, to Horton's amusement, helped to increase dramatically rank and file union participation.[30]

But fundamental differences continued to surface, and this was Highlander's last fling with the unions. In 1952, Zilphia told a meeting of the Montana Farmers Union that "the unions have become so reactionary and so complacent that they've lost their ideals, and I don't care anything about singing for people like that."[31]

Developments in the South were as much a reason for the change as Highlander's disappointment with the unions. By 1950, Grundy County, like much of the South, was emerging from the worst of its economic ills. Not every Southern worker had a full stomach or a decent-paying job, not all their children went to adequate schools, but more did than didn't. Since there was little indication that the unions would go beyond their current accomplishments, it was time for a change at Highlander.

Even the labor leaders longest associated with the school—and they made up a majority of the board of directors—agreed with Horton in 1952 that race relations should constitute the school's new direction.

6

. . . *for the first time at a Southern school* . . .

TWO WELLING SOCIAL movements, unions and civil rights, swept a reluctant South between Highlander's opening in 1932 and 1969. For many those were long and injured years. For Horton, and Highlander, they were reasons for being. The people who gave vitality to those powerful movements are almost organically meshed with three words: "We Shall Overcome."

In 1969, for Horton, the lone white man standing amidst a throng of blacks rallying in downtown Chicago to demand jobs, the words—the song—captured the prideful, self-confident first moments of a new day in American race relations, created mostly by blacks themselves. According to custom, as the song mounted, Horton extended his hands to those on either side of him. His gesture was ignored. Nine years before he had seen the song spark idealistic youth, black and white, to endure any pain in the belief that love, conscience, or the Constitution would end racism. Then no one's hand was disregarded. Still earlier, in 1946, when he had first heard the words sung at Highlander by two striking tobacco workers from Charleston, the song was as much a buoyant spiritual as a protest.

In those days, the tobacco workers had sung it to keep up spirits on their picket lines. The title and meaning had been transformed through Highlander, and Highlander in turn had been changed by those who had sung it through the years. Education at Highlander was lived out in tension between what is and what ought to be; learning was that which strengthened social forces in search of a liberating future out of a constricting present. Horton stood with his hands tucked under his arms thinking how the song's words symbolized Highlander's disengagement with the unions and its involvement with blacks.

As was the case in much of East Tennessee, except cities like Knoxville or Chattanooga, few blacks lived in Grundy County when Highlander began. As far as anyone at the school knew, only three families clustered together in the valley below Monteagle, sharing, if not exceeding, the neighboring whites' poverty. Local whites ignored them and kept separate from those families. The common Southern practice of prohibiting blacks from letting the sun set on their heads held strong. Even by the late 1960's, blacks who came into the county to work as maids or gardeners during the day had to leave by nightfall. The law was no better than folk custom. Tennessee had, since 1901, forbidden blacks and whites to eat, sleep, marry, or travel together.

Tuskegee Institute recorded six lynchings in the South the year Highlander opened, but knowledgeable blacks and whites knew the actual number was much higher. Vengeance, as opposed to justice, was swift for any black who violated either folk or formal law.

Even before Highlander opened, Horton, with his populist-socialist background, had hoped to bring black and white students together. In 1932, the climate was hardly favorable from the point of view of either blacks or whites. The Scottsboro case, in which nine black men—most of them from nearby Chattanooga—were charged with raping a white woman, still inflamed racist minds. When the Supreme Court ruled in *Powell* v. *Alabama* that denial of counsel in a capital case violated the due process clause of the Fourteenth Amendment, white passions reached new heights. Horton was disappointed, but not surprised, when, in answer to his request for help in recruiting black students, Professor J. Herman Daves of Knoxville College replied, "At this time we know of no student or graduate of our school who would be a good candidate or who would be desirous of enrolling with you." However, he added, "A number of us are extremely interested in your work."[1]

The reaction from Dr. P. A. Stephens, a physician and surgeon in Chattanooga, was similar. The most influential black man in Chattanooga, Dr. Stephens had been the first person to act on behalf of the Scottsboro men after their illegal arrest. He politely refused Horton's several invitations to join Highlander's board of directors. It was not until 1947 that he finally accepted. Horton went to Chattanooga personally to thank him, and Dr. Stephens told him, frankly, that he had joined "only after discussing with others Highlander's behavior and arriving at the conclusion you mean what you say as demonstrated by your practices."[2]

The Highlander staff failed to attract blacks as students on any significant scale until 1944. However, Professor Daves and his wife came to teach a course at Highlander. Resident students, including a few from Grundy County, had been studying labor problems and wanted to talk about blacks in the labor movement. The staff prepared the way by first talking with as many neighbors as possible, and by reporting in their sporadic community newsletter: "A few students who have families to support and live in towns where Negroes are unorganized, wanted firsthand information as to how Negro workers could be organized. Following a discussion, several people from the community said that the students should get the Negroes' side."[3]

Thus, in 1934, Dr. Daves and his wife became the first black people at Highlander to violate Tennessee's Jim Crow school law prohibiting blacks and whites eating together or staying overnight under the same roof. Students from Fisk University and Tennessee A & I visited in groups later. This law would be flouted repeatedly at Highlander.

Throughout the thirties, Highlander worked to open the labor movement to working people, regardless of race or sex. They were able occasionally to wedge open some closed doors. The union program was the major part of Highlander's educational effort, and the staff continually emphasized the practical damage of discrimination. If bosses could pit whites against blacks to keep wages low, then whites had to join blacks for the sake of both. Eventually, such discussions were more and more frequently led by blacks—labor leaders in the South or college professors.

Horton's experience with TWOC proved valuable. When he organized the union in McColl, a town with a curfew whistle warning blacks that they had fifteen minutes to get off the streets or be jailed, it was, at first, an all-white union. Of the 1,100 or more workers in the plant, about 250 were black men, working long hours and earning low pay for doing the worst jobs. After signing up a majority of the white workers, Horton sought out leaders in the black shops. The black workers were suspicious of him, but, finally, he was taken to a man who was never introduced by name and who said not a word during their brief meeting.

Horton said what he had to say: the union was for everyone; every black worker could join, and join the fight for a twelve-dollar minimum for forty hours; this would cut blacks' working hours from sixty to forty each week, and double their pay—if the union won. Then, he left. The next day, the man, still unknown to Horton, asked for membership cards.

The union made demands which the company refused. The plant was shut by strike. Blacks and whites went on the picket line without friction. When the company agreed to bargain, negotiating was done by Horton and Paul Christopher, son of a North Carolina textile worker and a Clemson graduate with a degree in engineering. During the final bargaining session, the company president told them, "These colored people work on my plantation and they work in my mill. They are good boys and I think we ought to do something for them. I understand how you Southerners feel about it, but I'm a Republican from Pennsylvania."

"No," Horton replied. "Don't do anything special for them. They'll be satisfied with what the rest get."

"You mean *they* are covered in the contract?" the president shouted, his face paling. "The minimum will double their wages and cut their hours. You don't mean to say you expect me to pay *them* twelve dollars?"

"See the contract," Christopher said. "That's what it says. You signed it."

The president blew up, swearing that he would fire the blacks before he would pay. To pay blacks that much was unreasonable and unheard of, he claimed. What seemed to bother him most, according to Horton, was the possibility that the contract would draw the scorn of fellow industrialists, and be a model for other locals.

Evidently, however, the desire to keep his mill running triumphed over the desire to save face. The next payday, every worker received the twelve-dollar minimum.[4]

Such tangible success was rare in the South during the thirties. For the most part, Highlander staffers helped set up organizations or joined with other groups seeking to resist or erode racism. Two groups are especially bound up in the history of Highlander: the All-Southern Conference for Civil and Trade Union Rights, and the Southern Conference for Human Welfare. One lasted a day; the other, a decade.

The All-Southern Conference for Civil and Trade Union Rights was called to counteract the tide of repression sweeping the South in the mid-thirties. Black Shirts and other groups similar to the Ku Klux Klan were coming into being. The conference was called by eight persons: Jim Dombrowski, administrative head of Highlander and secretary of the Conference of Younger Churchmen of the South; Lee Burns of the Bessemer, Alabama, Trades Council; Howard Kester, secretary of the Committee for Economic Justice, in Nashville, Tennessee; Gaines T. Bradford, publisher of the *Birmingham World*; the Reverend L. T. Baptiste of Birmingham; Robert C. Wood, secretary of District 17 of the International Labor Defense Committee; H. L. Mitchell of the interracial Southern Tenant Farmers' Union; and Myles Horton.[5]

Agreeing early in 1935 that "it is imperative to call a united front conference for mapping out ways and means to struggle against the growing reaction in the South," they invited representatives from all the progressive political, trade union, religious, interracial, and social organizations to attend a conference in Chattanooga on April 14, 1935.[6]

The first problem to beset the All-Southern Conference was Raleigh Crumbliss, a Chattanooga insurance agent who was head of the Americanism Committee of his American Legion post. He learned of the planned meeting and charged in a press statement that it was "communistic." The Odd Fellows, who had contracted with the conference for the use of their hall, canceled the agreement. Within days, the conferees had arranged with the black Pythians for the use of their hall. Crumbliss learned of that arrangement and told the press: "I consider this movement more important than the World War. During the war, the Germans were in uniform and we knew where to find them. In the present situation, we can't always locate the people back of these movements in America."[7]

That was it for the Pythians. They canceled, too. The conference finally found a room over the Villa DeLuxe beer garden in which to convene and were doing so about 10:00 A.M. on a placid spring Sunday. Suddenly, over fifty uniformed American Legionnaires, some carrying dynamite sticks, a number of Chattanooga police, and several local politicians charged the upstairs hall. They demanded that the nearly one hundred delegates leave immediately.[8]

The conveners agreed. The situation was desperate. They quit the place, but not before hitting on the idea of sending the vigilantes off on a wild goose chase. Loudly, before the entire assembly, the conference leaders declared that they would reconvene the meeting at a roadhouse in Summit, not far away, and told the delegates how to get there. Privately, as they left the hall, the delegates were urged to head for Summit, then take a side road to Monteagle and Highlander.

Excerpts from reports filed by Fletcher Knebel, the author and journalist who then worked for the *Chattanooga News*, tell what happened.

The Legionnaires, "determined the 'Reds' should not meet in Hamilton County, exchanged City for County officers, added an enthusiastic squad of ten men from the Labor Hall, and boiled out the highway, hot on the carmine trail," wrote Knebel.

Arriving at Summit, the contingent, not seeing any delegates at the roadhouse, "pulled up short for reconnoitering . . . and deployed over surrounding roads in a vain search for the Red prey . . . the men mulled about in the hot sun, questioned miscellaneous Negroes and laid worried plans for further quest."

Slightly-built Henry Sprinkle, a Methodist minister from Nashville, who was secretary of the General Board of Christian Education of the Methodist Episcopal Church, South, arrived on the scene, tardy but still trying to join the meeting he thought was in Chattanooga. He had three passengers in his car. After he stopped, Knebel describes the scene:

"What's all the fuss about?"

"We're looking for the Reds," said Wiley Couch, over 6 feet and bulky.

"You mean the All-Southern Conference for Civil and Trade Union Rights? asked Sprinkle.

"Reds is the word we use," said the County trustee.

"But what's the objection?" asked Sprinkle. "It's just a conference for . . ."

"Don't give me that," barked Couch, as he whanged Sprinkle sharply across the cheek.

Mr. Sprinkle, only slightly hurt, got back into his car and drove off. Before the vigilantes could mobilize to follow him, another car stopped at the crossroads. Innocent of any part in the All-Southern Conference, the driver told of "suspicious-looking" people gathering near Cleveland, Tennessee.

Five carloads of men sped off toward Cleveland, the seat of Bradley County, where one Legionnaire soon spotted what he thought to be the remnants of the ousted delegation reconvening on a vast, tree-shaded lawn. The five cars quickly surrounded the assembly, which, to the vexation of the Legionnaires, turned out to be the graduating class at Bob Jones College, the ultra-conservative religious school now located in South Carolina. The posse returned empty-handed to Chattanooga.[9]

Before the first and only All-Southern Conference ended that day at Highlander, the delegates had discussed and adopted resolutions calling for the outlawing of lynching and the death penalty for any conviction; seats on grand juries for blacks (a situation still not resolved in many Southern communities); immediate and unconditional pardon for the Scottsboro defendants; the reversal of the rape conviction of James Carruthers and Bubble Clayton, young black farmers from Blytheville, Arkansas; the dismissal of charges against six Burlington, North Carolina, textile workers and union leaders jailed in the aftermath of a dynamite blast; dismissal of anarchy and barratry charges against the Reverend Claude C. Williams and Horace Bryan of Arkansas; an end to a Florida union leader's attempt to break up efforts to build a representative tobacco workers union; the immediate release from "review" in Nashville of a grant of $7,000 to Highlander Folk Cooperative under the Federal Emergency Relief Act; and, finally, repeal of all anti-sedition and antiunion legislation previously passed by several Southern states and presently pending before the Alabama legislature.[10]

To the best of Horton's knowledge, the ill-fated, one-day conference was among the earliest attempts made in the thirties to form a Southern coalition of black and white religious, political, and labor groups.

In contrast, the initial convening of the Southern Conference for Human Welfare in Birmingham has since been called "perhaps the largest tent meeting of Southern liberals of all time."[11] Certainly, few exclusively regional events matched it in size: 1,250 official delegates gathered November 20, 1938, "like a cleansing flood, animated one and all by selfless purpose—to help the South through the democratic process of free speech and frank discussion."[12]

The conference represented the Southern wing of the Roosevelt coalition—liberal, respectable, responding as much to the highly-publicized National Emergency Council's claim that the South was "the Nation's No. 1 economic problem" as to the cries of an aching people who needed no official report to tell them that bad times hadn't gotten much better.[13]

The conference's founding force, Joseph Gelders, scion of one of Birmingham's few Jewish families, had turned to Eleanor Roosevelt for help when earlier plans for a conference on civil liberties in the South faltered. (Gelders' efforts had been prompted by a brutal beating he had suffered in September, 1936, apparently as the result of his work with the National Committee for the Defense of Political Prisoners.) Meeting with Gelders at Hyde Park, New York, Mrs. Roosevelt suggested that he widen the scope of the conference to include all the South's ills. He agreed, and she lent her considerable prestige to the project. On the way back to Birmingham, he stopped at Highlander to ask for the school's backing, which he got.[14]

Gelders assembled a host: Mrs. Roosevelt; blacks of world fame, including Mary McLeod Bethune, founder of Bethune-Cookman College in Daytona Beach, Florida, Dr. Benjamin Mays, president of Morehouse College in Atlanta, and Dr. F. D. Patterson, president of Tuskegee Institute; many of the region's widely-known white liberal churchmen, newspaper editors, and labor leaders; a sprinkling of politicians, among them Florida's Claude Pepper and Alabama's Lister Hill; officials of the WPA and other federal agencies, including the respected Aubrey Williams; Supreme Court Justice Hugo Black, who was given the first annual Thomas Jefferson Award as "the Southerner who had done most to promote human and social welfare"; and Southern patricians, including Dr. Frank P. Graham, president of the University of North Carolina, and Lucy Randolph Mason, descendant of George Mason, author of the Virginia Bill of Rights, who was herself working as the CIO's public relations director in the South. All told, there were scores of New Deal Democrats, sundry Socialists, six avowed Communists, and one or two admitted Republicans there.[15]

Jim Crow came, too. Police Commissioner Theophilus (meaning loved of God) Eugene "Bull" Connor, a law and order man long before his name became synonymous with American apartheid in 1963, was determined that Birmingham's law of racial separation should be maintained during the conference. Even the protocol surrounding the wife of a United States President failed to daunt him.

When Mrs. Roosevelt entered the conference hall, in which seating was segregated, she seated herself with blacks in defiance of both law and custom. A silence which had little to do with the opening prayer fell among the delegates. For an embarrassed moment, Connor's uniformed police were immobilized. One, however, knew his law and his duty. Going up to Mrs. Roosevelt, with the eyes of the delegates focused on him, he quietly pointed out the error of her ways. Her gesture made, Mrs. Roosevelt rose with what Horton recalls as "commanding dignity and moved to the lawful side of the aisle."[16]

The conference produced hundreds of recommendations that sought to support farming, end discriminatory freight rates, shorten working hours for women, and protect and widen civil liberties. The conference only blandly decried the segregation of its own meeting. Lucy Randolph Mason later said, the "conference was a people's movement, representing every strata of society from capitalist to sharecropper."[17]

As such, the conference could expect to draw fire and did, almost before the ink was dry on the last resolution. *Alabama*, the house organ for Birmingham's industrial leaders, declared that the conference sought "some sort of law . . . to equalize the economic, social and political condition of colored people with . . . the white race."[18] Many whites got the message and never returned to subsequent meetings.

However, because of its broad base of membership, and because of the skillful work of Gelders and Clark Foreman of Atlanta, the Southern Conference remained a force for social change in the South. Highlander's role in the group continued throughout its existence. In 1942, Jim Dombrowski left Highlander to become the conference's executive secretary. Under his leadership, the conference moved from its original mission of trying to liberalize the Democratic Party in the South to the more lonely task of speaking out against segregation.

In the summer of 1947, after a serious policy fight with the conference executive board, Dombrowski took over the administration of an offshoot organization, the Southern Conference

Education Fund, which outlived its parent. On November 21, 1948, SCHW's five remaining board members—Dombrowski, Foreman, Aubrey Williams, Mrs. Clifford J. Durr, and Horton—met in Richmond, Virginia, and resolved that "new political alignments have largely absorbed the political energies of the members of SCHW" and made "its continuation unnecessary and a duplication of effort."[19]

Eight years before, in 1940, Highlander had informed all the unions it served in the South that the school would no longer hold workers' education programs for unions which discriminated against blacks. Highlander had also reaffirmed its policy that any student with the ability to write who came with a recommendation from his or her local would be enrolled, regardless of race or sex. It had also used its extensive union contacts to insure that locals began opening their memberships to blacks.

The pressure paid off four years later. Paul Christopher, who had been promoted to regional CIO director and was on Highlander's board, organized a Highlander workshop for the United Auto Workers attended by forty union members, black and white, from every corner of the South. The workers held sessions on collective bargaining, the economics of the auto and aircraft industries, and UAW's postwar plans. They also organized a cooperative food store, wrote wall newspapers, washed dishes after meals, and sang rousing union songs.

With a dryness which hid Horton's pride in this unprecedented accomplishment, he noted in Highlander's 1944 annual report: "This session was historic because, for the first time, Negro and white delegates studied, worked and played together at a Southern school."[20] But there was more to it than a footnote in labor history. Black participants indicated their willingness to defy law and custom for economic advantage.

After this, Highlander could more easily urge other unions

to join the pioneering UAW. Support was soon developed from the Tennessee Industrial Union Council and the Southern Farmers' Union. Others followed.

The integrated workshops were not without incident, however. Old customs die hard. One black woman, after suffering a series of bitter insults, came to Horton in hot anger for permitting her to be made the target of ridicule. Horton told her what he believed: "If segregation is to end in the South and the nation, people as strong as yourself will have to find the means to end it. That you feel free enough to assail a white man at a white school is cause for renewed hope."[21]

Bob Jones, one of the first black UAW committeemen to attend a Highlander workshop, pointed out another reason blacks would use the school. "When I first joined [the union], I had an idea that there were a few people who didn't feel about Negroes like those I had been brought up with in Memphis. And when I came to Highlander, I was fully convinced there were such people. Here, it's just a matter of giving the CIO a chance to carry out its constitution . . . there is more religion in this union than in the average church."[22]

Highlander, then, was an affirmation. As growing numbers of rank and file members used the school, blacks joined Highlander's board of directors. Dr. Lewis Jones, a sociologist at Fisk University, was the first, in 1942. Dr. P. A. Stephens of Chattanooga and Mrs. Grace Hamilton, an official of the Urban League in Atlanta, became members in 1947. Dr. B. R. Brazeal, dean of Morehouse College in Atlanta, joined in 1949.

Four years later, Dr. George Mitchell, head of the Southern Regional Council in Atlanta and chairman of Highlander's board, told those gathered for the school's annual meeting: "The times call for some new unsung heroes. The next great problem is not the problem of conquering poverty, but conquering meanness, prejudice, and tradition. Highlander could become a place in which this is studied, a place where one could learn the art and practice and methods of brotherhood."[23]

His remarks reflected the trends of the previous fifteen years. The New Deal's accomplishments in labor relations had engendered some improvement in the overall economic condition of black people. In 1944, the U.S. Supreme Court ordered an end to segregation on interstate transportation. Three years later, U.S. Judge J. Waites Waring, descendant of eight generations of Charleston aristocrats, ruled that blacks must be allowed to vote in South Carolina's all-white primaries. (To back up his ruling, he issued an injunction banning any interference with voters by election officials and announced that he would sit in court on primary day to deal with any violators.) Charleston and the South were stunned.

These developments under the Roosevelt administration gave blacks hope of a fighting chance. Subsequent federal action added to their willingness to combat racism. President Truman's Committee on Civil Rights called for the elimination of segregation from American life. Truman, one year later, set up the permanent Fair Employment Practices Commission. At the same time, he took formal steps to end segregation in the military.

To Horton, however, what black people had done for themselves during the period seemed of greater significance than any governmental or private program. Individual blacks were beginning to speak up. Charles Hayes, a black packinghouse worker from Chicago, had tangled with a white organizer for the Texas Packinghouse Workers during a residential session at the school. The Texan had frequently called Hayes "boy," and blacks, in general, "nigrahs." Suddenly during a workshop discussion, Horton recalls, Hayes stood above the Texan and said,

"Look, this is a school. I'm going to try to educate you by telling you—don't say 'boy' or 'nigrah.' My names is Charles Hayes. Call us Negroes. Now, that is the education part. And if that doesn't work, then I'm going to beat hell out of you."[24]

Blacks' collective action had also been significant. In 1941, A. Philip Randolph of the Sleeping Car Porters Union threatened to bring 50,000 blacks to Washington to protest discrimination by manufacturers of war materials and in the federal government's training programs. After obtaining a pledge from Randolph to call off the march, Roosevelt ordered an end to the discriminatory practices. In 1947, the National Association for the Advancement of Colored People took the issue of North American racism to the United Nations, pointing out with damning clarity that the United States condoned at home the same practices it condemned in others and had waged a war to end.

All these actions, individual and collective, led Horton to conclude that the fastest way to teach white people about racism was to nurture the growing black willingness to stand and speak for themselves. But how to do it?

In his call for Highlander to concentrate on the South's racial problems, Board Chairman Mitchell had specifically urged the staff to explore the problems that might result should the U.S. Supreme Court, before whom the famous *Brown* v. *Board of Education* was then pending, rule to end segregation in public schools and/or enforce the separate but equal facilities decision. To that end, and to explore ways through which more black people could be encouraged to speak for themselves, Highlander announced two summer workshops on Supreme Court decisions and the public schools for "men and women in positions to provide community leadership for an orderly transition from a segregated to an unsegregated public school system in the South."[25]

In the summer of 1953, under the leadership of Paul Bennett, a graduate student at Howard University and a former Alabama Farmers' Union leader, the workshops attracted forty-three persons from across the South: white ministers, farmers, factory workers, and members of interracial groups. The workshop was the first attempt in the South to help local leaders desegregate their schools.

The uncertainty about the Supreme Court's direction, plus Highlander's own inexperience in the field, complicated the workshops. Nonetheless, guides for alternative action in local communities were outlined—and Highlander's staff learned.

Even these hesitant steps had effect. Mrs. Septima Poinsette Clark, later Highlander's director of education, has told in her book, *Echo in My Soul*, how one of her associates in the Charleston, South Carolina, black branch of the YWCA, Anna Kelly, felt after the workshop she attended: "She came home fairly bursting with enthusiasm . . . reported on the workshop . . . and at once began planning ways of getting across to our people the subjects discussed there, particularly those relating to desegregation; she also called in representatives from various clubs and planned a series of radio broadcasts. But she was especially interested in recruiting Charlestonians to attend forthcoming Highlander workshops."[26]

What Anna Kelly did is what Highlander had hoped would be a result of the workshops and illustrates the school's philosophy: work through local people as they seek to improve their own communities; work with an immediate, specific problem, with the hope that, when people facing the same problem are brought together, a social movement will emerge.

Despite limited success, the staff knew a few workshops did not constitute an adult education program, and were not enough to turn racism around. Moreover, they realized, Highlander was a predominantly white institution seeking to build from limited experience a program useful to Southern blacks. Thoughtful reflection didn't reveal many answers, just more confounding problems.

Highlander staff members were convinced that only a frontal assault on racism and its chief perpetrators, especially institutions, would bring results. Looking back, they realized that not only had Southern white supportive ranks failed to grow; they had, in fact, diminished. White Southern churchmen and most white churches simply forgot Christianity when asked to act for integration. White union men dropped from the barricades if an issue was of direct importance to blacks but only of secondary importance to whites. Highlander people knew of no teacher able to open a humanities textbook that was free of racist bias. They knew of few politicians and no governing body willing to support one man, one vote. The few they did see loomed so disproportionately large above the bleak landscape that they seemed stronger than they really were.

At first, the Southern Conference for Human Welfare seemed to provide hope. For a time, the conference constituted a liberal political force within the Southern wing of the Democratic Party. However, when the showdown over communism came within the organization, timid whites left the conference in droves. The issue was never communism. The issue was that Southern blacks and whites, in coalition, were using the conference to help blacks climb Jacob's ladder.[27]

The use of anticommunism to mask racism was exemplified by a rubber worker from Memphis, Tennessee. The man, once a president of his local, spread the word at the 1955 rubber workers' convention in Cincinnati, Ohio, that Highlander was "communistic." When questioned hard by other union members, he admitted that the only basis for his charge was that Highlander had been responsible for his local's being represented by a black man on the international executive board.

"If Josh Tools hadn't gone to Highlander and come back and

pushed himself on the union, we wouldn't be in the embarrassing position of being asked if we had no white members smart enough to serve on the executive board."[28]

Horton's dreams for militant unionism in the South were shattered by several factors. The idea of a working class never really developed as a concept or tradition in the United States, and workers seldom saw themselves as part of a struggle to build a better society. Those parts of the Protestant ethic enshrining individualism and self-advancement as good in the eyes of the Lord were undermining factors, too. If white workers could move from job to job seeking better pay, greater security, and shorter working hours, they undermined the idea that strong unions were the means through which to accomplish individual aims. Ultimately, however, the decisive barrier to unionism in the South was racism, raw and naked.

Highlander had encountered the communism-racism masquerade as early as 1940, when staff members had to stand armed guard around the clock to protect their lives and the school property from threatened assaults by the Grundy County Crusaders, a group of "One Hundred Per Cent Americans" formed in Tracy City by a coal company bookkeeper, C. H. Kilby.[29] The Crusaders told the press they were "working night and day" to send Highlander packing, not just from Grundy, but from Tennessee. Adopting as their slogan, "No ism but Americanism," they convinced Rep. Martin Dies of the House Un-American Activities Committee that he should investigate Highlander. Thereafter, FBI agents made frequent visits to Grundy County, asking neighbors pointed questions about blacks and Communists—always lumping the two together—and about where people ate and slept at the school.[30]

In December, 1940, two FBI agents came directly to Horton. He showed them around the grounds, took them to visit the cooperative nursery school, and told them how the labor schools operated. He showed them a copy of a speech he had made a few days before, condemning segregation and affirming the need for stronger trade unions and farm cooperatives. "By broadening the scope of democracy to include everyone," he had said, "and deepening the concept to include every relationship, the army of democracy would be so vast and so determined that nothing undemocratic could stand in its path."[31] One agent told him that most Southerners thought such views "communistic." Then he left, leaving no doubt in Horton's mind that he agreed. Such visits by the FBI and attacks by the Crusaders eventually eroded the solid relationships that Highlander had built among Grundy people.

Highlander and Horton had finally to acknowledge what they were reluctant to face: that whites, themselves included, had failed painfully to end white domination of black people. As individuals, they were, and would probably remain, crippled in their relationships with blacks by white institutions. No matter how well-intentioned a white shop steward might be in listening to the grievance of a black worker, he still had to resolve that man's difficulty in terms of a white-dominated union, a white-controlled company, a white world of capitalism. Neither the shop steward nor the black could act independently of what was, after all, Western civilization. Neither could Horton.

Only after arriving at this conclusion did Horton, as an individual, and Highlander, as an institution, begin to understand fully the implications of an encounter Horton had witnessed between an East Indian and an Englishman years before when he was a student at Union Theological Seminary.

He had been visiting International House in New York City, and he accidentally heard the Englishman—tall, blond, sturdy, and handsome—excitedly urging the East Indian—short, brown, slightly built, and equally handsome—to be patient and cautious in trying to end Britain's colonial rule of his native land. "The reactionary forces in your own Indian community and in the British colony will crush you otherwise," the Englishman had warned. The East Indian, who had remained silent during what was a much longer monologue than recorded here, quietly replied, "We look at the problem differently. I'm on the ground with my face in the mud. Your foot is on my neck, pushing. In this uncomfortable position, my attitude toward doing something to get up out of the mud in a hurry differs from yours. You are comfortable. I am not."[32]

Certainly Horton could say to a black man, "I want you to stand up," but that did not mean the man could rise. Regardless of Horton's personal convictions, white institutions kept the black man down, with his face in the mud. Blacks had known this all along. Horton was just beginning to learn. For example, try as they might, the staff could not keep the whites at integrated workshops from dominating black participants. Even whites with the best of intentions could not long work with blacks without telling them how to do what was supposedly good for them.

Blacks were forced to live in two worlds, one white, one black; forced to have words and ways for each; forced to support two sets of institutions, one black and of their own building, the other white and opposed to their interests.

Finally, despite his intellectual commitment to socialism and collective solutions, Horton always had been a firm practitioner of individualism. Passages he copied as a student from John Stuart Mill's essay *On Liberty* remain in his files today.

He who lets the world, or his own portion of it, *choose his* plan of life for him, has no need of any other faculty than the *ape-like one of imitation*. He who chooses his plan for himself, employs all his faculties. He must use observation to see, reasoning and judgments to foresee, activity to gather materials for decision, discrimination to decide, and *when he has decided, firmness and self-control to hold to his deliberate decision.*

If a person possesses any tolerable amount of common sense and experience, *his own mode of laying out his existence* is the best, not because it is the best in itself, but because it is *his own mode.*[33] (Italics Horton's.)

Individualism was a privilege for whites—one that they denied to blacks. In fact, Horton had been deluded by his belief in individualism into thinking that, once enough whites arrived at Highlander's position, the nation would move from paternalism to a system of equal treatment that did not destroy individual or group characteristics. But, he learned, there were two fallacies to his reasoning. First, individual blacks could be absorbed by white institutions rapidly. To be free individually, the black man had to acquiesce, to become *like* a white man. In helping token numbers of blacks become part of the Southern union movement, Horton had been dissipating, not encouraging, black individuality.

This led to the second fallacy. Horton still felt called upon to work out a solution to racism which blacks as a group might accept. But, he realized, he did not understand blacks as a group; before he could help them, they would have to clarify for him how they perceived themselves. His thoughts kept leading him, the individual, to conclusions that left him out. In the end, he admitted—and the admission contradicted at the same time it fulfilled his past career as an educator—that the blacks would have to make their own decisions on their own terms. Only in that way could integration become meaningful: letting the black man, and his people, be freely what they themselves wanted to be.

7

. . . to make the tongue work . . .

IN THE EARLY 1950's, two quite separate decisions made for different reasons resulted in the confluence of persons, time, and wherewithal to produce what Horton considers Highlander's most important contribution to the civil rights movement—and to the field of liberal adult education. The two decisions were to seek funds from sources other than unions and to answer a request to set up "night schools" in South Carolina.

In 1953, Highlander received a three-year grant from the Schwarzhaupt Foundation "to increase participation in local and national affairs, in stimulating interest in community problems, and in changing attitudes which limit democracy."[1] What, in essence, the grant allowed was unrestricted license to experiment in the field of adult education. From the standpoint of finances, at least, this was the first such opportunity in Highlander's history. By this time, work with unions was dwindling, and so were the funds usually derived from conducting their educational programs. The staff had been forced to search for new sources of support. Individuals who believed in the Highlander idea provided the bulk of the funding; foundations that weren't worried about the school's reputation, but looked instead for results, made up the remainder.

Highlander had tried two unsuccessful experiments in adult education by the time the second decision was reached. Schwarzhaupt funds had been used to try to spur participation in local affairs in predominantly white farming communities in Alabama and in East Tennessee. Internal factionalism had destroyed the Alabama project. The East Tennessee project had collapsed because the community had perceived no crisis. In each case, there had seemed little reason for whites to want to make democracy work any better: Eisenhower was president, the Silent Generation was just graduating from college, McCarthy was purging, and all seemed well, especially in the South, which was being ruled by the Byrds, the Byrneses, the Georges, and the Faubuses.

In 1955, one of Highlander's former students, Mrs. Septima Poinsette Clark, was "let go" by the Charleston School Board, in part for thinking that the U.S. Supreme Court decision in the Brown case applied also to her native city.[2] Mrs. Clark had been actively encouraging blacks to vote—another contravention of tradition for a black schoolteacher. However, her unpardonable transgression, in the eyes of white Charleston, had been her acceptance of social invitations to the home of Judge and Mrs. Waites Waring, patricians turned pariahs by the judge's ruling that South Carolina must let blacks vote. Mrs. Clark had taken meals with the Warings. Agitating was one thing; socializing, another. She had been fired and had subsequently been invited to Highlander as director of education. It was in this capacity that she had introduced the school to Esau Jenkins of Johns Island, South Carolina.

Set off from Charleston by the brackish Stono and Kaiwah rivers, Johns Island, after it had been securely taken from its original Indian inhabitants, had become a patchwork of lush plantations run by a handful of whites with the toil of black hands and backs. The island was segregated by race and was further sundered by language—the whites spoke Charlestonese, a Southern dialect strange even to other Southerners, while the blacks spoke mostly Gullah, a dialect that bore traces of an African Gold Coast language spoken before the days of slavery.

When Mrs. Clark had gone to Johns Island to teach in the thirties, long before bridges connected the island to the mainland, she had met a middle-aged woman who had seen only one white man in her life. The sight of him had terrified her, Mrs. Clark recalls her saying. In 1938, a black man had been shot dead for accidentally running over a white man's dog.

The island's 3,000 blacks fished and gardened when they could, but most of the time they worked in rich fields which were owned by others. Sickness, illiteracy, disease, and superstition were common. Education was scarce. Mrs. Clark was eighteen when she was assigned a two-room schoolhouse badly in need of repair and space. Over 130 students, ranging in age from six to sixteen, had filled the schoolhouse wall to wall. Mrs. Clark had been paid $35.00 a month. Down the island a way, a white teacher had taught three students in a well-furnished, well-kept schoolhouse—for $85.00 a month.

Life had changed by the fifties, at least for the whites. Bridges built across the rivers brought in Charlestonians, who subdivided the plantations and built suburban houses among the moss-draped oaks. Fewer blacks were needed to work fewer farms. They could only retreat into their isolation, one that deepened as the world went on faster and faster about them. It seemed that much of what most Americans called life would continue to pass them by.

On Mrs. Clark's second visit to Highlander in 1954, she brought along several people from the Charleston area, among them Esau Jenkins. He farmed and ran a bus line for the black islanders who had found work on the mainland, mostly in Charleston tobacco factories. Although Mrs. Clark and the others had come to a workshop on the United Nations, Jenkins wasn't much concerned about world government. In fact, he told Horton just that after the first morning's session.

"My immediate problem is literacy education," he said. "So many person were here [on Johns Island] can't read and write and I know this condition because I would have been almost in the same condition if I didn't go back to school." He asked Horton if Highlander would set up night schools for adults "to help them become better citizens."[3]

Over the years, Jenkins himself had tried to teach adults to read, but one man wasn't a school. Keeping black schools poor, and filling them to the brim with students, was the first step in disenfranchisement of blacks in South Carolina, and elsewhere in the South. Generation after generation of adults were unable to read or to do the simplest sums. The second trap whites devised to keep blacks powerless was directly tied to the first: if they couldn't read the state constitution, then they couldn't register to vote. That was the law.

Jenkins decided to try to get around these prohibitions. Several years later, he told Guy Carawan, who was on Johns Island for Highlander to develop a music program:

> I saw the conditions of the people who had been working on the plantations for many years. And I knew that they were not able to do things that would need to be done unless we could get people registered as citizens. I operated a bus from Johns Island to Charleston carrying people to their jobs. So I decided to get a group in the bus in the mornings and teach them how to read the part of the constitution that we have to read before we are able to become registered citizens.
>
> One of these mornings I was teaching the group to read the constitution, a woman by the name of Alice Wine said to me, "Mr. Jenkins, I would like very much to become a registered citizen, but I cannot read this constitution because I did not get but just so far in school, and I cannot pronounce these words. But if you are willing to help me, I will show you that I would be willing to vote in every election." So I decided to pay more attention to her, and I helped her at more times than I do the regular times when we have school in the bus, to get her prepared to register.[4]

Here was a powerful defiance of white Southern law and custom. Carawan went next to Mrs. Wine and recorded her words:

He (Jenkins) start to help me read and when I get to them hard words I feel like jump it. My tongue so heavy until I couldn't pronounce the words, you know. But he said to me, "No, the hard word is the things for you to learn." And so me and them girls (and some of the girls could read 'em—Dum-de-dum-dum-dum—right on through, right on through, but I couldn't do it), we tried 'em.

Then he take me up to a registration board on Society Street, and we get in line. Everybody read and get a paper, read and get a paper. And I be in line next to this girl, and she read and she stammer. And then the man put me for read, and I read those things just like I been know 'em. And I didn't know them thing, I swear.

Mr. Jenkins figure I going to fail. He been right outside there on the corner for listen. And when I come he said, "Miss Wine, you get it?" I say, "Yes, sir."[5]

By twos and threes, Jenkins had added a handful of blacks to the rolls of registered voters. This was no mean accomplishment, but, at that rate, he would be dead and in his grave before one-third of the island's black residents would be "able to do things."

With the Schwarzhaupt Foundation's money, Horton was able to spend six months visiting Johns Island, listening to the farmers, fishermen, maids, and field hands, in an effort to learn the ways of island life. How, he wondered, was Jenkins able to teach and drive a bus simultaneously? What was there in the learning experience of Miss Wine that could be used to develop an educational program? Why didn't the people of Johns Island learn to read at the state-supported adult literacy program that was offered on the island? He recorded his island interviews, and, as he drove back and forth between Johns Island and Highlander, he played the wire tape recordings back, trying to find answers to these and a host of other questions.

Gradually, he learned that the islanders were ill at ease in the adult literacy program for some simple, but not so obvious reasons. For one thing, they didn't fit into the classroom chairs, which had been designed for children. Not only were the adults who attended uncomfortable, but they were called "Daddy long-legs," and there was just enough deprecation in the nickname to cause embarrassment, just enough embarrassment to cause a prideful man or woman to quit. For another, they were being taught step-by-step, like children: a-b-c-d; the ball is red; New York is a big city. Over and over. They were being asked to delay reading a sentence until they could read letters. They were being asked to delay reading sentences useful to them until they could read sentences of dubious value, even to children. They could not read the constitution, which had to be read before a vote could be cast, until they could read about a world they had never even heard of: New York is a big city.

The few who had enrolled just stopped going to classes. The dignity of their adulthood and their reason for learning to read in the first place were being ignored.

Horton concluded that if Highlander was to respond to the request to "start a night school for adults," then that school should not be in a traditional schoolroom but should be in a setting, or settings, more familiar to adults. Moreover, the work of learning to read must be adult work and work that was a part of the islanders' own lives. Just as Jenkins couldn't fritter away his time talking about the United Nations, the other islanders couldn't solve their civic problems by talking about a nebulous New York City.

But who would teach them to read? The teachers who came over from the mainland were educated to teach children, not adults. Not only that, the two languages, Charlestonese and Gullah, meant that teachers and students had a hard time understanding each other. Jenkins had had no such problem. Obviously, then, the teacher had to be a peer and someone who could teach them to read what they needed to read, in this case, the South Carolina constitution. Highlander's experiences in the thirties with the successful teaching by Dolph Vaughn, the union leader, reinforced these conclusions.[6]

Mrs. Clark found a volunteer teacher, her niece, Miss Bernice Robinson, a Charleston seamstress and beautician, who had never taught before. Jenkins, in addition to being the link between the proposed school and the students, provided the place. In his spare time, he had started the Progressive Club Cooperative Store, a tiny enterprise selling groceries. Together with some neighbors, he partitioned off one end of the store and hung a light overhead. A blackboard was found, with some chalk and an eraser or two. Tables and chairs were adult size. The room's only ornament was a copy of the United Nations Declaration of Human Rights tacked to a wall. There were no textbooks.

In some respects, the start of the "night school for adults," which later became the Citizenship Schools, was for Horton like Christmas night, 1931: "get a simple place . . . move in . . . you're there . . . the situation is there . . . you start with this and let it grow. . . ."[7] Jenkins taught Horton how to link desire with dream, which, when coupled with an immediate reward, could produce a new way of teaching people. Two questions remained: Could the experiences in learning which took place on a bus jouncing back and forth to Charleston be transferred to a more routine setting and be effective for more people than those on Johns Island? If so, could that experience be used elsewhere?

Miss Robinson wrote within a few weeks:

> The school which we have planned for three months is in progress and the people have shown great interest. They are so anxious to learn. I have fourteen adults, four men and ten women, and there are thirteen high school girls enrolled to learn sewing. There are three adults that have had to start from scratch because they could not read or write. I start out with having them spell their names. About eight of them can read a little, but very poorly. So far, I have been using that part of the South Carolina constitution that they must

know in order to register. From that, I take words that they find hard to pronounce and drill them in spelling and pronunciation and also the meaning of words so they will know what they are saying. We have to give them some arithmetic. The men are particularly interested in figures. I have never before in my life seen such anxious people. They really want to learn and are so proud of the little gains they have made so far. When I get to the club each night, half of them are already there and have their homework ready for me to see. I tacked up the Declaration of Human Rights on the wall and told them that I wanted each of them to be able to read and understand the entire thing before the end of the school.[8]

At the end of three months—two classes a week, thirty-six in all, if none was missed—the fourteen students took the voting test in the registrar's office. For eight of them, that test was not a final examination, but a graduation into citizenship; they were registered. Before the first Citizenship School ended, its enrollment had more than doubled, from fourteen to thirty-seven, in contrast to the experience of the "regular" reading school. Most evenings when classes were held, thirty or forty young men and boys would jam into the front of the Progressive Club listening intently to what was happening beyond the partition.

Jenkins later told Carawan what happened next:

And then the people on Wadmalaw and Edisto Islands found out later the reason for Johns Island was so successful in registering Negroes. They ask me if it's possible to help them to get an adult school. So the next year when I went to Highlander, when it comes time for immediate problem again, I brought in Wadmalaw and Edisto, and they again say they will help if I can find a place and the teachers. I found the place, and today Wadmalaw registered more Negroes than ever registered in the history of Wadmalaw. In the 1964 election, Wadmalaw had about two hundred Negro votes for Johnson. Most of the white folks were voting for Goldwater, but Negroes voted enough to hold it in the Democratic column. That's the only area in Charleston County that went for Johnson.

The same thing is happening on Edisto and all over the county. In 1954, in the county, there were 'round five or six thousand Negroes registered. In 1964, almost fourteen thousand. So everybody is jubilant for the Highlander Folk School, who have helped them see the light."[9]

In 1959, partially as a result of the success of the Citizenship Schools, Highlander was facing an investigation by the Tennessee legislature and an uncertain future. To keep the Citizenship Schools going was one goal; to keep Highlander's principles intact was another. Arrangements were made to give the program—funds, funding sources, staff, and idea—to the Southern Christian Leadership Conference early in 1961.

Mrs. Clark and a minister whom Highlander had recruited to assist her, the Reverend Andrew J. Young, joined SCLC's staff, but Miss Robinson stayed at Highlander to run voter education workshops for both SCLC and SNCC. In 1963, Mrs. Clark reported that since the program's transfer to SCLC three years earlier, more than 26,000 blacks in twelve Southern states had learned enough reading to register. At that time, she noted, volunteer teachers were running more than 400 schools attended by 6,500 adults. In 1970, she estimated that nearly 100,000 blacks had learned to read and write through Citizenship Schools.[10]

Horton never entered a Citizenship School classroom as a teacher. As the idea spread, he discouraged other well-meaning whites from becoming involved. He felt that the presence of a white stranger in the class altered, even stopped, the naturalness of learning among black peers. He stuck to raising money to keep the schools going and helping to recruit and train teachers. Occasionally, though, whites wanted to visit the schools. Frequently, when they did, the worst possible reaction occurred: black men and women would quickly hide behind the roles whites had traditionally assigned to them, deferring and fawning. Not only did this hinder learning, but it continued the ruinous acceptance of white supremacy at the students' expense. Citizenship Schools were run by blacks from the start.

Horton believes that another factor in the success of the Citizenship Schools was that adults were respected as adults. They were asked to read dignified material, and to stretch their imaginations—the South Carolina constitution to secure citizens' rights, the Declaration of Human Rights to arouse hope for human equality. Teachers raised adult questions: Were they, as a people, responsible for their mean condition? Were they ignorant and unable to learn, as was said of them? Were they filled with sloth, treachery, or incompetence? Highlander encouraged teachers to stir up rebellion through such questions, to encourage blacks themselves to face and try to change the myths.

People learned enough to register, and they learned enough to live with a measure of dignity. American illiterates are kept in bondage beyond the legal or constitutional sense. Telephones are hard to dial; road and store signs are meaningless; routine forms are incomprehensible. To hands hardened to the plow, the fishing net, the hoe, or the jackhammer, even holding a pencil can be a chore. The Citizenship Schools' volunteer teachers were taught to teach the people how to hold pencils, read signs and labels, fill out money orders and forms from the Sears Roebuck catalog. Learning to read, write, and do sums became a practical matter, not just for elections, but for every day.

All wanting to read and write in order to vote and all dreaming of a better life, no one could outdo another in hopes. A Citizenship School would start off full of individuals who quickly became a group, helping one another learn to hold pencils, to say words, to make the tongue work.

The Citizenship Schools succeeded also because their cost was low. By using volunteer, nonprofessional teachers, by meeting in plain quarters, and by keeping materials simple and directly related to citizenship, it was possible to teach an adult for about eight dollars, excluding the cost to Highlander of recruiting and training additional teachers. Two years before the program was given to SCLC, Mrs. Clark and Miss Robinson had moved to Monteagle to run training workshops to train teachers.

Horton continued taking a single message across the South —black people must decide their own destinies. The Citizenship Schools illustrated how this could be done, but offered whites a supportive role. Horton told the all-black Southeastern Georgia Crusade for Voters in Savannah in the early 1950's, "I hope this will be the last time a white man tells you what to do, how to formulate policy, who should do what and when they should do it. White people should be used as technicians to help you accomplish what you say you want done to end segregation."[11]

8

. . . there assembled at Highlander . . .

BY THE MID-FIFTIES, Southern racists realized that many blacks had put on their traveling shoes, but they weren't always heading North.

Police in Haywood County, Tennessee, stopped a black minister for a routine check in 1956 and found pamphlets about voting rights in his car. He was arrested, jailed, and upon release several days later, he and his family were forced to leave the state on threat of death.[1]

In Elloree, South Carolina, L. A. Blackman, president of the local chapter of the National Association for the Advancement of Colored People, got word that a Ku Klux Klan rally had been called specifically to threaten his life. Blackman had been urging blacks in the community to vote. Scorning advice and defying history, he went to the rally. A hooded speaker was on the back of a truck haranguing the crowd about blacks and voting. When he finished, he asked if anyone had anything at all to say on the "subject of the nigger Blackman."

Blackman eased through the crowd, climbed up on the truck, and said without emotion, "I have been here seventeen years and I have no idea of leaving. I am going to stay here."

The astonishment was so great, the act so courageous, that the Klan speaker got down off the truck and left. The crowd evaporated.[2]

On Friday, December 1, 1955, Mrs. Rosa Parks, a soft-spoken seamstress, refused to move from her seat to the back of a bus in Montgomery, Alabama, when the bus driver demanded it. The whole world remembers what happened in Montgomery after that.

The more Southern racists pondered these and other defiances, the more they became aware of Highlander. The voting rights material found in the minister's car had the school's name on it. Blackman, they learned, had been to a Citizenship School. Only weeks before Mrs. Parks balked at the bus driver's orders, she had been in Monteagle. Highlander could not and did not claim any direct cause and effect relationship between students, school, and society. The idea of freedom was stirring among Southern blacks.

But the effect Mrs. Parks felt as a result of her experiences at Highlander can be noted: "At Highlander, I found out for the first time in my adult life that this could be a unified society, that there was such a thing as people of differing races and backgrounds meeting together in workshops and living together in peace and harmony. It was a place I was very reluctant to leave. I gained there strength to persevere in my work for freedom, not just for blacks but all oppressed people."[4]

Racists, however, drew a different conclusion. The notion that blacks themselves were taking the initiative and were dreaming of freedom from second-class citizenship and poverty was beyond the ken of most whites. Some conspiracy had to be behind these incidents, they reasoned. The available evidence led to Monteagle.

To celebrate its twenty-fifth anniversary, the school arranged a special weekend on Labor Day, 1957. Several hundred friends were invited. All told, about 180, mostly Southerners, came to renew old friendships, talk about the South, and share their thinking about how Highlander could strengthen its role in what everyone agreed was to be a gathering storm.

Aubrey Williams, publisher of the *Southern Farm and Home Magazine* and former president of the Southern Conference for

Human Welfare, and the Reverend Martin Luther King, Jr., head of the Montgomery Improvement Association, were keynote speakers. Ed Friend, a photographer, was sent from Georgia by Governor Marvin Griffin to learn as much as he could about the "fearful company."[5] The weekend proved to be memorable, not so much for what was said as for what was said later about it. Williams was not at all certain that good would triumph over evil in the South. King saw a day when racism would no longer keep men apart and thus prevent democracy.

Said Williams:

> When a governor of a state says, as Governor Coleman of Mississippi did recently, "We have no intention of complying with the decision" [by the Supreme Court on school desegregation], then, he, as chief peace officer of the state, is committing an act which I believe all reasonable men will regard as defiance of law, and rebellion, certainly in its incipient form. It is one thing for him to work and to advocate defeat of a civil rights bill, but it is quite another thing for him to defy the act and to plan with others who are also officers of the peace, open defiance of what has become law.
>
> The words and acts of publicly elected officials of the Deep South have, without question, placed us squarely and ominously on the road which leads to a vast public defiance of the federal laws, and the stuff out of which rebellions are made is definitely being planted.[6]

Dr. King was more hopeful:

> But in spite of all this, the opponents of desegregation are fighting a losing battle. The Old South is gone, never to return again.
>
> . . . the determination of the Negro himself to gain freedom and equality is a most powerful force that will ultimately defeat the barriers of integration. For many years the Negro tacitly accepted segregation. He was the victim of stagnant passivity and deadening complacency. The forces of slavery and segregation caused many Negroes to feel that perhaps they were inferior. But through the forces of history something happened to the Negro: he came to feel

that he was somebody. He came to feel that the important thing about a man is not his specificity, but his fundamentum; not the color of his skin nor the texture of his hair, but the texture and quality of his soul.

With this new sense of dignity and new self-respect, a new Negro emerged. So there has been a revolutionary change . . . ."[7]

No definite answers surfaced that weekend. There was no real, cohesive social movement yet in the South, just rumblings and eruptions. There was no organization—like an international union, for example—to which education could be tied. Highlander had to stay loose, keep learning, and continue making contacts with blacks through the Citizenship Schools, or in the way Highlander staff members usually made contact with people—by one person's introducing them to another.

Highlander was already in touch with many Southern leaders for change. The report on the Labor Day weekend at Highlander by undercover agent Ed Friend is one bit of evidence. Two hundred and fifty thousand slick copies of a brochure based on Friend's report, featuring his photographs, were subsequently sent throughout the South and the nation by Governor Griffin's Georgia Commission on Education, a tax-funded body he had set up to root out deviation from segregation. While the grammar is inaccurate, the tabulation of the people present is correct:

> there assembled at Highlander the leaders of every major race incident in the South, prior to that time since the Supreme Court decision. . . .
>
> There were representative leaders of the Tuskegee, Alabama, boycott, the Tallahassee, Florida bus incident, the Montgomery, Alabama bus boycott, the South Carolina–NAACP school teachers incident, the Koinonia inter-racial farm–Americus, Georgia, and Clinton, Tennessee, school incident among others.
>
> They met at this workshop and discussed methods and tactics of precipitating racial strife and disturbance.

The meeting of such a large group of specialists in inter-racial strife under the auspices of a Communist Training School, and in the company of many known Communists is the typical method whereby leadership training and tactics are furnished to the agitators. . . .[8]

In an Editorial Comment in the brochure, Governor Griffin stated, "It has been our purpose, as rapidly as possible, to identify the leaders and participants of this Communist training school and disseminate this information to the general public. . . . It behooves each of us to learn more of Communist infiltration and the direction of Communist movements. Only through information and knowledge can we combat this alien menace to Constitutional government."

Using the technique of guilt by association, the flyer described Dr. King as a representative of "the ultimate in 'civil disobedience.' It is doubtful that Reverend King could have carried on such a program [the Montgomery bus boycott] without leadership and financing." It said Dr. Charles Gomillion was "most vehement in his defense of Communists." Pete Seeger was "typical of the entertainer who gives his time and talent to the support of the Communist apparatus." Conrad Browne, who was to become Highlander's vice-president in a year or so, was a "resident leader of Koinonia Farm during the violence, boycotts and other incidents arising at this socialistic interracial community." As for Aubrey Williams, the brochure stated, "Few people if any have aided the Communist Party more in its conspiracy against peace between the races in the southern part of the United States. . . ."[9]

Friend had registered for the conference as a free-lance photographer. There were only a handful of newsmen present that weekend, among them Abner Berry, a columnist for *The Daily Worker*. He had registered as a free-lance writer, concealing his association with the official newspaper of the Communist Party of the United States.

In spite of his duties as host, Horton noticed that Friend and Berry chatted together frequently. Horton gradually realized that, when Friend took a picture, Berry usually inched his way into the group. Several times, Friend asked Horton to pose for a picture, and as the final arrangements were being made, Berry would suddenly appear beside him.

Matters came to a head when Horton asked Friend to photograph Aubrey Williams, Dr. King, Mrs. Parks, John Thompson, and himself for Highlander's annual report. Friend agreed. Just before he took the picture, Berry hurried in front of the group and stopped in the foreground. Friend clicked the shutter. Horton snapped, "I won't pay for that picture."[10] Highlander didn't pay for the picture with money, but it did in other ways. Friend's photograph became the most famous picture ever taken at Highlander, and it has been used in many ways ever since.

Soon, across the South, billboards using the photo started appearing with greater frequency than "Impeach Earl Warren" signs. Huge letters proclaimed that "King Attended a Communist Training Center." Postcards using the picture still circulate. Years later, when Horton was reelected to the board of the Council of Southern Mountains, one disgusted board member wrote his resignation on one of the postcards.

Governor Griffin's calumny backfired. The anniversary proved to be Highlander's highwater mark for publicity. Reaction came from around the nation. *The Christian Century* described Griffin's attack as work "shadowed through . . . distorting prisms . . . sad and sordid enough if it stayed south near whatever paranoid minds nurture such deceit."[11] On December 22, the *New York Times* carried a statement released by Highlander and signed by Mrs. Eleanor Roosevelt, Dr. Reinhold Niebuhr, Monsignor John O'Grady, head of the National Conference of Catholic Charities, and Lloyd K. Garrison, former dean of the University of Wisconsin Law School:

The attempt of the Georgia governor's commission to draw from the serious and fruitful deliberations of this gathering sustenance for the efforts of Southern racists to equate desegregation with communism evokes our strong condemnation. This kind of irresponsible demagoguery is obviously designed to intensify the difficulties confronting decent Southerners who might otherwise give leadership in the adjustment necessary for the desegregation which is inevitable. We deem it morally indefensible for any men or group to inflict upon such institutions as Highlander and upon such individuals as the respected leaders, both white and Negro, who attended the Labor Day Seminar, the damage to reputation and position which may result from wide distribution of this slanderous material.[12]

Press clippings kept by Highlander generally took the position expressed by the *Arapahoe Herald* of Littleton, Colorado, which noted in an October editorial, "The governor of the State of Georgia has fallen into a common error among Southerners. He believes that anyone who favors integration must be a Communist. That makes about 125 million Communists in the United States."[13]

Public reaction to the attack perhaps proved stronger than Governor Griffin had imagined. Georgia's Commission on Education quickly turned to other matters. But Horton realized that, as the surge for black freedom swelled, so, too, would resentment against Highlander. Without warning, the Internal Revenue Service revoked the school's tax-exempt status, an action which posed a far more serious threat than Griffin's broadside.[14] "We were intent on continuing whole," Horton says. "There was no compromise."[15]

In 1959, Governor Griffin's salvo was followed by a shot from Arkansas. Bruce Bennett, Arkansas' attorney general, came to Tennessee to warn the legislature of "subversion within its own boundaries," adding, "I would gladly come to Tennessee if invited to lend whatever help I could to close Highlander."[16]

The legislature needed little encouragement. Most of the

members had seen or heard of Governor Griffin's broadside and the billboards. Southern politicians generally agreed with what a Louisiana segregationist had told *The New Republic*, "The Communists and the NAACP plan to register every colored person in the South . . . using their votes to set up a federal dictatorship."[17] After expressing appreciation for Bennett's taking time away from his own fight in Little Rock, the Tennessee legislators adopted a resolution to investigate Highlander, then established a committee of three and appropriated $5,000 to "expose this evil."[18]

On February 21, 1959, Tennessee Senator Lawrence T. Hughes and Representatives Harry Lee Senter and T. Allen Hanover, with Attorney General Bennett to aid them, opened two days of hearings in Tracy City. Horton and the board realized that the school was fighting for its existence.

Much of the testimony was the sort of petty rumor that bad neighbors spread, such as the fact that few people had ever seen an American flag flying at the school. Mrs. Violet Crutchfield, register of deeds in Grundy County, testified that the school had not filed a charter in Grundy, as required by law. She was correct. Horton had filed the charter in Fentress County during the school's early uncertain days.

May Justus, Highlander's longtime neighbor and friend, was asked by the committee's lawyer, after he had shown her some of Friend's photographs, if she approved of blacks and whites dancing together. "I see nothing immoral about it," she said. "It's a square dance. I can look at television any time and see worse than that."

"Don't you know it's against the law for whites and colored to marry in Tennessee?" he retorted.

"Yes, sir, but I didn't know that a square dance was part of a marriage ceremony," she replied.

He changed the subject and asked about her knowledge of

Highlander's charter. "It says here one of your purposes is to train rural and industrial leaders. Have you ever issued any diplomas to rural and industrial leaders that you know of?"

"I didn't know diplomas were required for rural and industrial leaders."

Remarks of this nature won for her permission to stand aside.[19]

The investigators saved their main show for Nashville. Two days before driving there, Horton tried to register the school's charter in Grundy County. He was told that the committee had ordered Mrs. Crutchfield not to permit him to register the charter if he should try. "If the charter is wrong," he told the legislators on the third and last day of hearings, "I want to correct it, but apparently the committee doesn't want it corrected."[20]

Attorney General Bennett opened the proceedings in Nashville by drawing lines on a blackboard connecting Highlander to various groups or individuals who, in Bennett's words, "have been cited as belonging to various 'Communist front' organizations." Included on the list were Jim Dombrowski and Dean Gomillion, Anne and Carl Braden of the Southern Conference Education Fund, Lucian Koch, who was former president of Commonwealth College, Abner Berry, and Claude C. Williams, the Presbyterian minister who had urged Zilphia Mae Johnson to come to Highlander years before.

After producing his evidence, Bennett summarized: "If a barnyard goose is lured into a flock of wild geese, he may be excused only if he leaves the flock. But if he continues flying in formation with them, then he is a wild goose, no matter how loudly he may protest that he is not. I feel like that school has been flying in formation with a lot of people who have as their goal the destruction of the United States as we know it and the placing into power of a Communist conspiracy."

After Bennett's presentation, the legislators asked Horton to admit that he was a Communist. "Mr. Bennett has only proven that he can put names on a blackboard and draw lines between them," said Horton. Four-and-a-half hours later he was excused from the stand.

Earlier in the day, Ed Friend, who had come up from Georgia especially to tell of his weekend at Highlander, had shown a twelve-minute film he had made. Mostly, it showed blacks and whites leaving the school's library together, or swimming in the lake. When it was over Friend was questioned:

Q. Mr. Friend, was that a subversive meeting there at that time?

A. It was subversive sir, to the way that I have been taught to live in America.

Q. Explain that to the committee.

A. I have been taught by Southern tradition to keep the races separate. I was taught to go to Sunday School and Church. I was taught to respect the other fellow's habitat, and that is what I have always tried to do. Up here it seems like all of those things weren't even considered. It is the primary motive of this group to tear down the forces that were trying to keep the races separate in the South.

Q. Was it your observation that they were trying to bring about a condition of chaos and turmoil and strife among people?

A. Among the races, sir, between the races.

Q. It is true or not that this is the breeding ground for Communists under those conditions?

A. That is my understanding of it, sir.[21]

The hearings closed Friday, March 6, 1959. Even unsympathetic observers agreed with *The* (Nashville) *Tennessean's* editorial the next day: "[the] two-act drama . . . had some interesting casting and some dialogue in which the so-called 'villains' outperformed the so-called 'heroes'. . . . [But it] was pretty much the dud of advance predictions."[22]

Horton was not optimistic.

Six days later, the committee recommended that Albert (Ab) Sloan, attorney general for the Eighteenth Judicial Circuit in which Highlander was located, sue to revoke the school's charter. They made no finding in fact about alleged communism, but contended that "a great deal of circumstantial evidence . . . was unfolded before the committee . . . of long association with so-called communist front organizations. . . ." They did comment, however, "It is significant that no witness other than Myles Horton had ever seen the American flag fly over this 'school' in the 26 years of its existence, and he, only on a few occasions." Finally, they determined that Highlander was not a school. "No regular classes are held. They maintain no regular full-time faculty, no regular standard curriculum and do not carry on the usual activities as one would normally associate with school activities."[23]

Attorney General Sloan's indulgence lasted until July 31, 1959, when, about 8:30 P.M., he led twenty state troopers and sheriff's deputies, most of them in plain clothes, to Highlander in search of whiskey. Reporters and photographers from the *Chattanooga News–Free Press* came, too. Grundy County was dry. Possession or sale of whiskey, either store-bought or homemade, was illegal.[24]

Horton was in Europe serving as cochairman of an international conference on residential adult education when he got word of the raid. He hurried home to learn what had happened.

Mrs. Clark, in the midst of conducting a workshop on school desegregation, had been arrested and charged with illegal possession and sale of whiskey and with resisting arrest. The last charge was a result of her request to a sheriff's deputy to telephone a lawyer. Her request was refused. Her bankbook and wallet, containing identification and twenty-six dollars, were seized and never returned. Mrs. Clark, then sixty-one years old, had been a teetotaler all her life.

Three other persons, a New York City teacher, Perry M. Sturgis; a Quaker, Brent Barksdale, both teetotalers; and Guy Carawan, who was director of music at Highlander, were all arrested on charges of public drunkenness and of interfering with an officer.

Mrs. Clark had been showing a film when the raid started. Police had ordered the lights turned back off after they entered the center. Within minutes—once the initial shock was over—workshop participants had begun to sing "We Shall Overcome." They had added a new verse in the darkened room that night, "We are not afraid." Police found no alcohol in the main building, nor in any other school building. In Horton's home, however, they found an empty wooden whiskey keg, and, in a bottle, a half inch of gin. Horton's home was private property. As such, it was not subject to the search warrant. But police seized the gin and took it, along with their prisoners, to the justice of the peace in Tracy City. Charges were formally drawn against the four; they were fingerprinted and jailed in nearby Altamont. Their requests for blood tests were ignored.

Carawan said later that he could hear Mrs. Clark in the jail cell below him singing "We Shall Overcome" softly into the night. Miss Vera McCampbell, the school's neighbor, posted bond for them, and Mrs. Clark was released at 2:30 A.M. The others were held another eight hours, until "they sobered up."[25]

A few days later, Sloan told the *Chattanooga Daily Times*, "The members of the legislative committee gave me information mostly on integration and communism, and I wasn't satisfied I could be successful at that. I thought maybe this was the best shot and I think now I'll be successful."[26]

Later, he filed a petition requesting the county court to padlock Highlander as a public nuisance on the grounds that it was a place where people engaged in immoral, lewd, and unchaste practices, that it was the scene of loud and boisterous gatherings, that it engaged in the sale and consumption of intoxicating liquor, that it was operated in violation of a 1901 Tennessee law forbidding blacks and whites to go to school together, and that it was operated for Horton's personal gain.[27]

That was Highlander's situation when Horton decided the Citizenship School program should be given to the Southern Christian Leadership Conference—if that organization wanted it. If there was to be a trial, Horton and the others suspected that the court would find with Sloan. To keep the Citizenship Schools going was one important goal. To keep Highlander's principles intact was another. In July, 1961, SCLC opened its own Citizenship School training center in McIntosh, Georgia, at a church-related black community center.

Sloan got a temporary injunction. Highlander's main building was padlocked. But Horton told newsmen during a workshop in makeshift quarters, "You can padlock a building. But you can't padlock an idea. Highlander is an idea. You can't kill it and you can't close it in. This workshop is part of the idea. It will grow wherever people take it."[28]

9

. . . wind up your affairs . . .

JOHN THOMPSON, one of Highlander's first staff members, returned to Monteagle after the raid. He wrote rough notes on the five crucial days in November, 1969, when the school fought in court for the right to exist.

The legislative hearings last winter failed in their purpose to prove that Highlander is subversive. Then the Aug. 31 liquor raid found no liquor on school property and used a warrant so illegal that even this judge had to throw it out. Septima and 2 instructors are still under indictment for possessing liquor but the case is postponed until next year and will probably never be tried since the judge said the evidence was nil.

In last week's case the attorney general of this district (Ab Sloan) filed a bill against Highlander in a kind of shot gun approach: 9 charges, among them the charge the school sold liquor and other commodities; the charge that the school was run for Horton's gain and benefit; etc. In interviews this autumn he insisted the case had nothing to do with integration. But a week or so before trial he amended his bill to prosecute Highlander for violating an old Tennessee law forbidding whites and Negroes to attend classes together.

The case was held at Altamont, 25 or 30 miles from here. It went from Monday last week till the end of Friday. Our lawyer, [Cecil] Branstetter . . . opened with a brilliantly written demurrer outlining the constitutional issue since the integration issue had been added to the bill. We hoped if they should revoke the charter they would do it honestly because of integration and provide an issue that could be carried on up into federal courts. The judge over-ruled and a jury was chosen. While the prosecution played around with all the issues (introducing the integration issue more covertly and by constant innuendo rather than overtly) more and more they bore down on the charge that Horton had just set up a profit making device for himself and for 27 years has had no aim but to amass a fortune and gobble it up.

The state began by lifting the injunction and removing the padlock imposed in Sept. after the "liquor raid." Then they subpoened [sic] the CPA in Knoxville [Harry Herrell] who is the school auditor. He produced the audits of the school's accounts for the past 3 years and financial reports for its history; said that since he set up the school books 3 years ago they have been kept better than most corporations keep records; that the ratio percentage for salaries is much lower than in most corporations or institutions; and gave the school a clean financial bill of health.

The state insisted on a jury and the judge agreed. It took 6 hours or more to select 12 [jurors] out of 55 [called]. . . . 3 long term enemies of Highlander got on the jury. Also a cousin of a chief state witness in previous hearing; also a cousin of the sheriff; etc. . . . The Episcopal vicar in Tracy told us as soon as the jury was formed that we could never get a fair trial with that group. Every single juror admitted that he believed in segregation and if it was up to him an integrated school would not be allowed to exist in Grundy county. The judge [Chester C. Chattin] said, "But you could put your opinions in your pocket and forget them, couldn't you." So he ruled them competent. He seemed to believe in a kind of autonomous, voluntary schizophrenia.

The factual background of the property and profit issue is this: Myles worked from 1932 to 1954 without any salary, Zilphia worked from 1935 to 1954 without any salary; i.e. for subsistence only; and when the school bought the Glovier property Myles and Zilphia moved from their log cabin (without plumbing) into this old log house; then when Zilphia's mine-owner father gave her some money and later bequeathed more she put $12,000 of that money into building on the Glovier house until they finished the house they have lived in in recent years. The contractor who built the house testified that Zilphia paid him personally. We found many of the cancelled checks. . . . Then about 1954 the Board had insisted that they start paying a salary to Myles as well as to other staff members. The first year it was only $1,200. But in the current year it's on the books for $9,000. In 1957 without tax exemption they did not pay but made it up in 1958 (at rate of 7500) so his 1958 income tax returns showed $15,-

000 and the state tried to argue that he was getting $15,000 per year plus all kinds of other things. Then in '56 after Zilphia's death the Board realized that if Myles should die his kids [Thorsten and Charis] would be penniless since even the $12,000 equity in the house was legally the school's—i.e. built on school property. So the Board voted to transfer this equity plus a token of the twenty years without salary for Myles and 19 for Zilphia to Myles. They deeded him the house he lives in plus about 60 of the 200 plus acres here. Before this was done a committee was appointed to study and recommend; after they recommended they waited a year, got an attorney's interpretation and approval, etc. Then when the deed was made Myles started paying taxes on this place.

The School submitted Board minutes covering all these transactions. . . . But Sloan argued that Myles had come down in 1932 with the plot in mind to build up a fortune and then to cut the melon and eat up the slices himself. Of course this is a nice house but it has been used constantly for school purposes ever since 1954. The deed was just to give Myles some protection in case the school should be demolished or his kids if he should die.

* * *

The state produced a lot of witnesses to testify that candy bars, razor blades cokes, and on occasion beer had been sold at the school. The school had explained how and why this operation took place so they did not need testimony to prove it took place.[1]

Horton had explained why convenience items had been sold, and had testified to that effect at the earlier hearing:

I personally instituted a policy of having beer available for people who were there for conferences, the labor people who came, because I have always felt that we had no right to impose our students or ideas on other people in the community or neighborhood. . . . When groups would come [they would] pay for it as part of their expenses . . . and when they wouldn't, they had a rotating fund where people could contribute, put in some money in a box if they wanted to, and if they didn't want to, they didn't. . . . We used all the money to refill the ice box. This system operated up until, well, Mrs. Clark was against this kind of thing and the last few years there had been very little of that.[2]

Thompson's notes on the trial continue with an impression of the witnesses called by the state and by the defense.

Interestingly all the witnesses who were produced on this issue had had many jail sentences; all but one lived with someone else's husband or wife or was a well known bastard in the pure biological sense. In calling one woman witness the state made the mistake of calling Mrs. the man she lives with when the man had another legal wife nearby. The court room giggled and tittered. But these mountaineers do their sinning with a certain dignity. Even the sheriff when he raids moonshiners doesn't waste the confiscated liquor; he takes it around to treat his friends.

Because the charge implied that HFS is run not as a bona fide school but as a cow for Myles to milk we had a good many educators and ministers who are familiar with its program. Morris Mitchell (brother of George and Broadus) now president of the graduate school for teachers at Putney, Vt., was the most impressive. He is a man of great dignity, physically and spiritually; he is a man of values; he is urbane and calm and both his words and his speech are beautiful. He has been a prof at Peabody and Columbia and other good universities. He gave Highlander and Myles the highest praise and said a man of Myles' ability could be making a much larger salary in other places. Sandy [Dr. A. A.] Liveright of Chicago [the Center for Study of Liberal Adult Education] was also a very impressive witness since he is a big wheel in the whole adult education movement here and abroad. Also a doctor on the faculty at Michigan. Nearly a dozen Sewanee professors [including Scott Bates of the board]; Everett Tillson from Vanderbilt; Herman Long from Fisk; the National Council of Churches man in Nashville; the Unitarian minister from Nashville; Dr. F. D. Patterson formerly president of Tuskegee, now head of the Phelps-Stokes Fund in N.Y.

All our witnesses were educators and ministers who had been to Highlander many times. One Sewanee prof. had done adult education in the army and said he wished he had known Highlander's methods when he had that job. On the record the testimony was very impressive. The lawyer in identifying them asked them what schools they had attended, their degrees, their former teaching jobs, etc. Two or three had been college presidents and testified to salary scales and perquisites. But Ab Sloan in addressing the jury brushed them all aside by saying "And what did all those people who trooped in for Highlander really tell you? They just said 'Look at me. Look how smart I am.' That's all they told you." And the courtroom of farmers and miners and unemployed rocked with laughter.

Sloan proved to be an extremely clever demagog. He is a red-neck and ruthless but he knows his people; when he speaks it is the mighty Wurlitzer with all stops pulled out, from the tremolo to the roar of the mightiest diapason. He injected race again and again and again without being too specific. Reference had been made to Septima Clark. Sloan called her September Clark. . . . (and he pointed to her in the audience to make sure everyone saw she was a Negro) "Why she's a big ramrod out at Highlander." In addition to his exhibits he passed around the Gov. Griffin still picture of the folk dance where [a] white woman and a Negro man were caught close together. The jury all saw this before our lawyer did. It had no relevance to charges and the judge ruled it stricken from the record. But the jury had seen it. And so on all through.

The state danced on the edge of mis-trial many times but the judge protected them. Two or three days it looked like he was playing on their team. At other times it looked like he was trying to be fair. This is his first year as judge; the first chancery case he has ever tried . . . . Neither judge nor prosecutors seemed embarassed [sic] by much knowledge of the law. Our lawyer was much depressed by this angle of it and by the jury . . . .

Daily large groups of students from Sewanee and a good many profs came over. It was a good educational project for them. . . .

Myles kept his good humor and his sense of humor, enjoying the unbelievably crude and funny incidents as much as if he were not involved. He was also very good on the stand and gave Sloan much more than he wanted in his answers. Old Judge Rollings, formerly of that court, now past 90, nearly blind, traipsed and shuffled around the court room daily, walking up between lawyer and witness, sitting at lawyers' tables, but most of the time plying the audience trying to sell copies of a paper bound book on his views and life, his loves and hates, etc. He looked like a big bloated superannuated frog on his last crawl. Dogs wandered in and out. Women with crying babes at breast attended persistently. No flag of any kind hung in the court room—not even Confederate.

Outside the dingy court house and the nearby jail the autumn colors both on nearby maples and on distant hills were as beautiful as I have ever seen.[3]

Thompson's report also assesses the newspaper coverage of the trial: "The Banner [of Nashville] had a good reporter covering the case; the Tennessean [of Nashville] put a cub from Mississippi Univ. on it. The Chattanooga Times did a good job; the Free Press [of Memphis did] their usual hatchet job. And so on. The N.Y. Times had some coverage for friends in New York . . . ."[4]

Notes on the trial continue with Thompson's prediction about the outcome.

We were rather fatalistic from the time the jury was chosen. Sloan succeeded among other things in making any salary sound like "profit" and in blowing up the house deal and ignoring board authorization and all records. The jury was out less than an hour and were unanimous in saying "yes"—Horton had run the school for his own gain.

This was the only question put to the jury. The judge has to make his verdict interpreting the law. He does not have to agree with the jury. He has to consider the integration issue and the other issues. Our feeling is that for judge, jury, and prosecution the real commanding issue is integration but that probably the judge will not say so. It is so much simpler to destroy the school for fraud. His possible actions are: (1) To dismiss the case; (2) To declare the deed invalid and restore the property to the school—in which case we could operate; (3) To revoke charter of school but leave the deed valid—in which case we could operate by taking out another charter and continuing from Horton's house, adding cottages; (4) To declare deed invalid, revoke charter, and sell the whole thing in dissolution proceedings. If I had to bet on one it would be this last since their purpose is not just to punish Horton or to straighten things out but to get rid of the school.

Fri. night we had a Board meeting. The Board voted confidence in Horton and the staff and planned the next workshops. The judge gives our lawyers 30 days to file brief; the state 10 days to answer; so he can't officially make his verdict for 40 days. I think his mind is made up but he's going thru this ritual to make it look like a fair proceeding.

* * *

Late Saturday some old timers dropped in to assure Myles of their support and confidence. One man who came to our dances 26 years ago reminisced and deplored. He said, "I know I'm dumb. I've been in more jails than hotels. But I've been thru two world wars and Uncle Sam paid my travel. Those people at Tracy and Altamont are just plain ignorant. You've heard that ignorance is bliss. Well they've got too much bliss—that's all they've got. Why those people are so ignorant they don't know whether Jesus Christ was crucified or run over by a truck."[5]

Thompson's predictions proved correct. On February 17, 1960, Judge Chattin found that Highlander had sold beer and other items without a license, that the school was operated for Horton's personal gain, and that it had practiced racial integration in violation of Title 49, Section 3701, of Tennessee law forbidding such practice. He ordered Highlander's charter revoked and appointed a receiver to liquidate the property. He told Horton to "wind up your affairs."[6]

The school appealed the ruling to the State Supreme Court. That body upheld Judge Chattin's rulings, but threw out the violation of Title 49, Section 3701.[7] Integration was not an issue when the case was appealed to the U.S. Supreme Court which, on October 9, 1961, denied Highlander a hearing.[8]

Expecting the worst, Horton, weeks before, had applied for and received a new charter. On August 28, 1961, Highlander Research and Education Center, Inc., was opened in an abused, but still usable, Knoxville mansion overlooking the tin sheds of the Tennessee Marble Company plant.[9]

On a rainy, muddy December 16, nearly three thousand people trooped through the Summerfield property for an auction. The property had been badly vandalized; nonetheless, the sale of the school's effects—books, beds, typewriters, etc.—netted the state $10,000. Later, on July 8, 1962, the real property, including the house deeded to Horton and the one which had been purchased by his father and mother to live out their lives in, seven other residences, fourteen school buildings, 175 acres of land, and a private lake, was auctioned. The state made an additional $43,700.[10] No cent of compensation was ever paid to Highlander or to Horton or to his parents for the seizure of their private property. In an ironic footnote, lawyers from the Grundy area bought Highlander's library and turned the building into a private club.

Only the summer cottage originally given to Highlander by Dr. Johnson escaped the sale. Almost as if the state's vengeance had not been enough to satisfy the wrathful, the house had mysteriously caught fire and burned to its foundations between the first auction and the second.

10

... this is a movement for democracy...

THE STUDENT NONVIOLENT Coordinating Committee was the last group to use the Highlander Folk School at Summerfield. In August, just before the staff moved to Knoxville, SNCC workers from across the South gathered to talk about adding still another tactic to the nonviolent battle plan that had made SNCC, in its one year of life, the organization that Southern racists despised most. The audacious sit-ins, the Freedom Rides, the jails full of singing, would have seemed mild to segregationist whites had they known what SNCC, at Highlander, was talking about doing next. They proposed to couple direct action protests with voter registration drives and to carry this explosive mixture into the citadels of racism—Georgia, Alabama, and Mississippi.

Night riders attacked the school during this last meeting, probably more as a farewell send-off for hated Highlander than because of any knowledge of the SNCC meetings. Among those narrowly missed by rifle shots that were fired into the buildings was a bearded Howard University student, Stokely Carmichael, who had just gotten out of Mississippi's Parchman Prison.

The people, their reason for being there, the attack were all a fitting and appropriate fulfillment of Horton's early visions for Highlander. To answer the question of why SNCC was meeting at Highlander is to illustrate how education can be used for social change, how learning can be distilled from the ordinary experiences of people, and how, in John Dewey's terms, teachers can assume social leadership.[1]

There have been a good many providential accidents in Highlander's history, but the SNCC meeting wasn't an accident. For six years prior to the first sit-ins in 1960, Highlander, as part of its overall policy of seeking to make education serve Southern blacks, had held workshops in Summerfield. The workshops were started at the insistence of parents who had been to the school and had found it to be a place where, as one student put it, "You can live freedom."[2]

At first, the staff had let the college students join any residential workshop that might be in session, a training school for volunteer teachers in the Citizenship Schools, for example. The students were glib, and their easy answers, while they impressed the parents, constrained the adults from reaching their own appropriate and practical solutions to their problems. Horton concluded that "college-learned responses to complex community problems were, at best, oversimplifications."[3]

Therefore, the students were asked, in 1954, to set up and run their own workshops. They did. The first was held from October 29 through October 31 of that year and was called the College Weekend Workshop on Human Relations. It was mostly devoted to theoretical talk about the problems that the students faced. By 1959, when the workshop topic was "Campus Leadership for Integration," the students had begun to struggle with real social problems. At the end of this workshop, the participants, as was the practice, decided on a topic for the next year. It was to have been "The Role of Private Colleges in Criticizing the Social Order."[4]

Events in Greensboro, North Carolina, on February 1, 1960, changed the agenda. Four freshmen college students sat in at a dime store lunch counter from 4:30 P.M. to 5:30 P.M., when the store closed, without being served because they were black. The next day, about seventy-five students went back to the same lunch counter. They stayed two hours and weren't served. On

February 4, three white students joined the sit-in. On February 5, white students, Negro students, and members of the Klan vied for seats.

Within nine days after the first Greensboro sit-in, similar demonstrations had taken place in fifteen Southern cities in five states. By March 22, the Associated Press reported that a thousand blacks had been arrested during sit-ins. A social movement that had been fermenting for years had finally erupted.

On April 1, the Seventh Annual College Workshop opened at Highlander. Eighty-three students from twenty colleges came. Most, if not all, had sat in, and some had been jailed. Immediately after their arrival, they changed the workshop topic to "The New Generation Fights for Equality," and the Highlander staff realized that more than the workshop topic had changed.[5] "Our young have gone out in front," Septima Clark said, "and we must run to keep up with them. We must give them our support, but we must not attempt to wrest the leadership from them."[6]

The youthful leaders that would soon stir the nation were there: Lee Loder, Bernard Lafayette, Jr., Marion S. Barry, James Bevel, John Lewis, Diane Nash, Julian Bond—to name only a few.

"This is the first time since these protests started that people from a variety of places involved have gotten together," Horton said in welcoming them. "Something might come out of these discussions that will help further the thing you believe in. If, in your deliberations, you come to some conclusions—which we certainly have no interest in engineering—we will be glad to help you as you ask us to help. We're here to help you do what you decide to do, not to try to get you to join with us in doing something, because we don't have anything except a service to render."[7]

Consultants for the workshop agreed with Mrs. Clark and

Horton. They came to support, not supplant. They were the Reverend J. Metz Rollins, a Presbyterian church worker in Nashville; Thomas Dilkes, a professor of history at the University of the South; Perry Sturgis from the Collegiate School in New York City, who had been arrested in Sloan's raid on Highlander; and Dr. Herman Long of Fisk's Race Relations Institute.

Talk during the workshop's early hours centered around the beatings suffered at the hands of police. Students compared jails. They listened to reports about what was happening or was planned for the immediate future. Though prideful, their voices, even in the tape recordings made during the sessions, reflected tension. Before the first evening's discussion ended, they had spelled out problems the movement would wrestle with often in the days ahead: Was nonviolence a way of life or a tactic? Were they right to break the law? Should they ask others for support? What was the role of white students? How would they relate to divisions in the black community? Friday night opened with questions like these.

Saturday morning, Dr. Long, whose association with Highlander stretched nearly to its beginnings, expanded on the students' discussion of the previous evening: "adults . . . would probably not have taken action of this kind even if they had seen the possibilities in it," he said. "They probably would have had prestige positions and economic interests, or job interests, to protect. Furthermore, adults are essentially conservative. Mass demonstration is not impossible for them and some do participate in it, but it is not the method the adult community seems at present to believe is its final strategy for attack on discrimination. In this sense, this is a unique movement, especially suited to students."

He urged the students to clarify their aims, methods, and philosophy. "The method of nonviolence, for instance, needs to be clearly interpreted. The question of whether this movement is meant to force a testing of the existing law through existing legal procedures, or to dramatize injustice through mass demonstration reckoned to touch the conscience of the community," must, he said, be determined by the students themselves.[8]

Then Dr. Long suggested that they break into four groups: philosophy, communications, methods, and community relations—so that they could better talk about the issues they had raised and come to some conclusions. They agreed. Late Sunday afternoon, just before the participants left to go back to college, or to more protest, they gathered to share the tentative conclusions of the four groups. Up to this time, the students had taken only one break, except for meals: on Saturday night, with the help of Guy Carawan, they had staged a talent show and square dance. Carawan had taught a song many of them would carry around the world, "We Shall Overcome."

The Sunday afternoon gathering heard ideas and proposals advanced in ways that would become characteristic of SNCC. For example, the students' philosophy was summed up in three sentences: "We believe in democracy. We are using nonviolence as a method, but not necessarily as a total way of life. We believe it is practical." While the majority agreed that they wanted to end segregation within the nation's legal framework, they were unclear as to whether to continue deliberate violations of Jim Crow laws or to take the laws through costly court tests. A handful of them, mostly the students from Nashville, argued that nonviolence was a way of life. To them, there were laws higher than civil law.

The group considering communications urged that students not affiliate with any existing organization. They urged protesters to use the loose confederation of protest groups in South Carolina as a model, and suggested a similar structure for the entire South. Such a coalition, they argued, should not have a constitution, but should grow as it would. A headquarters would be useful in channeling money into specific communities or protests, but headquarters should do little more than direct the flow of funds.

Explicitly, they said that they were unwilling to have any support funds directed to any adult group other than the NAACP, "and only to this agency provided it will agree to distribute the gifts to student groups according to their need for court action."

They urged college newspapers to cover the demonstrations fully, and to exchange papers with each other across the South. They rejected as impractical the idea of a special sit-in newsletter. They encouraged student visits between Northern and Southern, black and white, colleges.

The methods group advanced four proposals: careful planning of demonstrations to increase the impact on a given community; economic boycotts, where practical; selective buying to show appreciation of stores that served blacks on an equal basis; and continued use of picketing. So far, their experience was limited to one form of direct action, the sit-in. Few of them knew that labor unions had used that technique years before, or even that the Youth Council of the Oklahoma City NAACP had conducted sit-ins two years before Greensboro. The students refused to be hamstrung by one method, or by a lack of alternatives. They were willing to use sit-ins, they said, "only as long as [they] proved useful."

The community relations group urged closer ties with adults, but it did not want any group or agency, black, white, or interracial, to take control of the student movement. It suggested that each sit-in group appoint a representative from the community to serve as a liaison between protesting students and adults, "but only as liaison." White students would be welcome. "This is a movement for democracy, and in a democratic movement, all are welcome and useful."[9]

In the months ahead, the roaming, impetuous, purposeful group called the Student Nonviolent Coordinating Committee gained strength. The name served, to Horton's way of thinking, to symbolize more a quality of independence emanating from the South's black belt than an organization. SNCC was a group characterized by easy humor, song, and poetry, yet it was tough-minded and fearless. SNCC was the embodiment of the dream of what could be in America, rather than what is, Horton felt.

Highlander and SNCC were tied in countless ways going far beyond those visible, countable meetings the students held at the school. Rosa Parks is one tie. On March 3 and 4, 1956, about eighteen months after she had been to Highlander for the first time and returned to Montgomery to spark the bus boycott, Mrs. Parks came back to Highlander to help the staff plan a series of workshops on public school integration. Parts of that session were tape recorded:

"Rosa," asked Horton, "tell us what's been going on in Alabama."

"Montgomery today is nothing at all like it was as you knew it last year," she said. "It's a different place altogether since we demonstrated, which marked the time of my arrest on the city line bus for not moving out of the seat I had already occupied. For a white person to take the seat I would have had to stand. It was not at all prearranged. It just happened that the driver made a demand, and I just didn't feel like obeying his demand. He called a policeman, and I was arrested and placed in jail, later released on a hundred-dollar bond and brought to trial on December 5. This was the first date that the Negroes set not to ride the bus. From December to this date they are still staying off the bus in large numbers, almost 100 per cent. Once in a while you may see one or two, but very seldom do you see any riding the city line buses. It attracted too much attention all over the nation and worldwide, you may say. There was attention even as far away as London. We had a correspondent at one of our meetings. There was a correspondent from even as far away as Tokyo, Japan. People all over the country have called in to see what's going on, what's being done, and what is the reaction of it."

"What you did was a very little thing, you know, to touch off such a fire," Horton said. "Why did you do it; what moved you not to move? I'm interested in motivations—what makes people do things. What went on in your mind, Rosa?"

"Well, in the first place, I had been working all day on the job. I was quite tired after spending a full day working. I handle and work on clothing that white people wear. That didn't come in my mind, but this is what I wanted to know: when and how would we ever determine our rights as human beings? The section of the bus where I was sitting was what we call the colored section, especially in this neighborhood because the bus was filled more than two-thirds with Negro passengers and a number of them were standing. And just as soon as enough white passengers got on the bus to take what we consider their seats and then a few over, that meant that we would have to move back for them, even though there was no room to move back. It was an imposition as far as I was concerned."

Horton turned to Dr. George Mitchell, chairman of the Highlander board and president of the Southern Regional Council, and said, "Why, suddenly, does somebody—who happens to be somebody we know and admire and are proud of—say, 'Now, this is it!'? It seems to me what has happened in Montgomery is a new high in American protest, in the sense of people using passive resistance instead of more conventional methods. Now why, in the first place, did Rosa do this instead of it just being another time when she'd move? And then, equally important, why did the fact touch off the tremendous response that it did in Montgomery? These are interesting questions. I don't know whether we can get the answers to them. You couldn't have the highest paid public relations people or the highest paid organizers in the country do this, you know, George. It's just the kind of job that you couldn't set up, plan, and carry out. We had heard last summer, when Rosa was here, that the Negroes in Montgomery were timid and would not act. In fact, some of the leaders in Montgomery wrote us to that effect. They said they couldn't get any interest stirred up there, that the Negroes wouldn't stand together. Then Rosa refused to move and, as a result of her arrest, something big happened. Was it an accident? How do you feel about it, Rosa?"

"None of us seem to know exactly, ourselves," she replied, "unless it was because this incident had been experienced by so many others—many Negroes had been subjected to this type of humiliation. I think they responded because each person had experienced something of the same thing."

Mrs. Beulah Johnson of Tuskegee Institute had an answer for Horton, also.

"You asked what has happened to Rosa. I think I can tell you what happened to her. It is the same thing that happened to me and that man on the L&N railroad. I was tired of insults. You know the law is on your side and you get tired to being run over. You say, 'Well, let's fight it out—if it means going to jail, then go to jail.' That's just the whole attitude. When you get tired, then you get tired of people asking you to get up and move. I'm pretty certain that that's just one of those days that happened to Rosa. There comes a time in your life when you just decide that you don't give a rap. Many of us have reached that point. I don't live in Montgomery, but I'm in Montgomery every week and I know the situation. Now that's what happened to Rosa here."

She continued, "It is not only the Negroes in Montgomery—but Negroes all over the country are sticking together. This is a new day. I think Langston Hughes wrote a poem—here's the essence: 'I'm comin', I'm comin' but my head ain't bending low/ 'Cause this is a new Black Joe.' I think it brings out very definitely the way Negroes are feeling today."[10]

Unknown to Mrs. Parks during the Montgomery bus boycott, or to Dr. King, who would emerge as an internationally known leader because of his efforts in Montgomery, a teen-ager, the third child in a family of ten, John Lewis, was listening and learning. He lived in Pike County, Alabama, some fifty-eight miles from Montgomery. His father was a small, but independent, farmer.

"We heard it on the radio," he told a Northern audience a decade later. "We saw people marching and people refusing to ride the buses. We saw it on television and read about it in the newspapers.

"The Montgomery bus boycott, perhaps more than anything else, had a real impact on my life. I had tried during elementary school and junior high school—in my own way, I think, and I don't know why—not to become filled with hate and bitterness against this whole system of racial discrimination. But at the same time, I resented it and wanted to do something about it. After graduating from high school, I wanted to get out."

Lewis did leave Alabama. He went to the American Baptist Theological Seminary in Nashville, where he washed dishes in the cafeteria and worked as a janitor to pay his way. Lewis also became active in the NAACP Youth Council and, when the Reverend Martin Luther King, Sr., came to Nashville to help start a chapter of the Southern Christian Leadership Conference, Lewis attended the rally.

Soon thereafter, Lewis started going to a workshop on nonviolence organized by the black pacifist, James Lawson, then on the staff of the Fellowship of Reconciliation. Lewis said later, "In a sense, the movement, the workshops, the philosophy, the discipline of nonviolence became much more important to me than going to class every day." Every Tuesday night, Lewis and other students from the seminary, from A&I State University, and from Fisk converged on a black church for role-playing, social drama, and reading about and discussing civil disobedience.

"I saw these young men, Jim Lawson and the Reverend C. T. Vivian, saying, in effect, that you must be consistent with truth, that you must take the same teachings, same theories, same philosophy of Jesus, Gandhi, and Thoreau and attempt to make them real. In our own way, we tried to do what we could to make them real."

These attempts included demonstrations at two Nashville department stores in November and December, 1959. Lewis later told an audience of Northerners:

> Thus, when the sit-ins in Greensboro, North Carolina, on February 1, 1960, occurred, these sit-ins did not reach the Nashville student community or the larger black community in a vacuum because we were prepared to use the philosophy, the discipline of nonviolence, to break down the walls of racial discrimination in the area of public accommodation.
>
> During those first days in February, 1960, I saw what you might call a social movement develop—a movement with a great sense of dignity, a great sense of pride. You had hundreds of young black and white students, many professors, most of them well-dressed, marching into stores and places of public accommodation saying, in effect, "We must all be equal. It's a question of human dignity."
>
> There was no violence. No one struck back. Later, when the violence came, it came from the opposition. And, when some of us first went to jail, our parents and teachers in so many instances became troubled. Like most parents, they saw jail as a bad thing. But we saw going to jail for standing up for what we were involved in as an attempt to dramatize to Nashville, to the South as a region, to the whole nation, that black people were tired of being denied the same constitutional rights, and that this was an affront to their dignity.[12]

Lewis came to Highlander Easter weekend with the group from Nashville and, like countless other SNCC workers, was in and out of the school many times over the next few years before he went on to become director of the Voter Education Project in Atlanta.

In many respects, Lewis symbolizes the spreading power of an idea conveyed through social education, as practiced at Highlander. The black community in Montgomery was divided before Mrs. Parks' defiance. Black ministers, as members of the community, were divided, too. The man generally credited with encouraging the unified backing of Mrs. Parks, and giving the protest its nonviolent character, is E. D. Nixon. Back in the 1930's, he and Horton had worked together trying to organize Alabama cucumber picklers. He had urged Mrs. Parks to go to Highlander. Another Highlander friend, Mrs. Virginia Durr, who had worked with the school since the days of the Southern Conference for Human Welfare, arranged a scholarship for Mrs. Parks.

Fourteen days after Highlander's Seventh Annual College Workshop, on April 15, 1960, more than two hundred student protesters converged on a jittery Raleigh, North Carolina, for a three-day conference at Shaw University. By this time, sit-in demonstrations had spread to twelve states and sixty cities. Hundreds were in jail. The reason for the conference was the Southern Christian Leadership Conference's hope that the sit-in demonstrators would coalesce into an arm of SCLC. Dr. King and James Lawson were keynote speakers on opening night.

Dr. King called for a nationwide campaign of selective buying. He urged the students to form an organization whose members would be dedicated to going to jail without making bail or paying fines. He urged them to take sit-ins to every Southern community. "Resistance and nonviolence are not in themselves good," he declared. "There is another element in our struggle that makes our resistance and nonviolence truly meaningful. That element is reconciliation. Our ultimate end must be the creation of the beloved community."[13]

Lawson spoke on the technique of nonviolence. "By appealing to conscience and standing on the moral nature of human existence, nonviolence nurtures the atmosphere in which reconciliation and justice become actual possibilities."[14]

The students who had been to Highlander had invited Guy Carawan to Raleigh to lead the singing. He closed the first evening's events with "We Shall Overcome." The whole audience sang. One newsman from Norfolk, Virginia, described the song as "a powerful, welling thing."[15] Jane Stembridge, a Virginian who had studied with Horton's mentor, Reinhold Niebuhr, wrote of the night, "It was hot that night upstairs in the auditorium. Students had just come in from all over the South, meeting for the first time. February 1 was not long past. There was no SNCC, no *ad hoc* committees, no funds, just people who did not know what to expect but who came and released the common vision in that song. . . . It was inspiring because it was the beginning, and because, in a sense, it was the purest moment."[16]

Music became one of the basic ways in which Highlander related to the black movement. What Zilphia Horton had done for the labor movement, Guy Carawan did for a time for the civil rights movement. Born in California of parents originally from the South, Carawan first visited Highlander in 1953. After traveling in western Europe, the Soviet Union, and China, he joined the staff in 1959. It was a hectic time. In Carawan's words:

Here I was . . . running around the South being invited to cities like Birmingham and Montgomery and Albany and Greenwood to lead singing and teach songs. I was surrounded by people who could sing circles around me. I had the job at Highlander of pulling together a body of songs that, rather than saying "Onward Christian Soldiers" or "The More We Get Together the Happier We'll Be," said instead things like "We Shall Overcome" and "Hold On."

Before long I was down at Nashville leading singing at mass meetings and at workshops. Nashville was one of the first towns in the South to have a real singing movement. You started off with one or two songs but as things began to spread, and it wasn't long—five years later—you ended up with at least a hundred songs that were well-known.[17]

Like Zilphia Horton, Carawan used music that grew out of immediate situations. It wasn't tacked on as entertainment; it was a way to fuse a commonality of purpose, to communicate beyond rational appeals. Carawan recalls, "I think I ran into C. T. Vivian for the first time in front of the mayor's office in Nashville. It was probably the first time that 'We Shall Overcome' was used at a mass gathering as part of that movement, and you could see tears in people's eyes. Singing really had that kind of impact."[18]

Carawan's work also took him to Johns Island where, in cooperation with Esau Jenkins, he organized a number of Sea Island Folk Festivals featuring the Moving Star Hall Singers and the Georgia Sea Island Singers. Their spirituals and their style of singing represented, perhaps, the oldest form of black folk culture alive in the United States. Because of Jenkins, Carawan was invited to attend the unique Christmas Watch Meeting:

When the hall had filled and quieted, the singing started. Some woman with a thick, rich, low alto started off in the corner and very soon was joined by some deep, resonant male "basers" from another corner. Then falsetto wails and moans sailed in to float on high over the lead. By the time the whole group of about sixty worshippers had joined in, each freely improvising in his own way, the hall was rocking and swaying to an ecstatic "Savior Do Not Pass Me By." This is a relatively modern hymn of white origin, but, in their style of singing, it was as old as any Negro religious singing in America today.[19]

Josh Dunson, a historian of music in the civil rights movement, has claimed that Carawan infused the struggle "with the hidden power of the Afro-American tradition" in song.[20] In 1964, at a Sing for Freedom Workshop organized by Carawan and Bernice Regan of the Student Nonviolent Coordinating Committee, at Old Gammon Theological Seminary in Atlanta, the Sea Island Singers joined over fifty musicians, mostly veteran "movement" blacks, from seven Southern states. Although they won a standing ovation for a subtle antislavery song, some young movement members, during a later workshop session, questioned why "old-timey" singers and songs such as gang-labor songs, children's party songs, spirituals, and shouts had been included. They were ashamed of what they called "down home" music. Bessie Jones, one of the Sea Island Singers, defended Moving Star Hall as an institution, saying that it was "the only place where we could say we did not like slavery, say it for ourselves to hear."[21]

Other, older participants, reminded the young people that their music would also be "old-timey" one day and that slave songs were being preserved to help black people know of their forefathers' strength and history.

The next year three young men, Willie Peacock, Willie McGhee, and Sam Block, each a toughened veteran of the struggle against racism, ran a two-day festival of Afro-American traditional music at Mileston, Mississippi. They put together buck-dancing, an art show, old secular and religious music, and a cookout, slavery style. Julius Lester, who had just left Highlander's staff to work with the Newport Folk Festival, said the event was the first one organized by blacks for blacks. Others would follow. Carawan's work with the movement was nearing its end by 1965. The swiftly changing social currents seemed to Carawan to be echoing a song he had recorded on Johns Island, "You Got to Move":

> I got to move, we got to move
> We got to move, we got to move,
> When the Lord get read', you got to move.[22]

Carawan, with his wife Candie, left the Sea Islands and the South to get two books published in New York, one a documentary on Johns Island; the other, songs of the Southern freedom struggle. After that they spent some time in Eastern Kentucky, trying to learn how music could be related to the grassroots struggles going on there at the time.

Explaining his decision to leave the South, Carawan said later, "A lot of these same people who, a few years earlier, had made up these songs and [done] a lot of singing, along with strategy and tactics and the real moving, decided 'We're too bitter to sing anymore.' "[23]

11

. . . one whispered word–freedom! . . .

FEW PLACES IN AMERICA are as hushed as sun-baked Mississippi towns on Sunday mornings after the white churches take in. In one such town, Winona, in 1963, almost two years after echoes of the last words spoken in Dr. Johnson's well-used Summerfield cottage had died away, the explosive nature of education for fundamental social change—the Highlander idea—ended a Sabbath stillness.

A bus heading for Greenwood, Mississippi, stopped in Winona for a short layover. On it were five black Mississippians returning to their homes in Ruleville from a Community Development and Voter Education Workshop on Johns Island, South Carolina. With them was a staff member of the Southern Christian Leadership Conference.

The Volunteer Training Center at McIntosh, Georgia, set up and run for SCLC by Septima Clark and the Reverend Andrew Young, until he became one of Dr. King's key aides, was proving so successful that it had run out of space, time to schedule, and staff to fulfill the requests to train literacy teachers.[1] Mrs. Clark had borrowed the Progressive Club, through Esau Jenkins, to hold a workshop for Mississippians recruited by SNCC volunteers in Ruleville. Rosemary Freeman, June Johnson, Euvester Simpson, Fannie Lou Hamer, and James West, all of Ruleville, and Annelle Ponder of SCLC had traveled to Johns Island and were coming home.

When the bus stopped in Winona, all but Mrs. Hamer got off, to go either to the rest rooms or the lunch counter, both supposedly open to them by federal law. They had barely set foot inside the station when Winona's chief of police and a highway patrolman whirled into the depot, ordering and shoving them outside. There would be no tradition broken in Winona that Sabbath, only federal law. Outside, the police pushed the travelers into a patrol car. When Mrs. Hamer stepped off the bus to ask what she could do for her friends, she, too, was hustled into the car, getting kicked as she stooped to sit.

At the Winona jail, the chief rebuked them for "raising hell all over the place."[2] Otherwise, no charges were docketed. The prisoners were separated into cells. Except for June Johnson. She was held out, interrogated briefly, then beaten bloody by the police. When she was brought back to a cell, Miss Ponder was taken out. Three men, two in police uniforms and one in plain clothes, beat her with their fists, open palms, blackjacks, and belts.

Meanwhile, the police had somehow learned that Mrs. Hamer, the wife of a sharecropper and mother of two children, had tried to register voters in Ruleville the year before. For that effort she and her family had been evicted from a plantation where they had worked for eighteen years.[3] Now, the Winona police apparently reasoned that she deserved further punishment. She was taken by a highway patrolman to a room where two black men, prisoners themselves, were ordered to beat her with blackjacks. They did so until, she said later, they could beat no more. Then the highway patrolman took over until he, too, was exhausted. Finally, Mrs. Hamer was dragged to her cell. West was the last traveler to be beaten.[4]

Word reached SNCC workers the next day in Greenwood, about thirty miles away, that some civil rights workers were in jail in Winona. Bernice Robinson was running a workshop in Greenwood for twenty-eight persons from Tchula, Batesville, Courtland, Itta Bena, Lamar, and Holly Springs. No one at the workshop or among the SNCC staff could find out for certain if there was any truth to the report. Rumors started easily in Mississippi during those days. The prisoners had not been allowed to telephone relatives or lawyers. It was Tuesday morning before a group of SNCC workers, including Lawrence Guyot, arrived at the Winona jail. A crowd, mostly members of the White Citizens Council, was waiting. When Guyot didn't "sir" a highway patrolman, he was immediately seized. His companions were ordered to leave town. The highway patrolman slapped Guyot around, then turned him over to the Citizens, who beat and kicked him until he couldn't lift his arms. His eyes were swollen shut.

The SNCC workers, who had been ordered to leave immediately, headed for Greenville and sent to Atlanta for legal help. All the prisoners except Guyot were released on Wednesday. Bernice Robinson, who went with the SNCC workers back to Winona, wrote:

> They were a horrible sight. Annelle Ponder's eyes were swollen and bloodshot from the beatings and one hip was swollen twice the size of the other. Mrs. Hamer had bruises all over her head, and her hips were bruised black. June Johnson's head was all bruised, and her lip cut. James West's face was swollen, and hips bruised. The other two weren't touched, but Lawrence Guyot, who had gone down Tuesday to get them out, was beaten so badly he couldn't use one of his arms and for several hours couldn't even be located. He was held incommunicado. He was finally released on Thursday. Annelle Ponder whispered one word as she left jail: "Freedom!"[5]

Winona was the second tragedy within days to strike at black defiance of Mississippi political tradition. On June 12, Medgar Evers was ambushed and killed from behind on the front lawn of his home as he returned from a civil rights rally in Jackson. Known, tested, and trusted leadership was being destroyed. But out of the Winona jail came new leaders to fill the void. Miss

Robinson alluded to the tragic process in her evaluation of the workshop she had been trying to hold in Greenwood.

The workshop was interrupted in several ways . . . but amid all the chaos, we were able to get in three full days of discussions on problems common to all of the communities represented . . . fear, lack of local leadership, lack of organization, police brutality, uninformed people, lack of news media . . . [and] at the end of the workshop each person expressed [himself] as being more determined to work at getting Negroes registered and to overcome the many barriers facing the Negro today.[6]

As the majority of the SNCC volunteers continued pressing their challenges to white racism across the South, a quiet, sensitive Harvard graduate, Robert Moses, was unobtrusively at work in McComb, Mississippi, on a strategy that eventually became the youthful organization's major thrust: "one man, one vote." Moses had been in touch with Amzie Moore, a respected veteran in the struggle for black self-determination who lived in Cleveland, Mississippi. Together, they worked out ways to teach blacks how to register. On August 7, 1961, as SNCC leaders were debating at Highlander what steps to take next, Moses, not yet a SNCC worker, opened the first voter registration school in Pike County, if not in the state.[7] Eight days later, sixteen persons went to the registrar's office after having patiently learned the voter registration form, and after having carefully studied questions related to the 285 sections of the Mississippi state constitution. Voters—prospective black voters, that is—had to answer the questionnaire and interpret the state constitution to the satisfaction of the white county registrar before they were allowed the franchise.

Six applicants passed the tests in Magnolia, the county seat, and were registered. Moses, who accompanied them, was arrested by a state trooper who had been in the registrar's office. He was charged with interfering with an officer, apparently because he had tried to write down the lawman's badge number. At his trial, he was found guilty and fined five dollars. He was sent to jail when he refused to pay.[8]

As soon as Moses got out of jail, he set up another registration school in neighboring Amity County. On August 29, he and two students set out for the registrar's office in Liberty. Before they got there, Billy Jack Caston, the sheriff's cousin, stopped them and commenced beating Moses with the butt end of a knife. He fell unconscious. The voter registration drive ended in Liberty. But, when Moses recovered, he filed charges of assault and battery against Caston, an unprecedented impudence.[9]

Word of Moses' struggle reached SNCC volunteers. Marion Barry came to McComb to hold several workshops on nonviolent direct action. Three days before Moses was beaten in Liberty, two teen-agers from Barry's workshop had sat in at a McComb dime store. They were arrested, found guilty of breach of the peace, and sentenced to thirty days in jail. The next day, five more students tried to sit in at the same dime store. They were arrested, convicted, and jailed eight months for breach of the peace. John Hardy, a SNCC volunteer, was pistol-whipped by the Walthall County registrar, then arrested for disturbing the peace.[10]

Still another sit-in demonstrator was given a year in the state school for delinquents for trying to eat at the McComb dime store. Up in Ruleville, two black SNCC workers were wounded by shotgun blasts fired through the window of a home where they were staying. The notion of combining nonviolent direct action with voter registration was being tested, and was under siege.

When Caston was brought to trial on Moses' charge, the

courthouse was packed with openly-armed whites. Moses and the two blacks who had been with him during the attack were kept in a back room out of sight until time for them to testify individually. Once their testimony was given, the sheriff had them escorted to the county line and let them go. He told them he didn't think it would be safe for them to be around when the jury reached a verdict. Moses learned the next day, *in absentia*, that the jury had acquitted Caston.[11]

White reaction to the voter registration and direct action campaigns reached a tragic climax on September 25. Herbert Lee, a black farmer and the father of nine children, was shot and killed for no apparent reason. E. H. Hurst, Caston's father-in-law and a state senator, was charged with murder but was exonerated by both a coroner's jury and a federal grand jury.[12]

Despite the violent setbacks, or, perhaps, because of them, Moses and Moore demonstrated the impact voter registration could have on a racist community, if actively and nonviolently pushed. In spite of the years of heavy migration to the North and the West, blacks were in the majority in twenty-one of Mississippi's eighty-two counties, a fact that had not gone unnoticed by those who practiced racist politics. But in 1962, only 24,000 of the potential 422,000 voting-age blacks were registered, and that was the way many whites wanted the statistics to stay.[13]

Earlier that year, James Forman, who had become SNCC's executive secretary, asked Highlander to run a second workshop on voter registration. He wanted to extend Moses' work into Alabama and Southwest Georgia. Some twenty SNCC volunteers, three of them white, including Bob Zellner, SNCC's first white field secretary, arrived at Highlander Research and Education Center in Knoxville on June 4.[14]

Immediately, the debate that had started at Highlander resumed. Direct action had many advocates. SNCC's leaders didn't want to abandon the tactic completely. But they had asked Moses to come up from Mississippi. With SNCC's approval, Highlander had also invited blacks who had experience in voter registration and elections: Hosea Williams, chairman of the Crusade for Voters in Savannah; Washington Butler, a city councilman in Oak Ridge, Tennessee, who was one of the few black elected officials in the South then; Esau Jenkins from the Citizenship School on the Sea Islands; and Dr. Lewis Jones, the Fisk sociologist. Bernice Robinson of the Highlander staff was discussion leader. If the SNCC leaders weren't going to take up voter registration as another nonviolent tool, the workshop's resources certainly indicated that they planned to examine its potential carefully.

The firsthand experiences recounted by Moses had a profound influence on the workshop participants, Horton recalls. What had been almost an either-or debate at Highlander flattened out in talk of both-and. In the end, the idea that Moses and Moore had worked out independently in Mississippi was adopted. The time for "one man, one vote" had come. Before leaving Highlander, each participant drew up a proposed plan for organizing registration drives. Here, the experiences of the resource persons were drawn upon. So, too, were copies of the voting laws in Georgia, Alabama, and Mississippi, compiled and mimeographed by the Highlander staff beforehand. But no workshop theorizing would be sufficient preparation for the reaction those young volunteers, and others, would encounter in the days immediately ahead.

Moses asked Miss Robinson to come to Mississippi to follow up on what the participants in the Highlander workshop would be doing in several communities, and to help extend the idea. She held voter registration workshops at Tougaloo College, Cleveland, Ruleville, Bolling, Marigold, and, finally, at the Mount Beulah Christian Center in Edwards, on the edge of the Delta, west of Jackson.

Only six persons came to the Mount Beulah workshop. The sheriff had brought heavy pressure on blacks in the area not to attend. The White Citizens Council demanded that the gathering be canceled. Talk had been heard of dynamiting the center. The six who came had a workshop. William Higgs, a white Mississippian who had graduated from Harvard Law School and returned home, talked with them about state, federal, and local government. The volunteers outlined plans for their own voter registration drives, and even held mock registrations. After the working sessions, they talked about the toughest problem—the fear, the widespread, justifiable fear.

After Mount Beulah, Miss Robinson wrote Highlander: "This fear is real. In Ruleville, Negroes must be off the street by the 12 P.M. curfew, or be arrested and held in jail until a fine is paid. In Greenwood, a Negro woman tried to register and was told by the clerk to leave her name and address, and that she would be called and told when to come back. She did, and the next morning a white couple who lived near her home came to her house and told her they would burn her house if she went back to register."[15] Higgs and three college students had been stopped by police after a meeting at Tougaloo and held incommunicado for twenty hours before being released.

But when Bernice Robinson returned to Mississippi in August, all six students from the Mount Beulah workshop were running their voter registration drives as planned. One had registered six of the seven persons he had prepared.

At SNCC's request, Miss Robinson came back into the state in 1963 to run three more week-long workshops. By then the situation had "hotted up," as the expression went. On May 6, she wrote back to Highlander: "At this time eight of the leaders in the voter registration movement in Greenwood were still in jail. On April 2, nineteen others were jailed for marching to the courthouse to register."[16] The home of a Greenwood family whose son had been working with SNCC had been shot into. Earlier, Greenwood police had set upon praying blacks in front of the Leflore County Courthouse with riot sticks and police dogs.

After this came the death of Medgar Evers. And Winona. It is little wonder that Miss Robinson wrote that the workshops had been "interrupted."

Before the summer's end, dozens of SNCC workers and demonstrators were locked up in Parchman Prison for two-month sentences, which became customary upon arrest and conviction for trying to register. Trucks were used to haul the protesters to the prison. Once there, cattle prods with electric shocks were used on inmates. Teen-agers told of spending over one hundred hours in the hot box, a cell six feet square, which would be jammed full of prisoners and heated during the day, cooled at night.[17]

By the end of June, over three thousand blacks from Greenwood and Leflore County had marched to the courthouse trying to register. Thirty succeeded. Some say the spirit of white resistance was broken in Greenwood; others say the drive was a defeat for the blacks. Horton believed that the drive was an ultimate victory in that many blacks overcame their fear of whites.

Horton's conclusions were borne out by black participation in Mississippi's mock election that fall of 1963. More than 83,000 blacks cast Freedom Ballots for Aaron Henry, a Clarksdale pharmacist and NAACP leader, for governor, and for the Reverend Edwin King, a Vicksburg native who was white chaplain at Tougaloo College, for lieutenant governor. The turnout demonstrated once and for all that Mississippi blacks would vote, if given the opportunity. Four times the number actually registered had voted.

On November 22, the day John Kennedy was shot and killed

from ambush, SNCC's James Forman wrote Horton from Atlanta: "There is no question in my mind that the increasing effectiveness of our operation is due in part to these workshops. By comparison, we have not had similar workshops in other areas where we have been working. This is a tragic mistake. We realize the extreme importance of on-the-job training and constant evaluation of what we are doing."[18]

The next year, Horton was asked by John Lewis and Forman to set up an educational program for SNCC. He agreed to serve in an advisory capacity, training staff to take over the responsibilities themselves. Within a few months, SNCC staffers were running workshops on their own, and by 1965, at Horton's urging, a SNCC department for education had been set up.

The spreading spirit of protest unleashed by four black college students in the winter of 1960 surged to a climax in the summer of 1964. COFO Summer, so named because a Council of Federated Organizations had sprung to life in Mississippi as a result of the mock elections, was to be the year racism would be finally harried from Mississippi.[19]

Planning for the campaign to bring thousands of volunteers into the state started at a gathering in Greenville from November 11 through November 17. Moses had asked Horton to run the workshops. Horton had politely refused on the ground that there were enough staff members from the coalition's groups who could, and should, run them. He agreed to serve as a consultant only.

Many, if not all, of the discussion leaders had attended earlier Highlander workshops, and together they pushed through the meeting's only major decision: to use COFO Summer to strengthen leadership among blacks who would be living in Mississippi long after the summer was over.

In May, Horton and others came to Greenville to lay final plans for the summer assault on Mississippi.[20] They spent much time considering how the Mississippi Freedom Democratic Party could challenge the all-white delegation to the national Democratic convention in Atlantic City, New Jersey, that August. Aaron Henry and Mrs. Fanny Lou Hamer, a congressional candidate, led discussions on the upcoming primary race, and the alternatives for blacks.

What COFO volunteers would face in trying to get blacks to participate in the electoral process was brought into sharp relief by SNCC workers who had already been volunteers in small Mississippi towns. Many rural blacks had no idea of the meaning of words like delegate or convention, let alone the significance of the challenge. Horton recalls attending one meeting in a remote community where, after two hours of patient explanation, a black man stood and hesitantly said, "I will volunteer to go to Jackson. I would like to see Jackson. I would like to be a delegate."[21]

The SNCC worker explained that he could not volunteer; his neighbors would have to elect him. Still the man didn't understand. Being a delegate to a convention was outside his experience, and the experience of most of those attending the meeting that night. Finally, a few white SNCC volunteers decided they could help the man understand. "They took chalk to a blackboard and drew diagrams to explain a convention," Horton recalls. "This confused the issue all but hopelessly."[22]

Another problem that was to have increasing significance surfaced. Many blacks were irritated by the idea that whites should have any part in COFO Summer. They argued that giving whites the chance to help register blacks would be another demonstration that the white man and the white man's ways were superior. They resented whites being given positions of leadership. They had seen whites grab off a lot of publicity, then leave for a high-paying job because of their work with blacks. If whites were to be in COFO Summer, they contended, they should not be leaders, but should do legwork or run mimeograph machines. The constitutional challenge should be made by blacks only.

Taking the other side were Lawrence Guyot, Mrs. Hamer, and Moses. All had become driving forces in the challenge. They all wanted to include whites. Guyot took the position that the white volunteers probably would be unlike any whites whom black Mississippians had ever seen. Relationships could be based on human individuality. That, he felt, would be positive for all concerned.

"If we are going to break down this barrier of segregation, we can't segregate ourselves," said Mrs. Hamer.[23]

Moses declared that Mississippi was dehumanized by racism. "The only way you can break that down is to have white people working alongside of you so then it changes the whole complexion of what you are doing. It isn't any longer Negroes fighting whites. It's a question of rational people against irrational people."[24]

The Greenville planning session had gone on for hours. It was after midnight. A final decision wasn't put off or avoided so much as it became understood, Horton felt, that the sense of the gathering favored white participation. The talk had been blunt, searching, honest, free of cant, but always sensitive to the other side. This was a characteristic of SNCC's decision-making process, Horton thinks. At the end, the conferees clasped hands to sing "We Shall Overcome."

The next morning, they were confronted with the "Communist issue." Aaron Henry, the state NAACP president, had been lukewarm to the idea of COFO Summer from the start. He told SNCC organizers that the NAACP Legal Defense Fund, Inc., would withdraw staff lawyers and financial backing from COFO if the group accepted assistance from the National Lawyers Guild, a group tainted in the minds of many Northern liberals because its lawyers had defended Communists.

Moses asked a heretofore silent Horton for his opinion. "I can only talk from our experience at Highlander. We have found that you decide what you want to do, decide what your program is, and then let anybody who will, help you accomplish what you want to do. We don't make judgments about anyone who wants to help, regardless of what other people might think. But you don't let anyone use your program or run your program for their purposes. You make the decisions. They help carry them out."[25]

Henry, sensing that he might not be able to control the outcome of the debate, added that the American Civil Liberties Union might also withdraw if the National Lawyers Guild participated. Again, at Moses' request Horton offered a rebuttal. "We have found if you have a good program, tied to the people, others will work with you in spite of your refusal to give in to their demands. The people you need working with you will come because your program is sound, and where the action is. Good people want to be where the action is. Those who stay away because you won't let them run your program or make your decisions for you probably wouldn't be of much value to you anyway." The kind of thinking they represent would have kept them from full, effective participation anyway, Horton felt.

Horton argued that the question wasn't whether an organization could work with Communists, but, instead, whether an organization could work with any group, some of whom might be called Communists. "If the so-called Communists will respect and help further the organization's goals, then let them in," he said. "In the end, it's a question of who can be defined *in*, not who can be defined *out*."[26]

The planners of COFO Summer accepted this position. The National Lawyers Guild joined. The Legal Defense Fund did not withdraw. To Horton, this was a practical demonstration of what Highlander had always defined as "independence."

In June, over seven hundred COFO Summer volunteers arrived at Western State College in Oxford, Ohio, for orientation. Mostly white, Northern, middle-class college students made up this small army. The National Council of Churches paid for the training session. COFO ran it. They tried to get across two points: expect violence; follow black leadership. Formal speeches by veteran activists like James Forman and Charles Morgan, the white lawyer who had been run out of Alabama and had joined the American Civil Liberties Union staff in Atlanta, were followed by informal discussions.

During one discussion, a student from an Eastern university declared his intention of challenging students at "Ole Miss," the state university at Oxford, to public debate on the merits of COFO Summer. He told the group, including Horton, that a debate would allow students to make up their own minds on the issues. It might even help Southerners understand why Northern students were coming to Mississippi.[27]

Lawrence Guyot, the discussion leader, choked back laughter and glanced incredulously at Horton. "I think it is an excellent idea," Horton said, without a blink. "However, I would make several modifications. Since many black people don't trust whites to bargain with other whites on their behalf any longer, I would suggest that you specify in the invitation that blacks be present in a public restaurant in a place like Greenwood for the debate."[28]

The student was pleased; he hadn't been put down. He was too naive to know that no white restaurant in Mississippi that summer would open for an integrated dinner debate. But Horton knew he would learn that soon enough.

As for expecting violence, and preparing for it, Mississippi's racists were to teach the volunteers better than the SNCC discussion leaders. On June 20, three volunteers left the session for Meridian. Two days later, word came back to Ohio that James

Chaney, Mickey Schwerner, and Andrew Goodman were missing. By chance, Moses and Horton were together when the word arrived. They knew instinctively the trio was "missing" only in the sense that their bodies hadn't been found. Moses had frequently talked with Horton about his own concern over involving other people with his ideals, perhaps, he had worried once, to the extent that the others might be killed. Late that night Moses wept.[29]

Later, standing in the ashes of Mount Zion Methodist Church, which had been burned to the ground by Longdale, Mississippi, night riders, Moses told mourners at a memorial service for the slain volunteers: "The tragedy here is the work of people who believed in an idea enough to kill for it. The problem of Mississippi is the problem of the nation and of the world. A way has to be found to change this desire to kill." He reminded the mourners that the day the bodies were found was the day the United States government started bombing North Vietnam. Ben Chaney, the eleven-year-old brother of the dead black man, his gaze intent on Sheriff Lawrence Rainey and Deputy Cecil Price, who were standing nearby, ended a brief eulogy by declaring, "I want us all to stand up here together and just say one thing. I want the sheriff to hear this good. We ain't scared no more of Sheriff Rainey!"[30]

COFO Summer would break many bonds of fear. Sheriff Rainey, Deputy Price, and others would eventually be tried for murdering the young volunteers. Price and six others would be convicted and sentenced to prison for varying terms. Rainey would be found "not guilty."

Before the murdered trio's bodies had even been found buried under an earthen dam near Philadelphia, Mississippi, eighteen students, three-fourths of them white Southerners, left Ohio for a second week of orientation at Highlander. Theirs was to be a special role in COFO Summer.

Sue Thrasher, one of the students, later wrote about the session at Highlander:

> The old stone house overlooking the river seemed a welcome respite from the chaotic nature of the orientation at Oxford. For days we sat around in the frumpy old meeting rooms discussing in confused and muddled fashion our battle plan. Some talked romantically about the possibilities for organizing poor whites and blacks into a working coalition. Others thought we would be lucky to find a few timid souls who might want to tell us in secret that they were in favor of our goals. Looking back now, I don't think it really mattered, for it wasn't until we had a "place" and a "situation" that we began to comprehend the depth of the racism and the fear of white Mississippians that summer.
>
> Toward the end of the week, we packed a picnic lunch and headed for the mountains. That afternoon as we were driving in the magnificent beauty of the Smokies, we heard the news on the car radio about the deaths of Goodman, Chaney, and Schwerner. I remember only the silence.
>
> Halfway down the mountain, we stopped for a pre-arranged visit with Florence and Sam Reece. Somehow or other as we sat around their living room that night, and listened to Florence sing "Which Side Are You On" and tell us how she had come to write it, and about the times she and Sam had helped to organize the miners in "Bloody Harlan," the iciness began to slip away. Before we left that evening, Florence and Sam had "rooted" us in our history, had helped us see ourselves as neither the beginning nor the end, but simply a part of a process.[31]

The work of the white volunteers in Mississippi that summer produced a few tangible results, and some important intangible ones, Horton feels. At a follow-up workshop held in Gulfport, the volunteers reported finding that community centers, Freedom Schools, and political education—the same devices used around the state among blacks—had produced positive results with poor whites. Slowly, and not in great numbers, poor white Mississipians began to work with the COFO volunteers, and began to move on their own to solve their problems. One white Mississippian actually joined the staff of COFO.[32] In part because of the students' efforts, the Human Relations Council in Jackson, a private group affiliated with the Southern Regional Council, formulated a statement urging moderation, which was printed in the local newspapers.

But essentially, Horton feels, the white students learned that blacks themselves had to gather together before the Sheriff Raineys in white America would know that racism was done for.

That fall, Horton joined the organizers of COFO Summer in Mount Beulah Christian Center to evaluate their accomplishments and to lay plans for a second summer assault on Mississippi.

Bob Moses assembled from the group about twenty-five movement veterans. Horton was the only white man asked to join them. They sat in the shade of the center's scattered, but stately, trees. Moses was vague and rambling. It seemed to Horton that he was saying aloud for the first time thoughts he had been silently mulling for a long time. He talked about the need to develop pride among blacks. Pride had to come before accomplishment, he said.

His listeners became restless. They were for action—direct action, voter registration, Freedom Schools, doing. "Doing" self-pride didn't seem to be of great interest to them, Horton recalls. But as Moses continued, they began to listen.

What did it mean, he asked, to have two SNCC workers, one black and one white, go into the rural areas to find that the timid, frightened blacks there would speak only to the white worker? What did it mean when they would go to the registrar's office only if a white worker assured them it was all right? What did it mean to find black children in Freedom Schools able to relate best to white volunteers? Why didn't blacks take open pride in the bravery of their own young men and women? Why wouldn't they believe their own kind? Why didn't they relate to their own?

As Horton took lunch that day, he thought of how Bishop Grundtvig had stirred the pride of dispirited Danes by encouraging them to act on their own real needs. He thought back to the time when Elizabeth Hawes had organized a union at the Liebovitz shirt factory in Knoxville. Highlander then was still trying to get its union education program off the ground, so Horton had gone to Knoxville to listen to the workers. He asked one new union member what the union contract had done for her, fully expecting she would say something about higher wages or shorter hours. "The most important thing in my life since the contract is that the foreman hands me the cloth he wants sewed instead of throwing it at me," she told Horton.[33]

He also remembered the Reverend C. T. Vivian, a leader in SCLC, during a visit to Highlander several years before the birth of SCLC, telling workshop participants that "black people had to qualify themselves." Vivian had clarified his remarks, which, though prophetic, were unacceptable to many blacks, by telling a long anecdote that Horton delights in recalling. For one thing, the story captures the relentlessness of white supremacy.

Whites, according to Vivian, would tell blacks, "If you'll get cleaned up, then you'll be more acceptable." And the blacks would go off to scrub their skins nearly raw, and starch their hair until the lye burned their scalps. When they returned, the whites would tell them, "If you get educated, then you'll be more acceptable." And off they'd go, earning degrees at the cost of food, family, and health, only to have the whites suggest, when they returned, that they get jobs as janitors, maids, or bootblacks.[34]

Vivian lived to see the day when his teaching wouldn't be scorned, and he would write in 1970, "One can sense an exciting new mood within new Black organizations. One can sense the relief which accompanies liberation from false presuppositions and false goals. . . . We could see that we would have to devise answers for ourselves."[35]

Horton, therefore, after the meeting at Mount Beulah and after watching countless blacks learning to "qualify" themselves, wasn't surprised to see Stokely Carmichael on television a year later shouting to all the world from Greenwood, Mississippi, "The only way we gonna stop them white men from whuppin' us is to take over. We have been saying 'freedom' for six years and we ain't got nothin'. What we gonna start saying now is 'black power.' Black Power!"[36]

Willie Ricks, a big-voiced SNCC field secretary, shouted from the crowd, "Black Power!" And the crowd of blacks roared back, "Black Power!"

Out of the persistence of American racism, out of the painful struggle, out of the hopes of black people came a shout for liberation, their shout. History was made.

During the years SNCC volunteers roamed the South challenging the status Crow, federal law was usually on their side. It was the local authorities—the sheriffs, local police, and judges, and, sometimes, the Federal Bureau of Investigation—that caused grief, bloodshed, and, ultimately, bitterness.

In August, 1961, only nineteen months after the Greensboro sit-ins had dramatized the smoldering willingness of blacks to demand what was right, there was hardly a trace of bitterness. Reflecting on that time a few years later, author Julius Lester wrote, "We had honestly believed that once white people knew what segregation did, it would be abolished. But why shouldn't we have believed it? We had been fed the American Dream, too. We believed in Coca-Cola and the American government."[37]

There was a debate within SNCC's leadership about tactics. The gathering at Highlander, for what would be the last meeting there, was the occasion for that debate, or at least one of the first times the question about tactics was thoroughly thrashed out.

Some of the volunteers had turned away from direct action. They were exploring ways blacks could gain a voice in government. If, they reasoned, government wouldn't enforce laws or live up to the letter and spirit of the U.S. Constitution, if government was cracking black heads for trying legally to participate in the life of a community, then it seemed that the best thing to do was to achieve a voice in government.

Horton recalls that advocates of this position wanted SNCC to begin voter registration campaigns. Their number wasn't large, but they were vigorous. The right to vote was being systematically denied to many Southern blacks. The number of black elected officials in the South, or the nation, could have been counted at that time on a callused hand. Opponents, the majority at the meeting, countered by saying that voter registration was reformist, that it was a white man's trick to separate SNCC from its most powerful weapon—direct, nonviolent confrontation. They pointed to earlier times when organizations like the NAACP had tried, and failed, to register black Southern voters.

In the end, Ella Baker, who had been responsible for pulling together the Raleigh meeting for the Southern Christian Leadership Conference and who had come to Highlander for the pivotal discussions, offered a compromise: do both; create two arms of SNCC, one responsible for continued direct action; the other, for voter registration. The volunteers agreed. Diane Nash was chosen to head direct action. Charles Jones was selected to work with the voter registration efforts.

Most of the conferees left Highlander committed to continuing what SNCC was deservedly known for—frontal assaults on racism's superficial, yet humiliating restrictions. One or two, Horton recalls, went off to McComb, Mississippi, where Moses and Moore were persistently and independently trying to register blacks. In McComb the seeds of COFO Summer took root.

When the Highlander property was seized, Horton knew for certain that blacks' deciding their own goals, and acting to secure those goals, was a more effective, powerful means of social change than moral persuasion. For years, Highlander, like so many other well-intentioned white institutions, and Horton, like countless open-minded whites in the South, operated on the principle that a moral democracy could be persuaded to eliminate racism, and its legal manifestation, segregation, if only sufficient illustrations of blacks and whites cooperating could be presented.

As long as Highlander operated on the principle of moral persuasion, the school was left pretty much alone—except, of course, for sporadic attacks by special-interest hate groups. But when blacks started qualifying themselves through the Citizenship Schools, and in other ways, and black voters started being counted, Highlander came under sustained attack by the states of Arkansas, Alabama, Georgia, and Tennessee. Highlander was helping nourish a political threat. The extent of the suppression of Highlander was a measure of the power of that threat.

12

. . . *a glimpse of the future* . . .

BY 1964, HORTON was trying to get Highlander out of the civil rights movement and into Appalachia, and to encourage the civil rights movement to become a means through which all oppressed people in America could effectively challenge their oppressors. It was slow work.

Gradually, ties with the Council of Southern Mountains were restored.[1] Horton and others arranged a conference for politically active miners in Hazard, Kentucky, in 1964.[2] A year later, four college students—Horton's son Thorsten, Sam Clark, John Chater, and Robert Flint—spent the summer living in Habersham, Tennessee, listening to people there, trying to hear what problems they faced.[3] Other forays were made into the coalfields and the hollows as time permitted. But, essentially, the school's space and time were still being pressed into service by the civil rights movement. There were the Southwide Voter Education Internship Project workshops.[4] The Southern Student Organizing Committee came into short but influential being, frequently using Highlander.[5] In 1965 alone, SNCC held an executive committee meeting, two labor workshops, a full staff meeting, and a poetry workshop at Highlander.[6] Highlander's own staff was crisscrossing the South in response to requests from civil rights workers for educational work.[7]

And Horton, as he traveled, was urging grass-roots members and leaders of the civil rights movement to go beyond their own immediate concerns and link up with all of the nation's poor; he dreamed of a massive social movement that would fundamentally alter America, and genuinely felt that the potential for such a movement existed. The last conversation he had with Dr. King in March, 1968, only days before the SCLC leader was slain, Horton recalled in a letter he wrote Andrew Young upon returning to Knoxville:

> I believe we caught a glimpse of the future at the March 14 meeting called by SCLC. We had there in Atlanta authentic spokesmen for poor Mexican-Americans, American Indians, blacks, and whites, the making of a bottom-up coalition, as I tried to impress on you and Martin as you were leaving for the airport.
>
> I realize all of you have been extremely busy, but I hope you have been considering the possibility of broadening the Washington Poor People's Campaign to encourage autonomous activities of the Mexican-Americans and other poor groups. This, as you know, would require not only sharing of planning but sharing of the publicity where the mass media will be primarily concerned with SCLC. Martin, and those of you close to him, will have to spearhead the putting together of grass roots coalitions for the Washington demonstrations. This could lay the groundwork for something tremendously exciting and significant. Just as it is fitting for SCLC to make ending the war in Vietnam a basic part of the program, it would be fitting now, it seems to me, for SCLC to provide leadership for a bona fide coalition. No other organization has this opportunity and therefore, this responsibility.[8]

America caught a glimpse of the future during the Poor People's Campaign; and what they saw was a coalition of ethnic poor united in a common cause. Highlander had a tent complex in the midst of Resurrection City. The tents became a place where strangers could get to know one another, talk strategy, sip coffee, or hear some music. The school followed up on contacts made during the campaign by holding annual five-day workshops where Mexican-Americans, blacks, Puerto Ricans, American Indians, and whites from Appalachia could talk about common problems.[9]

Much had changed in Appalachia since Highlander Folk School had settled there in 1932. For one thing, technology had come to the company store. Scrip was out. At least one store run by a coal company in Southwest Virginia had a computer to deduct automatically from a miner's wages what he and his family had bought the preceding week. Two hundred and fifty men had once been needed to mine as much coal as one automatic auger could pull from the earth in a day's time. Strip-mining had come, too. And the corporations had learned how to get more out of Appalachia by the 1960's. Profits had been slim for most companies in the thirties. In 1965, Virginia Coal & Iron Company, headquartered in Philadelphia, reported a total revenue of $2.9 million from mining and leasing Appalachian land, and a net income of $1.9 million. That represented a sixty-five per cent profit, the largest of the year for any American company.[10]

As capitalism thrived in Appalachia, so did welfare. Welfare had become a major Appalachian industry; dependency, a way of life. In Southern Appalachia alone—the 190 counties in Georgia, North Carolina, Tennessee, Virginia, Kentucky, and West Virginia—nearly one-half of the 1.6 million families lived at, or below, the federally-defined poverty level; slightly over 25 per cent had incomes of less than $2,000 annually; another 13 per cent had incomes of less than $3,000.[11]

After decades of attention from well-meaning public and private agencies, a once proud and independent people had become dependent, controlled, channeled, and managed. Gentle and paternalistic voices, with governmental responsibility for the region's poor, lectured the mountain people with good advice, expositions of their problems, and ideas for solutions. The silent listeners got food stamps, a welfare check, maybe a free school lunch for a child; they also counted on being humiliated and made more dependent. One Appalachian told Horton, "We've been bruised so long and told to shut up so often that we try to stay out of sight."[12]

Highlander set out to intervene in the problem of dependency and end it through education. The first steps were halting and limited, often wedged in between the dramatic rush of events in the civil rights movement.

In March, 1964, before COFO Summer started, Highlander held a workshop on "Appalachian People and Their Problems," the school's first effort to acquaint white college students with problems in the white world that often were as pressing as those in the black, but were less glamorous in those days. The meeting laid the basis for what emerged later as the Southern Student Organizing Committee. SSOC was short-lived, but became, before disbanding itself, the South's New Left.

In December, 1964, after COFO Summer, representatives from fourteen organizations met at Highlander, formed the Appalachian Economic and Political Action Conference, and pledged to encourage an alliance between jobless, underpaid Negroes and whites in Appalachia and unite the two groups in solving their common problems. They also pledged to help people develop their own organizations which would act to redress grievances, to demand better jobs or income, to elect candidates favorable to equal opportunity, to seek proper education, medical care, and housing, and to understand the economic and political situation in which poor people find themselves.[13]

That alliance, formed as it was from the top, lasted only a little longer than the All-Southern Conference for Civil and Trade Union Rights, but it was a start. Others were also turning their attention to Appalachia: a few politicians, but powerful ones, became involved; a so-called National War on Poverty started; the Appalachian Volunteers came and went; church groups by the score arrived. Their numbers neared the dimensions described as legion.

Frequently, the natives were rankled by the well-intentioned volunteers. One Appalachian, Jim Branscome, then barely out of Berea College, wrote Horton in 1968:

> I have grown very weary of the apocalyptic politics among certain young organizers in Appalachia who expect somehow all our ills to be overcome in a very short time by some crash program or new movement nostrum. I am convinced that only programs which have a long term goal, a proper understanding of the Appalachian people, and a vision of what kind of social order that we must have to live with any sort of dignity in the last half of the 20th century are of any benefit. And my contention of course is that there are no answers to these questions at present and that we must simply sit down and begin to talk to each other, not playing "one up" because we've read Marcuse or Cleaver or whoever, but simply admitting that none of us know the answers to our most perplexing questions. Only when this happens do I see any prospect for helping Appalachians. This unacknowledged dialogue of non-equals that so many people are carrying on with mountain people must come to an end.[14]

To end the "dialogue of non-equals" was also, of course, Highlander's goal. By 1969 there seemed to be emerging from all the experimentation a way to accomplish it, or at least to get started. In March, the president of the Tennessee Community Action Programs, Cliff Ingram, asked Horton to hold a workshop on small-group self-education for the Community Action Program directors. Horton set forth two stipulations: that every CAP director bring along a poor person at the expense of the agency, and that no participant be told in advance of the program's nature. Ingram agreed.

Shortly thereafter, fifteen CAP directors from Tennessee and an equal number of poor people arrived at the hotel at

Montgomery Belle Park, south of Nashville. Ingram explained to the CAP directors that Horton had been asked by Early Padgett, of Mineral Springs, Tennessee, to talk with the poor people they had brought—separately—about small disscussion groups.[15]

After commandeering the hotel's most comfortable lounge, Padgett and Horton met with the fifteen guests. Although they came from different parts of Tennessee, poverty was a common denominator, as was the fact that each visitor was the object of some CAP director's concern. When Horton asked them to name their problems, they recited a familiar litany: how to get people out to meetings; how to get them to listen and to speak up once they got there; how to get them to do something after they left; how to help a man who had been out of work and let down by do-gooders for so long that he no longer had the heart for anything; how to deal with community leaders who said poor people couldn't do any better.

As they talked, it became evident that the poor people were being asked their own ideas about running a "war on poverty." They were being stimulated to think what they would do. Clinton Francis, a mountaineer from Newport, Tennessee, suddenly said, "I came here with part of the answers to questions I'd been asking officials a long time. I got the other part from the people right here." Francis asked for the names and addresses of everybody at the meeting so that they could exchange progress reports.[16]

Before the session started Horton had asked Padgett not to describe the community discussion group he had organized until the others had exhausted their own ideas. But after Francis' burst of excitement, Padgett couldn't contain his own.

Like most communities on the Cumberland Plateau, Mineral Springs had once been caught up in the coal boom, he said. By the late 1960's, however, only a few truck mines were still operating; miners who could find work farmed, logged, or worked in small industries relocated from the North. After attending a Highlander workshop in the fall of 1968, Padgett returned home determined to start a community workshop in Mineral Springs.

A jack-of-all-trades who had quit school after the third grade, Padgett made his living as a carpenter, plumber, electrician, and doer of odd jobs. He had gotten people together who had never been "involved" before: miners, farmers, housewives, loggers, and a few young people. They ranged in age from eighteen to seventy. Padgett had invited only poor people to his first meeting in November, because they "might not feel free to speak out" if teachers, missionaries, or social workers were present. "It was time for poor people to decide what they wanted to do in their own communities," he told the Montgomery Belle Park session.

The first meeting had been held in an old schoolhouse, and Padgett had explained the idea of a community group where each person would have a chance to talk about his ideas and problems. "I told them, 'Don't talk about money. We don't have any, so let's not even talk about it. Let's talk about what we could do if we had as much money as we needed.'"[17]

There had been no parliamentary rules and no proper chairman. Padgett had started people talking by asking one man what he thought about the community. Then the group had discussed the man's opinion. When talk or interest lagged, Padgett had turned to another person and asked the same question. The group had soon warmed to talking without a chairman; they had become frank with each other, more deeply involved. Padgett had talked less and less, and the people had talked more and more.

By the second meeting, they had gotten down to specific

community needs: a school for retarded children, new roads, better schools, a program to train the unskilled and unemployed for new jobs.

At the third meeting, they had made a decision together: to ask the county school superintendent to come and talk to them about a school for retarded children. At the next meeting, with the superintendent present, and before he could make any opening remarks or a speech, the group had started asking him questions. Their vigor had sprung from a sense of solidarity: *they* had talked it over, had made a decision, and the superintendent was at *their* meeting as a result.

Once the dialogue had started that night, Padgett said, many people had found that their ideas were just as good as the superintendent's. They had spoken as equals to a man they had previously thought was "above" them, an expert. The superintendent, they had learned, had as many problems as the people did. And the superintendent had learned, too. He had learned that there was a group of poor people interested in their school and in his job. They had begun to work together to find ways to get a school for retarded children.

Padgett told the workshop participants at Montgomery Belle Park "the idea was so different and new" that CAP officials "as far away as the state of Washington were talking about it." His account had a great effect on the workshop participants, and by the time the sessions ended that weekend, most of the poor people had come to think of themselves as discussion leaders. They were determined to hold community workshops for poor people only.

To this end, they sent Clinton Francis to the CAP directors who were meeting in another room. He bluntly announced: "The poor people have decided they don't want you in their meetings any more unless they ask you. We want more meetings like this one [the poor for the poor] every two months."[18] They got their way. What had been tested before, proved itself again. Highlander's Appalachian Self-Education Program, as it was called, could function with results.

Mike Clark, a young man from the North Carolina mountains who joined Highlander's staff in 1968, wrote a staff report eighteen months after the Montgomery Belle Park meeting:

> Although we have the broadest contacts with community people of any organization in the six Appalachian states, we have still been limited by the relatively small number of community groups that function democratically. Much of our time over the past year has been spent broadening the contacts and trying to expose as many poor people as possible to these ideas.
>
> I have moved into Middle Tennessee on the edge of the Cumberland Plateau to work with several poor people's organizations which do function with a democratic orientation. They still have major problems, but they feel a need to involve all their members in decision-making and that need is the important thing right now. I have two main goals: first, to help set up local centers where people from several counties can come to hold their own workshops; and, secondly, to help set up ways by which community people can visit other community people across state and county lines. Both these needs came up during our last workshop at Highlander. People began to plan ways they could travel cheaply. The plan they eventually developed was for the visitor to arrange his own transportation and the community where he was visiting would take care of room and board.
>
> While this may sound like a relatively simple thing, it's a giant step forward for many of these people. They are beginning to say, "We don't want to depend on outside funds or organizations. We want to do things on our own."[19]

As has so often happened at Highlander, the plan for travel didn't work out, but the underlying ideas of independence and self-determination were developed in other ways. For example, Charles Maggard, who had been a coal miner like his father before him, turned to Highlander after watching the War on Poverty hurt more Appalachians than it helped. His idea was simple—help younger mountain people learn from the struggles of previous generations by encouraging them to meet and talk with men and women who had brought the union movement into the mountains in the thirties or who had fought against the destruction of their land when strip mining started in the late fifties.

This part of the story about how the Highlander idea is being used has no ending. It's still in process. But a footnote, of sorts, should be added. Highlander reinforced its commitment to continue working in Appalachia when, on February 11, 1972, the school moved from Knoxville twenty-five miles east to New Market, Tennessee, to a hillside farm overlooking the Smoky Mountains. Knoxville's urban renewal program was taking the house on Riverside Drive and demolishing it in the name of progress.

On May 28, 1973, Lewis Sinclair of Knoxville, an economist for TVA who was chairman of Highlander's board, wrote the school's supporters that Horton had resigned as a full-time staff member at the board's annual meeting in April, and that Mike Clark had been named to take over direction of the school as president:

> Despite the fact that Myles is past the normal retirement age, many of us on the board were not sure if he should step down from a position of active leadership within the school at this time.
>
> However, his announcement came at the end of our annual meeting, after detailed reports on the current program were submitted by staff members. These reports, and the development of Highlander's residential facility at New Market, convinced us Myles was correct. Many of us have been concerned about how the school would continue when Myles did decide to retire. We are now certain that the new staff can continue the Highlander idea for many years to come.[20]

Horton added a note of his own:

My retirement does not mean inactivity. Those of you who know me personally understand that I will remain active and involved in issues wherever I am. Mike Clark has asked me to take full responsibility for the development of our multi-racial program. This assignment will take up a great deal of my time and energy. In addition, I will be living on the Highlander farm and will be taking part in many of our program activities at the request of our staff.[21]

13

... *Mr. Marshal, take him out* ...

HORTON HAS BEEN PORTRAYED as a heretic for most of his adult life; Highlander, as both the result and the source of heresy. This would tempt some to cast Horton and the school in a heroic mold, badgered by men with small minds and governments with mean ways. Others would be tempted to report the attacks and the attackers as travesty, thus putting authority in a bad light and perhaps getting a few laughs, perhaps a few advocates. Yielding to those temptations would obscure this point: the badgering, the attacks came, mostly, from people who were acting out of conviction and from governments that were touchy about any challenge to their traditional ways. Few, if any, of Highlander's educational programs or of its staff's adventures have been popular. As for laughter, there was plenty of that at Highlander, but it seldom lasted long.

Horton could find amusement in his first encounter with the law, his arrest for "coming here and getting information and going back and teaching it." That episode, in isolation, was comic. What subsequently happened in Wilder was not. Horton learned soon after going to Wilder for the first time that Barney Graham, the union leader, had been marked for murder. He even knew the names of the men hired to kill him. Yet when Horton and Dr. Alva Taylor, professor of Christian ethics at Vanderbilt, went on April 22, 1933, to see Tennessee's governor to urge him to protect Graham's life, the governor said he could find no constitutional grounds on which to act, that the law was "on the side of the Co. and guards."[1]

Graham was killed eight days later. The two men who were charged with killing him, Jack (Shorty) Green and M. O. (Doc) Thompson, the same two men Horton and Dr. Taylor had named to the governor, were acquitted by a jury from which miners had been excluded. The ground was self-defense, despite testimony by Deputy Sheriff Dick Stultz that Graham had never fired a shot from the pistol found six inches from his hand. The safety was on, Stultz testified. Other witnesses had seen Green put the weapon near Graham's hand after he fell.[2] This experience taught Horton not to trust that the state, at least not the state of Tennessee, would serve as an impartial arbiter.

The consequences of Horton's Wilder arrest didn't end at the moment of his release. At the time, Highlander urgently needed funds to keep going. Horton had arranged with some high schools and colleges to make several paid speeches, either about his experiences in Denmark or about the school. After the arrest, every invitation was canceled. Friends of long standing had extended the invitations, but the same friends had jobs and families to protect. By the time Wilder subsided, Horton and Highlander were in trouble.

And it has been trouble ever since, though not without some benefit. Horton learned to use trouble to Highlander's advantage. A case in point is the way the Grundy County Crusaders were handled.

Horton first learned of the Crusaders when a Nashville *Tennessean* reporter called him early in November, 1940, to tip him off about a statement he had just received from the newly-formed group. The Crusaders were an amalgamation of the Junior Order of United American Mechanics, the American Legion, the Veterans of Foreign Wars, the Tracy City Parent-Teacher Association, and the United Mine Workers of America, Local 5881. Under the slogan "No Ism But Americanism," they had announced a mass march on Highlander for Tuesday, November 12, "to check firsthand on oft-repeated charges the school was an undesirable influence in the county."[3]

Thanks to the reporter's tip, Horton and the staff were able to prepare. First, they determined the sources of the Crusaders' charges. One source turned out to be a pamphlet titled *The Fifth Column in the South.*[4] Written by Joseph P. Kamp, vice-chairman of the right-wing Constitutional Educational League, the pamphlet included among other "charges" a photograph of a hundred-dollar check, made out to Highlander and signed by Eleanor Roosevelt, as "evidence the White House help[ed] support Fifth Column activity in the South.[5] The other source of accusation was C. H. Kilby, a bookkeeper and secretary of Tennessee Consolidated Coal Company, who for two years had worked to organize the Crusaders.

Leon Wilson, librarian at Highlander, later explained how Kamp's pamphlet was used against Highlander:

> Distribution of *The Fifth Column in the South* in the Grundy area appears to have followed the usual course. Just before formation of the Crusaders, copies flourished like weeds, especially among the coal miners. At least one influential resident of Tracy City received his copy directly from the absentee owner of the coal company, E. L. Hampton of Nashville.
>
> Alvin Henderson, cashier of the Tracy City First National Bank, and Kilby's Man Friday, passed out to the newspapers a photograph of the hundred-dollar check given Highlander by Eleanor Roosevelt [which the bank had received for deposit]. Asked if he did not consider this a violation of banking ethics, Henderson declared he felt it his duty to attack the school every way possible and that ethics were not involved since he had acted not as the cashier of his bank but as a private citizen . . . ."[6]

To counter the Crusaders, Highlander first sought support from labor. Paul Christopher, Tennessee CIO director, and other union men who had been working with the school, urged Tennessee labor leaders to consider the Crusaders' diatribe an attack on organized labor. They did so, and sent telegrams of support to the press. Kilby's march on Highlander never came off. The governor of Tennessee persuaded him that he and the Crusaders would be legally liable should any loss of life or property result. Instead, Kilby and a committee of seven met with Horton and the staff on neutral ground, St. Luke's Chapel at the University of the South in Sewanee. The Highlander people brought all the school's records, including lists of its contributors, students, and visitors, and offered them for inspection. None of the hundred people in attendance accepted the offer to inspect the records. The Crusaders, on the other hand, could produce no evidence of un-Americanism.[7]

The Crusaders unwittingly helped to develop broad support for the school. Highlander rode out their attack with its principles intact. The lesson was a valuable one for both students and staff. The miners and woodcutters that Highlander was working with at the time learned who their own enemies were, and thus consolidated their mutual aims. When the third national convention of the CIO met, it condemned the defamation of Highlander as "an attack on the progressive labor movement of the South," then unanimously approved a resolution endorsing the school, its aims, and programs.[8]

Backers appeared from nowhere. One man Highlander had never heard of until the Crusaders' threat wrote to offer the school 180 acres of land in Hamilton County, Tennessee.[9] Financial support was given by people who didn't fully agree with the school's work but who nonetheless believed with James Madison that the mechanics, farmers, and artisans should vote their interests. Civil libertarians defended Highlander. Whether or not they agreed with the school in principle, they defended its right of free expression as essential to the democratic process.

The Crusaders' was the first carefully organized effort to put Highlander out of business and, as such, helped prepare Horton for later, more serious attacks.

The IRS has twice revoked Highlander's tax-exempt status on the ground that the school had violated the provisions in federal law under which nonprofit educational institutions operate. The first revocation was on February 20, 1957, for "activities prior to 1951 which attempted to influence legislation." The IRS specifically cited Highlander's statement of purpose as a violation of law: "Our purpose is deliberately to use education for the realization of certain social and cultural values. We do not consider other education any less propaganda, because its teachers are ignorant of the fact that they are supporting an unethical status quo, than our approach which consciously seeks to bring about a more just social order."[10]

After no little expenditure of energy and funds, Highlander's appeal was upheld and the tax-exempt status returned.[11] The IRS again attempted to revoke the favored tax status on charges that Highlander had influenced legislation and had participated in elections by sending Horton to the New Politics Convention in Chicago in 1968, and by conducting workshops for black candidates in Mississippi. An appeal of its action, which was taken May 25, 1970, resulted in the exempt status again being returned to Highlander. Still a third IRS investigation of the school was launched in 1971. It, too, ended with the school's tax exempt status intact.[12]

As could be expected, Horton clashed with the government during the McCarthy era, specifically with Senator James Eastland of Mississippi. Just as Joseph McCarthy saw a Red behind every government door, Eastland, in Horton's view, saw a Red behind every black. For three days in 1954, Eastland, representing the Jenner Internal Security Committee, conducted hearings in New Orleans to prove that Communism had been "masquerading behind the facade of a humanitarian educational institution." He referred to the Southern Conference Education Fund, on whose board Horton had once sat.[13]

There was speculation in New Orleans that Eastland was probing "the Communist conspiracy in the South" because he faced a tough re-election fight in Mississippi. This view seemed to be supported by the fact that he came alone, leaving behind in Washington a committee full of vigorous Red-hunters. A related theory held that the Dixiecrats, who seemed to be losing the courtroom battle to maintain legal segregation, saw McCarthyism as a way to intimidate any white Southerners willing to establish even casual contacts with blacks.

Whatever the reasoning behind Eastland's move, he made sure that the events would be played out on his terms. At the start of the proceedings, he declared that cross-examination would not be allowed. Congressional procedure made no provision for such questioning, he explained to a packed courtroom. As for rules, he said that he would announce them as occasion required.[14] Then, with a stout cigar wedged into one side of his mouth, and with his counsel, Richard Arens, near at hand, he banged his gavel for the hearings to come to order.

Two witnesses, Paul Crouch and John Butler, provided the basis of the committee's charge that SCEF was a "Communist organization." Butler said he was a member of the Communist Party from 1941 to 1943 while at the same time serving as president of Local 121 of the Mine, Mill, and Smelter Workers in Bessemer, Alabama. He attempted to link James Dombrowski with the party. Dombrowski was SCEF's secretary at the time of the hearings.

Butler's testimony was weak and inconclusive, presented in a barely audible monotone. Even Richard Arens asked him once or twice to speak up.[15]

Crouch was another matter. A professional witness in dozens

of Smith Act trials, deportation cases, and congressional hearings, he was then nearing the end of a career as "consultant" for the Department of Justice.[16] Born the son of a Baptist preacher and teacher in North Carolina, Crouch had moved away from the South in 1921. He had joined the United States Army and the Communist Party, apparently at about the same time. Four years after enlistment he had been sentenced to forty years in prison for advocating the overthrow of the government while trying to organize a Communist League among soldiers at Schofield Barracks in Hawaii. He had served two years in Alcatraz when his court-martial was reviewed and his sentence ordered reduced.

Between his release in 1925 and his break with the party in 1942, he crisscrossed the United States as a Communist organizer. After his break, he became an informer, testifying most notably in the perjury trial of Harry Bridges, the West Coast longshoremen's leader. Crouch's part in bringing about the government's conviction of Bridges (later reversed) made him particularly valuable to Eastland.

When Crouch stepped down from the witness stand the first day of hearings, Dombrowski seemed to be in trouble. On the stand himself, Dombrowski refused to name the contributors to SCEF, then almost immediately found himself defending Highlander:

> . . . I came into Tennessee from a theological seminary and I joined an educational institution and it was branded by the press and vigilantes tried to destroy it, and it was a religious organization primarily trying to carry out, as I understood, the Judeo-Christian tradition of a socialist gospel and doing it. All these charges were unfair and untrue, and I have learned from bitter personal experience that you must judge a man or a program in terms of the Bible by its fruit, not by what he does or says.[17]

To that Eastland responded: "These agencies [HUAC and

the FBI] have investigated it [Highlander] and found it was a front for a conspiracy to overthrow this country. Its program was a fraud. That was a front. That was not its program. Its program was the destruction of America."[18] So much for Dombrowski's veracity.

Aubrey Williams, publisher of the *Southern Farm and Home Magazine*, and SCEF president, was called on the second day of the hearings. Like Dombrowski, he refused either to invoke the Fifth Amendment or to name SCEF contributors. Then Butler was called back to the stand. In audible testimony, he said that he had attended a Communist Party meeting in 1942 at which Williams had been present. Williams denounced the accusation as a lie and challenged Butler to repeat it to newsmen after the hearing. "I'll sue him the minute he does," Williams shouted. Butler didn't repeat the charge.[19]

Williams was later called back to the stand and was being questioned when Eastland, without warning, decided to permit Crouch to be cross-examined. Clifford Durr was counsel for Williams and Horton. Durr was a former member of the Federal Communications Commission and a Rhodes scholar who had lectured on law at Princeton. His wife, Virginia, had been subpoenaed to appear before Eastland. When Crouch took the stand, Durr, after lengthy cross-examination, asked him:

"Can you prove you are not a Communist?"

Crouch said that he could. Arens leaned from the bench. "Is Mr. Durr a Communist?" he asked Crouch.

"I do not know whether he still is a Communist or not," Crouch replied.

"You say I was a Communist at one time?" Durr asked.

"Yes, sir."[20]

Durr then asked to be sworn as a witness. He denied the allegations and demanded a perjury investigation. Then, returning to his role of cross-examiner, he sought to pin Crouch down as to exact dates and exact meetings when he, Durr, was supposed to have been in the company of Communists. Crouch could supply no dates. The second day ended.

Horton was called as the first witness on the third and final day. When he arrived in court with Durr, the two men were ushered into an executive session with Eastland in private chambers. Horton balked at answering any question in private. He demanded both an open hearing and the right to read for the record a prepared statement he had already distributed to spectators and press.[21]

Eastland agreed that Horton's prepared statement would be part of the record. However, when they returned to the courtroom, Horton was on the witness stand for barely five minutes when Eastland ordered him thrown out.

The exchange, as recorded in the hearing record, sheds considerable light on Eastland's methods:

MR. ARENS: Is Mr. James Dombrowski affiliated with the Highlander Folk School?

MR. DURR: Mr. Chairman, I submit that Mr. Dombrowski himself has already testified on that.

SENATOR EASTLAND: Is that any reason why this witness should not answer?

MR. HORTON: Couldn't I give my reasons why I don't want to answer?

SENATOR EASTLAND: No, I do not want your reasons. Do you decline to answer the question?

MR. HORTON: I would like to state my reasons as to answering your question as to whether I decline or not.

SENATOR EASTLAND: Do you decline to answer the question?

MR. HORTON: Mr. Chairman, you listened to an ex-communist who is a paid informer. Why don't you listen to the testimony of an ordinary American?

SENATOR EASTLAND: Wait a minute.

MR. HORTON: Why don't you listen to an American citizen talk?

SENATOR EASTLAND: Answer my question. Do you decline to answer the question?

MR. HORTON: Mr. Chairman, I would like to state that history attests to the fact that—

SENATOR EASTLAND: Wait a minute. Mr. Marshal, take him out of the room.

MR. HORTON: I decline to answer.

SENATOR EASTLAND: All right. Take him out of the room.[22]

With hammerlocks, two marshals took Horton outside the courtroom and threw him to the marble steps. Behind him Eastland was saying, "We are not going to have any self-serving declarations."[23]

What Horton had intended to say was that he would testify freely about his own actions, but that he would not discuss any other person or issue raised by the committee. He refused to recognize the constitutionality of the committee or the right of any public official to require him to express his opinions under the threat of punishment for failure to do so. "If the First Amendment insures freedom of speech," Horton said in his prepared statement, "it must likewise insure freedom to remain silent." And his statement continued: "The hysteria spread by your committee and others like it has substantially contributed to the fiction that the only dynamic force in the world is Communism. This I deny. Communism has never tempted me because I believe in Democracy, a powerful concept worthy of mankind the world over. You know, if you have made any effort to find out, that I have never been a member of the Communist Party. I am fearful only of the results of our own timidity in advancing democratic principles."[24]

The statement never appeared in the official report of the hearing.

Horton had scarcely regained his footing when another uproar took place in the courtroom. Crouch had returned to the witness stand to disclaim any intent to attack the integrity of President Roosevelt, Mrs. Roosevelt, Mr. Justice Black of the Supreme Court, or the Southern Conference for Human Welfare. However, at the end of his long, virtually uninterrupted oration, he declared that "Mrs. Virginia Foster Durr, Justice Black's sister-in-law [and wife of Horton's attorney], had full knowledge of the conspiratorial nature, according to the detailed reports . . . ."[25]

That was too much for her husband. Jennings Perry, writing in *I. F. Stone's Weekly*, reported that Durr ran around the railing in front of the witness benches. "You say that about my wife!" He threw himself at Crouch, threatening "to kill him with my bare hands." He was gently restrained by the marshals who had earlier, "with evident relish manhandled Horton from the room." Perry reported that Durr was taken to the hospital because of a heart condition.[26]

So ended the Eastland hearings. A reporter subsequently asked fellow newsmen covering the hearings, "On the basis of what you have seen and heard here, who of the principals represents the greatest threat to American ideals?" There were four votes for Eastland, two for Paul Crouch, one each for Jim Dombrowski and Max Shafrock, a Miami contractor who had also been a witness.[27]

For his part, Horton learned from the Eastland hearings that government may be more difficult than any private foe. His experiences during the Tennessee legislative investigation and the subsequent court proceedings which closed the Highlander Folk School reinforced his conclusion. And finally, The Knoxville City Council's action after the school located there did little to change his mind.

At the time, the city council was dominated by a wealthy groceryman, Cas Walker, who felt that no such tainted outfit as Highlander should be allowed within the Knoxville city limits. Accordingly, he pushed through the council an ordinance requiring that all educational institutions wishing to be established in the city be approved by the council.

Shortly after the ordinance was on the books, policemen started coming to Highlander with copies of it and with warrants. Horton and the staff ignored them. They knew that such legislation could not be made retroactive. But the move by Walker served its purpose: Knoxville's racists were aroused.

The Ku Klux Klan marched on the school in full regalia. Crank telephone calls came in day and night. Mrs. Walter McCormick, who years before had been a student at Highlander and was then serving as the school's secretary and bookkeeper, kept a Bible handy for responding to the calls. Once, when an anonymous voice asked, "How many little mulattoes have you got running around down there?" she replied without pause, "I don't know. How many have you lost?"[28] On another occasion, students attending a SNCC workshop had ice picks jabbed into their tires, sugar dumped into their gasoline tanks, and paint smeared on the bodies of their cars.

Other parts of Tennessee were no less resentful of Highlander than Knoxville. In 1963, Highlander arranged to use a piece of mountain property in Blount County. That summer one of the most serious attacks ever made on the school's students occurred there. The property was at the edge of the Smoky Mountains National Park, high on a mountain overlooking much of northeastern Tennessee, near Maryville, home of the grand dragon of the Tennessee klan. Highlander was holding a work camp on the property to help young whites from the North and South get better acquainted with black youngsters involved in civil rights activities in Birmingham. The camp was under the direction of Robert and Mary Gustafson, a young married couple who had come south especially to work there.

After attending a meeting in Oak Ridge on June 19, the group of twenty-nine was awakened at two in the morning by shouts and flashlight beams jabbing the darkness. It was the Blount County sheriff and a host of deputies. Without benefit of warrant, they rounded up everyone and took them to the Blount County jail. Long after sunrise, eight youngsters were charged with disorderly conduct; one was also charged with possession of liquor; the Gustafsons, with contributing to the delinquency of minors. Gustafson was also charged with possession of liquor.[29] The rest were released without charge. Two days before the trial was to begin, the work camp's single cabin and several tents were burned to the ground about 3:00 A.M.[30]

At the trial, the judge refused to admit defense evidence that no search warrant had been obtained, that the raiders had trespassed on private property, and that the "liquor" was actually water, tested and proved to be such by one of the Oak Ridge scientists. One deputy testified he had seen a girl running out of a tent "putting on a brassiere. She had on pajama bottoms and, I believe, a pajama top."[31]

Another told of finding a black boy sitting on the bed of a white girl. Both were fully clothed, he testified, but they had been talking together. That was it for the court. Seven of the eight were convicted. Charges against the eighth, a girl of fifteen, were dropped by the court, but she was ordered taken into the custody of juvenile officials, then later released.[32]

Of course, all appealed to the State Supreme Court. Highlander's lawyer was Edwin Lynch, a native of Blount County, and, up to the time of trial, a promising local politician trusted for his orthodoxy. The local prosecutor confidentially approached him with a "deal": the white students would be pardoned without blemish on their records if the black students accepted their convictions without further court challenge. Lynch and Highlander refused. Then, to the amazement of all, the General Sessions Court in Blount County suddenly voided all the convictions. The county's case was too weak for further prosecution.[33]

Several days after the convictions were voided, Lynch and his wife, Doris, were dining with Horton and his second wife, Aimee, in a Maryville restaurant. Horton was suddenly grabbed by the owner and given a brutal, painful beating before Lynch could pull him away. A few days after that, Lynch was formally told by fellow Maryville barristers that he would face disbarment proceedings if he sought to continue his practice in Tennessee. Aware of the resentment against him and certain that the proceedings would be started, Lynch closed his office and found employment in the state of New York.

But trouble for Highlander has come not only from the state and private groups, but sometimes from those with whom the school was supposedly conspiring. For example, at the same time labor unions were being mercilessly Red-baited for trying to protect their workers, some of those unions were Red-baiting Highlander, demanding that the school disavow this or that union as "communistic." The AFL attacked Highlander for supporting the industrial unions and the CIO; the CIO attacked the school for refusing to disavow the Mine, Mill, and Smelter Workers, among others. The same situation was true in the school's fight against racism. Blacks were Red-baited for associating with the NAACP, CORE, and SNCC. CORE, for instance, had been dominated since its inception in the forties by Northern white liberals who, remembering that Highlander had been branded "communist" in the thirties, would not associate with the school.

By and large, Highlander has always ignored such quibbles

over definition. Horton and his staff have refused to waste time labeling people or groups. Highlander has been ruthless only when a group sought to control the school's program for its own benefit. One day Horton got two letters denouncing the school activities that had been reported in a newsletter sent out only days before. Both irate letters were written the same day, but by different persons in different cities, unknown to each other. One scolded Highlander for taking "the Moscow line." The other repudiated the school for "following the reasoning of the socialists." Horton, cantankerously, took both letters and their envelopes, put them into new envelopes, and, without comment, sent the Socialist's attack on the school's alleged communism to the Communist, and the Communist's attack on its alleged socialism to the Socialist. Neither he nor Highlander ever heard from them again.

14

. . . and teach every man to know his own . . .

WHAT IS THE HIGHLANDER idea, disassociated from the events through which it has evolved since Ozone? What sets the Highlander approach apart from that of other adult education? How would someone "do" another Highlander? First it must be recognized that Highlander's goal dictates methods, measurement, and evaluation. Horton is the first to admit that he doesn't fully understand the results accomplished through Highlander—any more than any educator can say with certainty what the cause and effect relationship is between school and society, scholar and citizen.[1]

Obviously, Highlander seeks a society governed by natural human relationships, not dogmas of race or creed or nationalism. Too, Highlander aims for a society organized on the basis of voluntary association and mutual cooperation, rather than limited democracy and authoritarianism. The ideal of educating for citizenship in a fully free democracy is vastly different from the ideal of educating to serve a state, as different, in fact, as a school that aims to educate mathematicians is from one that aims to produce bookkeepers. One is dynamic; the other, static.

Highlander's original purpose—educating for a revolution that would basically alter economic and political power relationships to the advantage of the poor and powerless—has not been achieved. Poverty, repression, racism, and the denial of full democratic rights for all continue to plague the South's people. However, these ills are now generally recognized as endemic to any capitalist nation, not just to one region in America. Highlander may have contributed something to this wider understanding of social injustice, but clearly, there has been no second American Revolution. In any case, while American society may not have changed, neither has Highlander's purpose. The people—poor, adult Southerners; the place—the South; the broad concepts of democracy, brotherhood, mutuality, and united social action limit or qualify Highlander's methods. The school is specific about its mission, whom it is for and with, where it is, and why. It is deliberately vague about its governing concepts, letting the people it serves and the times in which they live define precisely what brotherhood, democracy, mutuality, and united social action mean. These ideals change as people change. Highlander changes with them and avoids learning dictated from specific theory, learning that, by nature, would curtail freedom.

There is only one axiom that never changes at Highlander: *learn from the people; start their education where they are.*[2] This is easier said than done. Most of Highlander's staff over the years, like Horton, have been highly-educated intellectuals who identify with Niebuhr's assertion that the responsibility of the socially-concerned intellectual is to leaven out society. Because they have been educated, or taught, and have been in school much of their lives, and because Highlander was a school, they taught—until people taught them otherwise. They had to learn that the people who came to Highlander were the educational authorities—not the staff; the people knew what they needed to know. Esau Jenkins didn't care to learn about the United Nations but wanted to learn about reading for voter registration, an *immediate* problem he and countless others faced in the South.

Highlander had to learn also that ideology, no matter how firmly grounded in objective reality, is of no value if it is separated from a social movement of struggling people. Thus Highlander itself had to become a process through which people could find purposeful and democratic unity with others to solve their collectively-defined problems. Education, then, had to develop naturally from the people themselves, from the ways they could and would learn, and had to be reinforced constantly. An educational program at Highlander isn't one workshop; it is years of process.

In this sense, Highlander has sought to be popular. The school has identified with the poor and has worked hard to be in touch with their daily lives, learning their customs and speech. The school has had to become an educational experience for the poor, both *in* and *in terms of* their own culture.

Poor people have been encouraged to find beauty and pride in their own ways, to speak their own language without humiliation, and to recognize their own power to accomplish self-defined goals through social movements built from their own kind and kin. Music plays a critically important part in this process. Seldom do people gather at Highlander without someone around to make music.

People learn about unity by acting in unison. They learn about democracy by acting democratically. Each time they act in democratic unity, as a result of Highlander experiences, they both strengthen their capacity for such action and demonstrate the process of education. Talking about this process distorts it, and is one step removed from the essential element—people themselves, doing. Writing about the process is two steps removed. Education at Highlander is a synthesis of person, group, time, place, purpose, and problem. Words and sentences, spoken or written, tend to order this synthesis and give it logic by making it a sequence, when, in fact, it is not and cannot be sequential or logical.

Even so, methods used at Highlander can be discussed. One is an objective, social approach to problem-solving. An individual's conscious process of critical thought begins in response to a perceived difficulty. Put another way, when people find themselves in a bind, they usually try to work out a solution. Some seek self-serving and individualistic solutions to their problems. Historically, education in America, more often than not, has taught people that, when the conflict between themselves and a problem lessens or disappears, the problem is solved. Critical, conscious thought about the causes of the problem, or who else may be affected by it, often stops at this point.

However, some individuals recognize also that their problem is one shared by others; thus, their individual problem is not solved for them until it's solved for all. Once Horton and Highlander realized that society would not be changed by individuals acting alone or by radical political analysis alone, Highlander sought to educate people away from the dead end of individualism and into the freedom that grows from cooperation and collective solutions. For example, workshop discussions that elaborate on what individuals have done by themselves are skipped over lightly. But when individuals talk about what they and others like them have done together to solve their problems, these discussions are examined in detail.

Independence is another element of Highlander. At first glance, this may seem to contradict what has just been stated. Not so. Horton quickly learned that solutions for the South's problems devised in New York City, or by anyone not directly faced with the problems, have no real application. The people Highlander works with won't try the solutions of outsiders. Education that suggests that everyone should conform to some specific ideology, Holy Writ, or political cause is unacceptable to poor people. They won't swallow it. So Highlander has a reputation for cranky independence—one that it maintains with care and pride. To teach freedom, a school has to be free. In this way, Highlander has avoided indoctrinating, and both disciplining and being disciplined. Some social critics argue that the people must be taught in order to be free; others argue that they must be free in order to be taught. Highlander agrees with the latter view, but only in an active sense: that is, once free, the people will learn, and will teach others, including Highlander.

Highlander's staff has learned to avoid telling people how to relieve their problems and has concentrated on helping people look to themselves to find their own potential *and their own* solutions. When Highlander has succeeded at this difficult task, the staff have been teachers who, as Joseph K. Hart said, were able "to teach their own capacity to learn."[3]

Once the early blush of idealism wore off and the Highlander staff, Horton included, stopped trying to save the South from itself, they learned to focus the school's limited resources on one educational program at a time. To develop leadership for a social movement requires a concentration of educational effort. One or two residential workshops producing one or two leaders is not enough. Changing political and economic conditions require a constantly-renewed leadership if a social movement of the poor is to survive and accomplish its goals. Highlander learned during both the labor union movement and the civil rights movement that the opponents of change, public or private, can destroy leadership among the poor, one way or another, almost as fast as leadership can emerge.

Highlander commits itself to five or ten years of single-minded effort on any given program. Educational activities are ignored that do not directly help new leadership for a specific social movement to emerge. There are only two exceptions to this rule: first, the school holds workshops for sympathetic groups who, once stimulated, might become directly involved in the work of a social movement; and second, they hold workshops that, though educationally sound, may have little or nothing to do with Highlander's own program but that pay for themselves, making it possible to continue the school.

To the uninformed, the residential workshop seems to be the central element in what happens at Highlander. These workshops are often misunderstood on at least two levels: first, they are only the most visible part of a process; second, they are not informal bull sessions.

At workshops, staff and participants talk about what is happening in their communities and what people there are doing about their problems. Deliberately, there is a relaxed atmosphere and a lack of routine, but this exterior hides a high level of purpose. No adult comes to a Highlander workshop unless he is already active in his community, and, because of this activity, feels the need to learn more. These are emerging leaders, people who in one sense are free and can teach and learn. Participants are invited directly—in person, and only seldom by letter—by former students or staff. Intimacy is important. To invite a poor person to leave the security of home and come to a place with a "bad reputation" requires a high degree of trust between the person invited and the person inviting. Highlander is usually familiar in some way to participants long before they come to a residential workshop. As a result, any workshop group tends to be homogeneous at the outset. The workshops themselves are vigorously nonacademic experiences in which every conventional learning device is discarded or used in some entirely new way by the people themselves. This is so because most people who attend are either offended or frightened by schools, and, more important, because their educational needs fit no traditional academic pattern.

Baffled by education without assignment or examination, without the learned talking and the unlearned listening, some critics have described Highlander's residential workshops as anti-intellectual, where the exchange of anecdote passes for education. This criticism overlooks several facts. Highlander is dedicated to helping develop the fulfillment of democracy, not to preserving academic discipline. What is learned at Highlander is usually tested in real life under the eye of an oppressor, not in the classroom under the eye of a tutor. Finally, educational work at Highlander is not done once or twice, then forgotten. An educational program that evolves through experimentation, such as the Citizenship Schools, is repeatable, and that makes it a program, which becomes more vital when tied into a social movement. "That's when Highlander's education perks," says Horton.

The residential workshop consists of a problem, people, and a place. The problems and the people have been described. The place—Highlander—is kept comfortable and homelike. Horton may not have realized the importance of low-keyed informality when he and West persuaded Dr. Johnson to let them use her house. They simply used what they had. Slowly the staff came to realize that this homey feeling was important—plain, well-used furniture, no desks or folding chairs, no bell, no cafeteria line, no tin trays, nothing to suggest an institution. Discussions are as likely to take place in the dining room as in the meeting room. Furniture is light and can be moved around. Food is served family style.

Still, Highlander is not a home. For one thing, participants have no job to go to, so they can relax. For another, there is an atmosphere of excitement during a workshop; strangers come and go, ideas and dreams dominate the talk. One person said that Highlander was a place where he could "actually live in wholesome friendship with other groups who were interested" in common problems and unafraid to look for solutions.[4]

During a Highlander workshop, the poor talk, and the experts talk when questioned by the poor. This is usually a new experience for both. Ordinarily, if poor people even go to public meetings where their problems might be dealt with, middle-class people, who are more accustomed to meetings and better able to express themselves, dominate. Poor people tend to be shut out, even though they may feel as strongly about the problems as anyone. Not so at Highlander. Workshop resource persons who fail to recognize that they are to talk only when asked will be told to "shush" by a staff member, quickly, politely, and firmly. College students, who frequently desire to attend workshops, are not allowed, unless they have had previous experience with community work and people.

Historically, Highlander workshops have fallen into two distinct categories, each relating to the stage of development of a social movement. If a movement is gathering force, the workshops tend to be broad and loose in range, usually without a specific topic. During these workshops, a feeling of commonality is established; isolation is broken down. For most of the people Highlander works with, just talking out loud and having someone consider their ideas seriously takes getting used to. Being with strangers and hearing new ideas is often hard. For example, Highlander held a workshop in 1970 attended by militant blacks, Puerto Ricans, Indians from six nations, Mexican-Americans, and people from Appalachia. The force with which each group presented its problems and expressed its determination to end those problems, coupled with the antagonisms among the ethnic groups, nearly overshadowed the fact that no one of them was free to determine its own destiny, and all were poor. There was a lot of talk about Black Power, Latin Power, Red Power; so much, in fact, that one Appalachian resident left in fury and tears. Later, he said that what had both infuriated and frightened him was "that they were talking about something I'd been thinking about for years and had done nothing about."[5] He went home determined to do something about problems as he saw them in Appalachia and has since been described by one national newspaper as a driving force in the region.

As movements gain momentum, however, more concrete information becomes essential. Thus, second-phase workshops require a greater use of experts, but only those whom the people themselves have decided they want to learn from. In this stage, the majority of Highlander's workshops are devoted to the presentation of specialized information requested by people active in the struggle.

In either workshop situation, Highlander relies on the tested concept that all learning is self-acquired and that people will learn, and put to effective use, only what they themselves determine is necessary. No matter in what stage of development a social movement stands, workshop discussions concentrate on ways in which the poor can gain for themselves both self-determination and pride in self. Highlander has never sought to help people get used to poverty or powerlessness—"education for adjustment," as it might be described.

Without violating the principle of *starting where the people are*, the workshop discussion leaders or the staff will deliberately reinforce talk in the group that points to united action. At the same time, free discussion is mandatory. Views opposing collective action must be examined. Otherwise, Highlander would fall into the trap of telling people what is good for them. The Highlander staff, however, continues to work only with those people who act collectively in their own communities after workshops.[6] This follow-up procedure reinforces the commitment to effective problem-solving by the people without relying on the experts.

The process of peer group learning prevents a Highlander workshop from becoming a meaningless exchange of anecdotes. As soon as each person has had a turn at telling of his or her community problems and what solutions, if any, have been tried, the floor is opened for questions and talk by everyone. Since workshop participants usually share common regional backgrounds and common economic and social experiences, they are likely to find that they also share common problems—although they may never have met before.

As a consequence, the discussion of solutions will apply to most people present and usually holds the interest of all. In this way, also, solutions come from the people, not the experts; they come from the bottom up, rather than from the top down. The search for solutions becomes, itself, a group process. Without saying so, Highlander provides an experience in group problem-solving. The group stretches the imagination of every individual in it and becomes the vehicle for introducing the concept of collective power. When this happens, the "seeds of fire" are unearthed. Lectures, textbooks, and examinations have nothing to do with the emergence of this phenomenon. Only people can produce and experience it.

What ought to be, rather than what is—that is Highlander's mission. From two words—*ought* and *is*—arises the tension out of which people will learn and act. Horton has come to believe that people will struggle to improve the future and to build for a dream. There is nothing new in seeking to use education as a means through which self-concept is affirmatively changed. Highlander has learned that poor people can affirm themselves and, simultaneously, learn the power of self in social unity with others. Finally, Highlander has learned that poor people are the only ones who can teach these things effectively.

This is the idea Horton first saw at Ozone but was unable to put into words. Accidental learning, if you will, was systematically made into a tool poor people could, and would, use to erase inequities. In many ways, this is what Thomas Paine talked about in *Agrarian Justice* when he said, "It is only by tracing things to their origin that we can gain rightful ideas of them, and it is by gaining such ideas that we discover the boundary that divides right from wrong, and teaches every man to know his own."[7]

There is one other major element of Highlander that needs elaboration. Just as the goal dictates Highlander's methods, the goal also determines who will be on the staff and what they will do. Oppressed people quickly spot and reject paternalism. During each of the school's major programs, the staff has been chosen because of prior experience related to the job at hand, and not because of a theoretical understanding of the problem.

There is some staff continuity from program to program. This prevents the repetition of mistakes. Horton has also provided continuity. Highlander's records show that almost every staff member has been wise enough to know that he or she did not need to know all the answers; most have been able to bring answers from the people. Highlander relies heavily on part-time staff and resource people who agree with the school's policies and can put their special knowledge to work accordingly.

The staff, not the board of directors, is responsible for raising funds. The board is selected only on the basis of interest in education. This policy is maintained to insure that Highlander's statements of activities made to potential donors are accurate and firsthand and that funds are raised solely on the basis of direct program needs. Highlander has never been endowed, and, by 1970, nearly 80 per cent of its income was given by individuals. While the board sets broad policy, the staff, in implementing it, actually shapes educational forms at Highlander. This is evident from the preceding descriptions of the staff's responsibilities before, and during, workshops but can be seen more clearly in what has come to be known at Highlander as "staff follow-up period."

The real measure of Highlander's effectiveness—perhaps the only valid one—comes when a workshop participant returns home. Many never become active. Others become devoted to fundamental social change. With the latter, staff members concentrate their energies after workshops. For example, if a workshop participant returns home determined to confront a particular problem but learns that he needs more specific information, the staff helps him arrange a local workshop, complete with appropriate resource people. Or, if a workshop participant finds himself challenging a local power structure, Highlander will help him find the necessary legal or financial aid. But in every case, the person or group needing help must decide how and when the help shall be forthcoming. Self-education is not a rescue mission. The staff, in these situations, must continue to be sensitive enough to help people make and carry out their own decisions, not to take them over.

On the surface, the idea Horton learned from poor people in Ozone would seem one that was disarmingly simple and that would be welcomed immediately. The notion of founding a school for poor people in a democratic America would appear to contain no troublesome prospect. But Joe Begley of Blackey, Kentucky, a Highlander "graduate," said it this way: "We're a sad, itty-bitty weepin' willow people. We've been taught to say yes. When you say no, that's a real chop-blocker."[8]

Notes

CHAPTER 1

1. Myles Horton, President Emeritus, Highlander Research and Education Center, Inc., New Market, Tenn. Daily personal interviews with Horton at his home between January 1, 1970, and June 30, 1970, provide the principal source of this book's narrative. This source will hereinafter be referred to as Horton Interview.

2. *Ibid.*

3. *Ibid.*

4. C. Vann Woodward, *The Burden of Southern History* (New York: Vintage Books, 1960), p. 28.

5. Thomas B. Brooks, *Toil and Trouble, A History of American Labor* (New York: Delta Books, 1964), p. 145. See also: "South Loses Five Leaders," *The Christian Century*, LVI (September 7, 1939), 1075; John E. Edgerton, letters to Highlander Folk School, 1933–1935, Highlander Papers (Social Action Collection, State Historical Society of Wisconsin), Box 11, folder 10.

6. See William James, *Pragmatism* (New York: Longmans, Green and Co., 1907), p. 282; Merle Curti, "William James, Individualist," *The Social Ideas of American Educators* (3rd ed.; Paterson, N.J.: Littlefield, Adams & Co., 1965), p. 454.

7. John Dewey, *The Quest for Certainty* (New York: Minton, Balch and Co., 1929), p. 253.

8. John Dewey, *Reconstruction in Philosophy* (New York: Holt, 1921), p. 155. See also: John Dewey, general correspondence, 1933–1935, Highlander Papers, Box 10, folder 18; Aimee Horton, "The Highlander Folk School: A History of the Development of Its Major Programs Related to Social Movements in the South, 1932–1961" (Ph.D. dissertation, University of Chicago, 1971).

9. Young Men's Christian Association Creed, Highlander Papers, Box 30, folder 7.

10. Horton Interview.

CHAPTER 2

1. Quoted in Horton Interview. See also: Abbott Kaplan, general correspondence, Highlander Papers (Social Action Collection, State Historical Society of Wisconsin), Box 17, folder 12.

2. Horton Interview.

3. Reinhold Niebuhr, letter to Horton, February 27, 1933, Highlander Papers, Box 22, folder 1.

4. Niebuhr, "Build a New Party!" *The World Tomorrow*, XIV (January, 1931), 19.

5. "Statement of Purpose," *The World Tomorrow.*

6. Horton, letter to Niebuhr, July 6, 1966. Highlander Papers, Box 22, folder 1.

7. John Dewey, *Democracy and Education* (New York: Macmillan Co., 1916), p. 319. See also: Niebuhr and others, "Letter for the Southern Mountain School" (mimeo.), May 27, 1932, Highlander Papers, Box 22, folder 1.

8. George S. Counts, "Education—For What?" *The New Republic*, LXXI, No. 911 (May 18, 1932), 12–15 and No. 912 (May 25, 1932), 38–40.

9. Joseph K. Hart, *Light from the North: The Danish Folk High Schools—Their Meanings for America* (New York: Henry Holt & Co., 1926), p. 144.

10. Eduard C. Lindeman, *The Meaning of Adult Education* (New York: New Republic, Inc., 1926), p. 166.

11. *Ibid.*, pp. 153–54.

12. Horton Interview.

13. *Ibid.* See also: Horton, "Notes on Brookwood Labor College," n.d., Highlander Papers, Box 37, folder 9.

14. Horton Interview.

15. This version was transcribed from a paper typed by Horton about 1930. Copyright 1926 and renewed 1954 by Langston Hughes. Reprinted by permission of Alfred A. Knopf, Inc. A slightly different version of this poem appears in *Selected Poems*, by Langston Hughes (1968), p. 275.

16. For a brief summary of Park's position see Ralph H. Turner, *Robert E. Park on Social Control and Collective Behavior* (Chicago: Phoenix Books, University of Chicago Press, 1967), p. xiii.

17. Lester F. Ward, *Dynamic Sociology* (New York: D. Appleton Company, 1833; reprint, New York: Greenwood Press, 1968), II, 546. See also: *ibid.*, pp. 541–633, *passim.*

18. Horton Interview.

19. *Ibid.*

20. *Ibid.*

21. *Ibid.*

22. Horton, "No Hunger in Denmark" (undated article from *Chattanooga News, circa* Summer, 1933), Highlander Papers, Box 41, folder 15. See also: Horton, "Folk High Schools" (undated article from *Chattanooga News, circa* Summer, 1933), Highlander Papers, Box 41, folder 15; Denmark trip correspondence, lectures, articles, diaries, notes, and songs, 1931–1934, Highlander Papers, Box 41, folders 16–18.

23. Hart, *passim.* See also: John C. Campbell, *The Southern Highlander and His Home* (New York: Russell Sage Foundation, 1921), p. 281.

24. Hart, p. 85.

25. Niebuhr, letter to Horton, March 26, 1931, Highlander Papers, Box 22, folder 1.

26. Horton, letter to Paul Hansen, April 12, 1932, Highlander Papers, Box 41, folder 15.

27. Horton Interview.

28. Hart, pp. 148–49.

29. Horton, "Christmas Night, 1931, Copenhagen, Denmark," Highlander Papers, Box 41, folder 16.

CHAPTER 3

1. Niebuhr, letter, May 27, 1932, Highlander Papers (Social Action Collection, State Historical Society of Wisconsin), Box 22, folder 1.

2. James Dombrowski, *The Early Days of Christian Socialism in America* (New York: Columbia University Press, 1937).

3. Lillian W. Johnson, "Beginning of the Cooperative Movement in the United States," *The Tennessee Union Farmer*, November 7, 1947, pp. 5–6.

4. Two years later, on October 20, 1934, the State of Tennessee issued a Charter of Incorporation to Highlander Folk School, listing as incorporators Myles Horton, Elizabeth Hawes, James Dombrowski, Rupert Hampton, and Malcolm Chisholm, who also were the school's first board of directors.

5. "Summary of School Activities, 1933–1934" (mimeo.), Highlander Papers, Box 12, folder 2.

6. Charles Allred, *Grundy County, Tennessee: Relief in a Coal*

Mining Community (Knoxville, Tenn.: Tennessee Agriculture Experiment Station, University of Tennessee, 1936).

7. Dombrowski, "Fire in the Hole" (MS in Tuskegee Institute, Tuskegee, Alabama, *circa* 1941). See also: Fran Ansley and Brenda Bell (eds.), "Mining Insurrections/Convict Labor," *Southern Exposure*, I, Nos. 3 and 4 (1974), 144–59.

8. Myles Horton and Don West, "New Year's Greetings from the Highlander Folk School," Highlander Papers, Box 1, folder 1.

9. "Cavalry on Way to Mine, Snow Falling," *Nashville Banner*, November 19, 1932. See also: "Trestle Blown Up in Wilder Section," *The* (Nashville) *Tennessean*, November 18, 1932; "Mine Union Official Blames Company Guards in Dynamiting of Wilder Bridges," *Knoxville News-Sentinel*, December 3, 1932; "Use of Army Property by Guard Angers Neal," *Chattanooga Times*, November 25, 1932.

10. Horton Interview.

11. Affidavits sworn by citizens include Isaac Wilson, coal miner, Wilder, Tenn., before Ira Scroggins, Notary Public, Wilder, Tenn., May 15, 1934; G. D. Howard, coal miner, Wilder, Tenn., sworn before Ira Scroggins, May 21, 1934; C. M. Stevens, Fentress County, Tenn., before Ira Scroggins, October 29, 1934; and Tom Hall, highway worker, Overton County, Tenn., before J. R. Copeland, Notary Public, Twinton, Tenn., May 21, 1934. Copies of each in Highlander Papers, Box 76, folder 15.

12. John Greenway, *American Folksongs of Protest* (New York: A. S. Barnes & Co., 1953), p. 159.

13. Press release by American Civil Liberties Union, New York, July 22, 1934, Highlander Papers, Box 5, folder 14.

14. Greenway, pp. 160–61.

15. Greenway, p. 162.

16. "State Police Hold Suspect at Wilder," *Chattanooga Times*, November 25, 1932. See also: "Teacher Tells Church of Arrest at Wilder," *Knoxville News-Sentinel*, November 29, 1932; "Guard Officer Angered by Charges of 'Horton' " (*sic* quotes), *Chattanooga Times*, November 20, 1932; "Communications, Editor's Note," *The* (Nashville) *Tennessean*, December 1, 1932.

17. "Union Chief Shot in Back, Says Doctor," *Knoxville News-Sentinel*, May 2, 1933. See also: "Slayer of Wilder Strike Chieftain

Indicted, on Bond," *Chattanooga Times,* May 3, 1933; "Another Charged With Murdering Barney Graham" (fragments of a newspaper clipping), May 19, 1933, Highlander Papers, Box 76, folder 17.

18. Della Mae Graham, "The Ballad of Barney Graham, a Wilder Striker," Highlander Papers, Box 76, folder 15. See also: Eleanor Kellogg, "Strikers Blues," and Thomas Lowery, "Little David Blues," Highlander Papers, Box 76, folder 15.

19. Tennessee Valley Authority office memorandums, November 3 and November 7, 1933, Highlander Papers, Box 76, folder 15. See also: Arthur E. Morgan, general correspondence, Highlander Papers, Box 21, folder 16.

20. Willie Lehr, "Open Forum," *Cumberland Outlook* (Tracy City, Tenn.), January 6, 1933.

21. Horton, letter to Dombrowski, *circa* January, 1933, Highlander Papers, Box 61, folder 11.

22. Horton Interview.

23. Aimee Horton, "The Highlander Folk School" (Ph.D. dissertation, University of Chicago, 1971), p. 61.

24. Highlander Papers, Box 52, folder 10.

25. Horton Interview.

26. Will L. Brown, letter to President Franklin D. Roosevelt, May 3, 1934, Highlander Papers, Box 53, folder 4.

27. Aimee Horton, p. 61.

28. "Edgerton Hits Fund for Reds," *Knoxville Journal,* March 31, 1935. See also: "Relief Grant to Radical School Stirs Citizenry," *Chicago Daily Tribune,* March 26, 1935.

29. "Sunday Condemns U.S. Relief Grant, Denounces Highlander Folk Cooperative," *Chattanooga Times,* May 4, 1935.

30. Edgerton, letter to members of Tennessee Manufacturers Association, June 28, 1934, Highlander Papers, Box 11, folder 10.

31. Horton Interview.

32. Highlander Papers, Box 59, folder 9.

33. "Highlander Folk School Summer School Report and Summary of Other Educational Activities, September 1933–1934," Highlander Papers, Box 1, folder 3, p. 7.

34. "The Fighting Eaglet" (mimeo.), No. 1 (June, 1934), Highlander Papers, Box 52, folder 10.

35. Hilda Hulbert, "Excerpts from a Diary Kept during Strike," February 1935, Highlander Papers, Box 15, folder 24.

36. "Don West and Myles Horton Barred from County School Buildings by Orders of the Chairman," *Cumberland Outlook*, December 15, 1932.

37. Dr. Lillian Johnson, letter to Dombrowski, January 22, 1935, Highlander Papers, Box 16, folder 18.

38. Johnson, letter to Horton, *circa* April 1954. Highlander Papers, Box 16, folder 19.

39. Dorothy Thompson, "Criticism of HFS," *circa* August 1934, Highlander Papers, Box 27, folder 25.

40. Elizabeth Hawes, untitled notes, *circa* 1934, Highlander Papers, Box 14, folder 28.

41. Horton Interview.

42. Joseph K. Hart, *Light from the North* (New York: Henry Holt & Co., 1926), p. xiii.

43. Horton Interview.

44. *Ibid.*

45. *Ibid.*

46. Horton, "Mountain Men," *circa* 1937. Highlander Papers, Box 63, folder 4, pp. 10–14.

47. *The Finances and Management of Government of Grundy County, Tennessee* (Nashville, Tenn.: Tennessee Taxpayers Association, Inc., 1934).

48. Horton, "Mountain Men," p. 15. See also: "The Highlander Fling" (in "WPA Workers Organize," September, 1936, mimeo.), Highlander Papers, Box 53, folder 2, p. 2; Lewie Vaughn, "My Work in Grundy County" (in "We the Students," mimeo., circa 1939), Highlander Papers, Box 53, folder 1, p. 69.

49. Horton, "Mountain Men," p. 15.

50. Minutes of the joint meeting of Executive Committees from three Hod Carriers' and Common Laborers' locals of Monteagle, Palmer, and Tracy City, Tenn., at Miners' Hall, Tracy City, July 11, 1936, Highlander Papers, Box 52, folder 12.

51. "WPA Strikers Ask F.D.R.'s Aid," *Chattanooga Times*, March 12, 1937.

52. "Berry Charges Reds Feed Relief Workers," *Chattanooga News–Free Press*, March 13, 1937.

53. Horton, "Mountain Men," p. 17.

54. "County Highway Commission Gives Its Side of Controversy," *Grundy County Herald*, January 19, 1939.

55. "WPA Workers End Grundy 'Sit-Down,'" *Chattanooga Times*, February 17, 1939. See also: "WPA Investigates Grundy Situation," *Chattanooga Times*, February 15, 1939; "Monteagle, Tenn., February 6, 1939" (untitled notes, author unknown), Highlander Papers, Box 53, folder 5.

56. Horton Interview.

57. "We the People" (mimeo.), February 10, 1939, Highlander Papers, Box 53, folder 7.

58. "Settlement Reached in Grundy," *Chattanooga Times*, February 21, 1939.

59. Nels Anderson, letter to Horton, December 31, 1940, Highlander Papers, Box 53, folder 4.

CHAPTER 4

1. H. E. Lawson, note to Horton, June 7, 1937, Highlander Papers (Social Action Collection, State Historical Society of Wisconsin), Box 64, folder 1. See also: "Lumberton Has Another Strike," *Charlotte Observer*, June 7, 1937.

2. "Child Labor Violations Aired in Robeson Courts," *News & Observer* (Raleigh, N.C.), June 2, 1937.

3. Horton, letter to Robert Wohlforth, La Follette Civil Liberties Committee, United States Senate, May 20, 1937, Highlander Papers, Box 64, folder 2.

4. Horton, "Facts regarding the walk-out of the employees of the Jennings Cotton Mill at North Lumberton, N.C.," July 28, 1937, Highlander Papers, Box 64, folder 1. See also: affidavit of S.C. Anderson, Highlander Papers, Box 64, folder 1.

5. Horton Interview.

6. "Robeson Sheriff Asks State Help to Prevent Disorder Cotton Mills [*sic*]," *Charlotte Observer*, June 10, 1937.

7. "NLRB to Open Lumberton Probe Today," *Charlotte Observer*, June 9, 1937. See also: "United States of America before the National Labor Relations Board, Fifth Region, in the Matter of Mansfield Mills, Inc., and Textile Workers' Organizing Committee, Case No. V-C-78," Highlander Papers, Box 64, folder 2.

8. Hubert Henry, Manning Mills, Lumberton, N.C., telegram to O. J. Stewart, Clinton Cotton Mills, Clinton, S.C., July 1, 1937, Highlander Papers, Box 69, folder 1.

9. Horton Interview.

10. "End Labor Hearing—Delay Verdict at Lumberton" (undated Associated Press newspaper fragment), Highlander Papers, Box 64, folder 1.

11. "Mill Employee Charged with Assault on Labor Organizer," *The Robesonian* (Lumberton, N.C.), June 25, 1937.

12. "Non-Strike Workers at East Lumberton Guarded by Officers," *Charlotte Observer*, June 30, 1937.

13. *Textile Workers' Organizing Committee and Myles Horton*, individual, v. *Mansfield Cotton Mills, Inc.*, et al. Judgment. Superior Court, Judge N. A. Sinclair, Robeson County, N.C., June 30, 1937. Highlander Papers, Box 64, folder 2.

14. Affidavit, Lt. A. T. Moore, State Highway Patrol, in Superior Court, Robeson County, N.C., July 1, 1937, in the case, *Textile Workers' Organizing Committee and Myles Horton*, individual, v. *Mansfield Mills, Inc., Dewey Griffin, Vera Lamb, Mark Page*. Highlander Papers, Box 64, folder 2.

15. Horton Interview.

16. "25 Strike Cases Are Nol Prossed," *The Robesonian*, July 16, 1937.

17. "Strikers Crowd Welfare Office; Seek WPA Help," *The Robesonian*, July 9, 1937.

18. "Receive Supplies From WPA For Striking Families," *The Robesonian*, July 12, 1937.

19. Horton, letter to James Dombrowski, August 12, 1937, Highlander Papers, Box 64, folder 11.

20. Horton Interview.

21. Horton Interview. See also: "Jennings Mill Employees Go Back to Work," *The Robesonian*, August 2, 1937.

22. Horton Interview.

23. Agreement of Textile Workers' Organizing Committee and Mansfield Mills, January 29, 1938, Highlander Papers, Box 64, folder 1.

24. Horton Interview.

CHAPTER 5

1. Zilphia Horton, ed., *Labor Songs* (Winston-Salem, N.C.: The Industrial Leader, 1939), Introduction. See also: records of labor drama tours, Highlander Papers (Social Action Collection, State Historical Society of Wisconsin), Box 58, folder 2; music, 1939–1950, *ibid.*, Box 65, folder 5; songs, *ibid.*, Boxes 69 and 70; sacred harp class, 1941, *ibid.*, Box 73, folder 9; iconographic collection of 250 tapes and discs (unprocessed), State Historical Society of Wisconsin.

2. Jim Pierce, personal interview with the author, March, 1974.

3. Highlander Folk School, "Five Plays About Labor" (mimeo.), August, 1939, Highlander Papers, Box 56, folder 14.

4. "Education to Play Big Role," *Hosiery Worker*, Vol. XV (May 13, 1938).

5. Theodore Brameld, ed., *Workers' Education in the United States: Fifth Yearbook of the John Dewey Society* (New York: Harper and Brothers, 1941), pp. 98–101, 146–47, 162.

6. John Handcock, "No More Mourning" (sung by Zilphia Horton; transcribed from wire recording by author), private papers of Myles Horton, New Market, Tenn. Hereinafter referred to as Horton Papers.

7. Huddie Ledbetter, "Bourgeois Blues" (sung by Zilphia Horton; transcribed by author from wire recording, circa 1941, Horton Papers. See, for a different version, Moses Asch and Alan Lomax, eds., *The Leadbelly Songbook* (New York: Oak Publications, 1962), p. 24.

8. Zilphia Horton, transcription by author from wire recording, Horton Papers.

9. Zilphia Horton, *ibid.*

10. Zilphia Horton, letter to Myles Horton, July 23, 1936, Highlander Papers (Social Action Collection, State Historical Society of Wisconsin), Box 15, folder 14.

11. Horton Interview.

12. *Ibid.*

13. *Ibid.*

14. *Ibid.*

15. "Summerfield News" (mimeo.), April 15, 1956, Highlander Papers, Box 73, folder 1.

16. *Ibid.*

17. Horton Interview.

18. Mary Lawrence, *How to Build Your Union* (New Orleans, La.: CIO Industrial Union Council, February, 1942), Introduction.

19. Highlander Folk School annual report (mimeo., Monteagle, Tenn.: Highlander Folk School, 1945), Highlander Papers, Box 1, folder 5, p. 3.

20. Lawrence, *How to Build Your Union*, Introduction.

21. Lawrence, "A Study of the Methods and Results of Workers' Education in the South," *circa* 1947, Highlander Papers, Box 18, folder 14.

22. Lawrence, "A Study of Workers' Education," p. 89.

23. W. D. Moore, *60 Million Jobs* (Southern CIO School, 1945), p. 6.

24. Dwight Macdonald, *The Root Is Man: Two Essays in Politics* (Alhambra, Calif.: The Cunningham Press, 1953), p. 27.

25. Horton Interview.

26. John A. Fitch, "The CIO and Its Communists," *The Survey*, December 1949, pp. 642–47. See also: Horton, "Memo: To Highlander Executive Council Members," September 1949, Highlander Papers, Box 41, folder 2.

27. Stanley H. Ruttenberg, letter to Horton, July 5, 1949, Highlander Papers, Box 41, folder 1.

28. *Ibid.*

29. Board of Directors, Highlander Folk School, "Statement of Policy," November 1949, Highlander Papers, Box 1, folder 8.

30. Horton (ed.), "Instructor's Materials" (mimeo., Chicago: United Packinghouse Workers of America, n.d.), Highlander Papers, Box 74, folder 10; Horton (ed.), "Instructor's Manuals for Shop Steward Training" (mimeo., Chicago: United Packinghouse Workers of America, n.d.), Highlander Papers, Box 74, folder 11.

31. Horton Interview.

CHAPTER 6

1. William M. Seaman, letter to Horton, December 11, 1933, Highlander Papers (Social Action Collection, State Historical Society of Wisconsin), Box 25, folder 2.

2. Quoted in Horton Interview.

3. Charles S. Johnson, Director, Department of Social Sciences, Fisk University, letter to Horton, January 10, 1935, Highlander Papers, Box 16, folder 15. See also: Zilphia Horton, "Community Reaction to Negroes at Highlander," *circa* 1946, Highlander Papers, Box 15, folder 14, p. 2.

4. Horton Interview.

5. "Call" (Monteagle, Tenn.: All-Southern Conference for Civil and Trade Union Rights, February 4, 1934), Highlander Papers, Box 31, folder 7.

6. *Ibid.* Subsequent events caused the date of the conference to be set for May 26, 1935.

7. "Forum Scores Effort to Stop Labor Meeting," *Chattanooga News*, May 17, 1935. See also: "Legion's Probe of School Discussed by Cook Here," *Chattanooga News*, April 6, 1935.

8. "Radicals Quit When Put Out of Third Hall," *Chattanooga News*, May 27, 1935. See also: Raleigh Crumbliss, "Twas a Famous Victory," *Chattanooga News*, May 30, 1935.

9. "Radicals Quit," *Chattanooga News*, May 27, 1935.

10. Minutes of the All-Southern Conference for Civil and Trade Union Rights (typed), May 26, 1935, Highlander Papers, Box 31, folder 7.

11. Edwin Yoder, Jr., "The Harmory of Confederacy" (review of *And Promises to Keep: The Southern Conference for Human Welfare, 1938–1948*, by Thomas A. Krueger), *Saturday Review*, (June 10, 1967), p. 66.

12. *Ibid.*

13. Thomas A. Krueger, *And Promises to Keep: The Southern Conference for Human Welfare, 1938–1948* (Nashville, Tenn.: Vanderbilt University Press, 1967), p. iii.

14. Horton Interview.

15. Krueger, p. iii.

16. Horton Interview.

17. Lucy Randolph Mason, *To Win These Rights* (New York: Harper and Brothers, 1952), pp. 159–63.

18. Krueger, p. 37.

19. *The Southern Patriot*, VII (January, 1949), p. 4.

20. Highlander Folk School annual report, (mimeo., Monteagle, Tenn.: Highlander Folk School, 1944), Highlander Papers, Box 1, folder 5, p. 4.

21. Horton Interview.

22. Zilphia Horton, "Bob Jones Speaks His Mind" (mimeo.), *circa* 1947, Highlander Papers, Box 61, folder 6.

23. Report of the Special Highlander Executive Council meeting, April 27–28, 1953, Highlander Papers, Box 1, folder 8, pp. 1–3.

24. Horton Interview.

25. Highlander Folk School Workshop announcement, n.d., Highlander Papers, Box 3, folder 1.

26. Septima Poinsette Clark, *Echo in My Soul* (New York: E. P. Dutton & Co., 1962), p. 121.

27. Horton Interview.

28. *Ibid.*

29. The Joint Legislative Committee on Un-American Activities, State of Louisiana, *Activities of the Southern Conference Education Fund, Inc. in Louisiana* (Baton Rouge, La.: State of Louisiana, 1963), I, 23. See also: records of Grundy County Crusaders, 1940, Highlander Papers, Box 31, folders 3 and 4; "Dies to Get Evidence on 'Folk' School," *Chattanooga News–Free Press*, Nov. 29, 1940.

30. Leon Wilson, Highlander staff member, letter to John J. Lynch, Federal Bureau of Investigation, October 1, 1941, Highlander Papers, Box 33, folder 7. See also: records of FBI investigation, 1950–1951, Highlander Papers, Box 33, folder 7; "FBI in the Tennessee Hills," *St. Louis Post-Dispatch*, March 21, 1951.

31. Myles Horton, untitled notes, Highlander Papers, Box 42, folder 10.

32. Horton Interview.

33. John Stuart Mill, "Essay on Liberty," *Harvard Classics*, ed. Charles W. Eliot (New York: P. F. Collier & Son Co., 1909), L, 263, 273.

CHAPTER 7

1. Summary of application to the Schwarzhaupt Foundation, Inc., from Highlander Folk School, Monteagle, Tenn. (typed), Highlander Papers (Social Action Collection, State Historical Society of Wisconsin), Box 51, folder 1. See also: Leo Gerngross, President,

Emil Schwarzhaupt Foundation, Inc., letter to Myles Horton, June 4, 1953, Highlander Papers, Box 51, folder 1.

2. Clark, *Echo in My Soul* (New York: E. P. Dutton & Co.), p. 117.

3. Quoted in Horton Interview.

4. Guy and Candie Carawan, *Ain't You Got A Right To The Tree of Life?* (New York: Simon and Schuster, 1966), p. 167. See also: Guy Carawan, untitled notes on work in South, 1959–1965, Highlander Papers, Box 8, folder 9.

5. Guy and Candie Carawan, *Ain't You Got a Right?*, p. 167.

6. Dolph Vaughn, "Dolph Vaughn Reports–1938," Highlander Papers, Box 53, folder 6, *passim.* See also: Mary Lawrence, "Report on Community Program, September, 1938–August, 1939," Highlander Papers, Box 2, folder 5.

7. Horton Interview. See also: William A. Price, "Freedom's Language Debated in the South: 'Dialect vs. Correct English,' " *National Guardian*, July 3, 1965, p. 5.

8. Bernice Robinson, letter to Septima Clark, January 20, 1957, as quoted in Horton, letter to Carl Tjerandsen, Consultant, Schwarzhaupt Foundation, February 16, 1957, Highlander Papers, Box 67, folder 3.

9. Guy and Candie Carawan, *Ain't You Got a Right?*, p. 168.

10. Septima Clark, report on Southern Christian Leadership Conference Citizenship Education Program to Highlander Folk School Board of Directors, May 14, 1965, Highlander Papers, Box 67, folder 4.

11. Horton Interview.

CHAPTER 8

1. Septima P. Clark, "Champions of Democracy" (mimeo., Monteagle, Tenn.: Highlander Folk School, 1956), Highlander Papers (Social Action Collection, State Historical Society of Wisconsin), Box 9, folder 12, p. 2. Minister deliberately unidentified.

2. Clark, p. 4.

3. Rosa Parks, "Reply to Follow-up Questionnaire on Workshop on Desegregation," May 20, 1956, Highlander Papers, Box 22, folder 22.

4. Highlander Folk School Workshops on School Integration,

August, 1956 (author's transcript of a tape no longer in existence). See also: Rosa Parks, "Report on the Montgomery, Alabama, Passive Resistance Protest" (mimeo., March, 1956), Highlander Papers, Box 22, folder 22; Mrs. Clifford Durr, Montgomery, Alabama, letter to Highlander Staff, January 30, 1956, Highlander Papers, Box 11, folder 1.

5. "Highlander Folk School, Communist Training School, Monteagle, Tennessee" (Atlanta, Ga.: Georgia Commission on Education, 1957), Highlander Papers, Box 76, folder 7, p. 4. Hereinafter referred to as "Communist Training School." See also: "Twenty-fifth Annual Report," Highlander Folk School, October 1, 1956–September 30, 1957, Highlander Papers, Box 3, folder 1.

6. Aubrey Williams, "The South Plays With Fire" (mimeo., Monteagle, Tenn.: Highlander Folk School, September 2, 1957), Highlander Papers, Box 76, folder 6.

7. Martin Luther King, Jr., "The Look to the Future" (mimeo., Monteagle, Tenn.: Highlander Folk School, September 2, 1957), Highlander Papers, Box 79, folder 6, p. 4. See also: King's remarks in transcript, "Meet the Press," March 28, 1965 (Washington, D.C.: Merkle Press, Inc.), Vol. IX, No. 11, p. 8.

8. "Communist Training School," p. 1.

9. "Communist Training School," pp. 2–3.

10. Horton Interview.

11. "Georgia Invades Ohio" (unsigned editorial, *The Christian Century*, October 30, 1957 (reprinted by Highlander Folk School), Highlander Papers, Box 34, folder 5.

12. "Leaders Defend School in South," *New York Times*, December 22, 1957.

13. "125 Million U.S. Reds" (unsigned editorial), *Arapahoe Herald* (Littleton, Colo.), October 16, 1957.

14. "Twenty-fifth Annual Report," p. 4.

15. Horton Interview.

16. "Shut Highlander Folk School, Advice of Arkansas Leader," *Chattanooga News–Free Press*, January 30, 1959. See also: "Arkansas' Attorney General Proposes Closing Highlander" (mimeo., letter from Dr. B. R. Brazeal, Chairman, Highlander Executive Council, and Horton, to supporters and press. February 2, 1959), Highlander Papers, Box 34, folder 10.

17. "Literacy—Louisiana Style," *The New Republic*, CXL (March 9, 1959), 9.

18. House Joint Resolution No. 26, Legislature of Tennessee, adopted January 29, 1959, Highlander Papers, Box 35, folder 1. See also: "Bill Revised on Highlander," *Memphis Commercial Appeal*, February 3, 1959.

19. Investigation of Highlander Folk School, Grundy County, Tennessee, before the joint Legislative Investigation Committee, Nashville, Tennessee, 1959, *Public Hearings*, II, 484–85.

20. *Ibid.*, p. 481.

21. *Ibid.*, pp. 447–48.

22. "Probe 'Drama' Lays An Egg," *The* (Nashville) *Tennessean*, March 7, 1959.

23. Committee report to the members of the 81st Session of the General Assembly of the State of Tennessee at Nashville, Tennessee, March 6, 1959, p. 11.

24. "Police Raid Interracial Meet at Tenn. School," *Jet*, August 20, 1959. See also: "Liberal School in Dixie Fights for Existence," *Milwaukee Journal*, August 30, 1959; Clark, pp. 3–12, 206–9.

25. Guy Carawan, interview with author, August, 1971.

26. Newspaper fragment, *Chattanooga Daily Times*, August 3, 1959, Highlander Papers, Box 34, folder 10.

27. "Officials to Ask Highlander School Padlock at Court Hearing Saturday," *Chattanooga News–Free Press*, August 27, 1959.

28. "Hold Workshop Despite Padlock," *Chicago Defender*, October 10, 1959.

CHAPTER 9

1. John Thompson, "Untitled notes, November 9, 1949," Highlander Papers (Social Action Collection, State Historical Society of Wisconsin), Box 34, folder 6.

2. Horton Interview.

3. Thompson, "Untitled notes, November 9, 1959."

4. *Ibid.*

5. *Ibid.*

6. "Tennessee Legal Action," *Southern School News*, VI (March, 1960). See also: "Judge Chattin Rules Against Highlander F. S. on

All Points," *Grundy County Herald*, February 18, 1960; "Unjustice in Tennessee," *St. Louis Post-Dispatch*, April 10, 1960.

7. *Highlander* et al. v. *The State of Tennessee*, ex rel. *A. F. Sloan* in Supreme Court of Tennessee. Included in Sloan, *Reports of Cases Argued and Determined in the Supreme Court of Tennessee* (Nashville, Tenn.: Rich Printing Co., 1961), CCVIII, 242; and Highlander Papers, Box 34, folder 7.

8. "Supreme Court Rejects Appeal," *Knoxville News-Sentinel*, October 9, 1961.

9. "Horton Granted Right to Open School in Knox," *The* (Nashville) *Tennessean*, October 8, 1961.

10. "Highlander Sale Gets High Prices," *Chattanooga Times*, December 17, 1961.

CHAPTER 10

1. John Dewey, *Democracy and Education* (New York: MacMillan Co., 1916), p. 22. See also: Dewey, letters to Horton, September 27, 1933, and October 12, 1940, Highlander Papers (Social Action Collection, State Historical Society of Wisconsin), Box 10, folder 11.

2. Woodrow Cooper, Tuskegee, Alabama, letter to Horton, May 28, 1955, Highlander Papers, Box 38, folder 2.

3. Horton Interview.

4. Report of 1959 College Workshop, Highlander Folk School (mimeo.), Highlander Papers, Box 71, folders 2–18, Box 72, folders 1–18.

5. Septima P. Clark, Seventh Annual College Workshop (tape recorded; transcription by author. In files of Highlander Research and Education Center, Inc., New Market, Tenn.). Hereinafter referred to as Seventh College Workshop.

6. *Ibid.*

7. Horton, Seventh College Workshop.

8. Dr. Herman Long, Fisk University, Seventh College Workshop.

9. Seventh College Workshop. The various student speakers are not identified by name.

10. Rosa Parks, Planning Session on School Desegregation at Highlander Folk School, March 3 and 4 (tape recorded; transcribed

by author. In files of Highlander Research and Education Center, Inc.).

11. John Lewis, address given at Loop College, Chicago, Illinois, Spring, 1970 (tape recorded; transcribed by author. Tapes in possession of Department of Adult Education, Loop College).

12. *Ibid.*

13. Dr. King as quoted by Carawan in interview with author, August, 1971. See also: Howard Zinn, *SNCC: The New Abolitionists* (Boston: Beacon Press, 1964), pp. 25–33.

14. Lawson as quoted by Carawan in interview with author, August, 1971. See also: Zinn, p. 33.

15. Robert C. Smith. *Virginian-Pilot* (Norfolk, Va.), April 20, 1960.

16. Zinn, p. 33.

17. Carawan, "Work in the South," Highlander Papers, Box 8, folder 9, p. 4.

18. *Ibid.*

19. Carawan, "Spiritual Singing in the South Carolina Sea Islands" (mimeo.), n.d., Highlander Papers, Box 67, folder 7, p. 3.

20. Josh Dunson, *Freedom in the Air: Song Movements of the 60's* (New York: International Publications, 1965), p. 43.

21. Quoted by Carawan in interview with author, August, 1971.

22. *Ibid.*

23. *Ibid.*

CHAPTER 11

1. Horton Interview.

2. Pat Watters and Reese Cleghorn, *Climbing Jacob's Ladder* (New York: Harcourt, Brace and World, Inc., 1967), p. 365. See also: pp. 363–75, *passim.*

3. Horton Interview.

4. Watters and Cleghorn, p. 372.

5. Bernice Robinson, activity report, June 15, 1963, Highlander Papers (Social Action Collection, State Historical Society of Wisconsin), Box 24, folder 13. See also: letters and field reports, Highlander Papers, Box 24, folder 13; activity reports, Highlander Papers, Box 35, folder 6.

6. Robinson, activity report, June 15, 1963.

7. Horton, letter to Robert Moses, October 10, 1962, Highlander Papers, Box 21, folder 21. See also: Howard Zinn, *SNCC: The New Abolitionists* (Boston: Beacon Press, 1964), p. 58.

8. Horton Interview. See also: Zinn, p. 76; records of Student Nonviolent Coordinating Committee, Highlander Papers, Box 71, folders 10–18; Box 72, folders 1–18, *passim*.

9. Zinn, p. 69.

10. Zinn, pp. 70–71.

11. Zinn, p. 69.

12. Horton Interview. See also: Zinn, pp. 72–73.

13. "Voter Registration in the South—1962, 1964, 1966" (mimeo., Atlanta, Ga.: Voter Education Project, Southern Regional Council, *circa* 1967), Highlander Papers, Box 80, folder 11. See also: records of workshops on registration and voting, 1956, and 1958–1960, Highlander Papers, Box 79, folder 4; records of voter registration project, Highlander Papers, Box 72, folder 18.

14. James Forman, letter to Horton, April 19, 1962, Highlander Papers, Box 27, folder 8.

15. Robinson, activity report, June 15, 1963.

16. Robinson, letter to Horton, Highlander Papers, Box 24, folder 13.

17. Horton Interview.

18. Forman, letter to Horton, November 22, 1963, Highlander Papers, Box 27, folder 8.

19. Records of COFO Community Project Workshops, 1964–1965, Highlander Papers, Box 80, folder 14.

20. See field reports, Council of Federated Organizations, Highlander Papers, Box 41, folders 5 and 6.

21. Horton Interview.

22. Horton Interview.

23. Quoted in Horton Interview.

24. Quoted in Horton Interview.

25. Horton Interview.

26. *Ibid.*

27. *Ibid.* See also: field reports, Council of Federated Organizations, Highlander Papers, Box 41, folder 7.

28. Horton Interview.

29. *Ibid.*

30. *Ibid.* See also: William Bradford Huie, *Three Lives for Mississippi* (New York: WCC Books, 1965), p. 231.

31. Sue Thrasher, "Radical Education in the Thirties," *Southern Exposure*, Vol. I, Nos. 3, 4 (Winter, 1974), p. 210.

32. Horton Interview. See also: records of Gulfport Workshop, Highlander Papers, Box 41, folder 5.

33. Horton Interview.

34. Quoted in Horton Interview.

35. C. T. Vivian, *Black Power and the American Myth* (Philadelphia: Fortress Press, 1970), pp. 65, 116.

36. Horton Interview. See also: Julius Lester, *Look Out, Whitey! Black Power's Gon' Get Your Mama!* (New York: Grove Press, 1968), p. 97.

37. Lester, p. 11.

CHAPTER 12

1. Records of Council of Southern Mountains, 1960–1965, Highlander Papers (Social Action Committee, State Historical Society of Wisconsin), Box 9, folder 24.

2. Records of conference at Hazard, Kentucky, March 26–27, 1964, Highlander Papers, Box 72, folder 20.

3. Records of Appalachian Project, Highlander Papers, Box 32, folder 9. See also: Frank Adams, "Highlander Appalachian Project, Summer, 1965" (mimeo.), Highlander Papers, Box 32, folder 9.

4. Records of Southwide Voter Education Internship Project, Highlander Papers, Box 71, folder 4.

5. Records of Southern Student Organizing Committee. Highlander Papers, Box 71, folders 2 and 3.

6. Records of Student Nonviolent Coordinating Committee, Highlander Papers, Box 72, folders 5–9.

7. Highlander Folk School annual reports, 1960–1970, Highlander Papers, Box 1, folder 7.

8. Horton, letter to Young, March 15, 1968, Highlander Papers, Box 30, folder 5.

9. Staff reports on Multi-Ethnic Workshops, and related papers, 1969–1974, *passim.* In files of Highlander Research and Education Center, Inc., New Market, Tenn.

10. Miscellaneous papers and statistics of Appalachian Commit-

tee for Full Employment, 1965, Highlander Papers, Box 5, folder 19.

11. Reports of Appalachian Economic and Political Action Conference, November 7, 1964, Highlander Papers, Box 32, folder 7.

12. Horton Interview.

13. Resolution of Appalachian Economic and Political Action Conference, *supra.*

14. James Branscome, letter to Horton, *circa* January, 1968. In Branscome's personal papers.

15. Horton, report on Poor People's Workshop, Montgomery Belle Park, Tennessee, March 15–16, 1969. In files of Highlander Research and Education Center, Inc.

16. *Ibid.*

17. *Ibid.*

18. *Ibid.*

19. Mike Clark, field report, n.d. In files of Highlander Research and Education Center, Inc.

20. Lewis Sinclair, letter to supporters, May 28, 1973, p. 1. In files of Highlander Research and Education Center, Inc.

21. Horton, letter to supporters. In files of Highlander Research and Education Center, Inc.

CHAPTER 13

1. Dr. Alva Taylor, letter to Horton, May 3, 1933, Highlander Papers (Social Action Collection, State Historical Society of Wisconsin), Box 27, folder 16. See also: "Governor Told of Strike Killing," *New Leader*, May 10, 1933.

2. "Union Chief Shot in Back, Says Doctor," *Knoxville News-Sentinel*, May 2, 1933. See also: "Officers Freed in Killing of Wilder Union President," *The* (Nashville) *Tennessean*, September 7, 1933.

3. "Grundy Group Plans Protest of Folk School," *The* (Nashville) *Tennessean,* November 9, 1940. See also: "Grundy Citizens Plan 'Visit' to Folk School," *Chattanooga News–Free Press*, November 12, 1940.

4. Flyer of Constitutional Educational League, Inc., of New York, N.Y., n.d., Highlander Papers, Box 86, folder 6. See also: American Jewish Congress, New York, N.Y., "Digest of the Anti-Semitic and Anti-Democratic Press in the United States" (confidential memo,

September 4, 1942), Highlander Papers, Box 86, folder 6, pp. 1–5.

5. "Communist School Receives White House Aid" (undated article from *The Fiery Cross*, publication of the Ku Klux Klan), Highlander Papers, Box 33, folder 5.

6. Original document not available. Statement corroborated by the author in telephone conversation with Wilson, January 22, 1974.

7. "Folk School Told to Leave Grundy County," *Chattanooga News–Free Press*, November 13, 1940. See also: summary of meeting between the staff of the Highlander Folk School and the committee from the Grundy County Crusaders, St. Luke's Chapel, Sewanee, Tennessee, November 12, 1940, Highlander Papers, Box 33, folder 4.

8. "Labor Leader Attends Parley," *Covington* (Kentucky) *Post*, November 29, 1940.

9. Nemesius Nielsen, letter to the "Free Press Forum," *Chattanooga News–Free Press*, November 26, 1940.

10. H. T. Swartz, Director, Tax Rulings Division, Internal Revenue Service, U.S. Treasury Department, Washington, D.C., letter to Horton, February 20, 1957, in files of Highlander Research and Education Center, Inc., New Market, Tenn.

11. *Ibid.*

12. Mike Clark, President, Highlander Research and Education Center, Inc., memo to the members of the Board of Directors and Land Trust, November 30, 1973, in files of Highlander Research and Education Center, Inc.

13. United States Senate, 83rd Congress, 2nd Session, Subcommittee to Investigate Administration of the Internal Security Act of the Judiciary Committee, Hearings on the Subversive Influence of the Southern Conference Education Fund, Inc., March 18, 19, 20, 1954 (Washington, D.C.: Government Printing Office, 1955), p. v.

14. *Ibid.*, pp. 4–5.

15. *Ibid.*, pp. 44–50.

16. *Ibid.*, pp. 11–12.

17. *Ibid.*, p. 74.

18. *Ibid.*

19. *Ibid.*, p. 118.

20. *Ibid.*, pp. 133–48.

21. Horton Interview.

22. U. S. Senate Hearings, pp. 150–51. See also: "Witness Ejected at Hearing," *New York Times*, March 21, 1954.

23. U.S. Senate Hearings, p. 151.

24. Horton, untitled statement (mimeo.), Highlander Papers, Box 33, folder 8.

25. U.S. Senate Hearings, p. 154

26. *I. F. Stone's Weekly*, March 20, 1954.

27. "Next to the News," *Chattanooga Times*, March 23, 1954.

28. Mrs. Walter McCormick, Secretary, Highlander Research and Education Center, Inc., Knoxville, Tenn., personal interview with author, August, 1965.

29. "Hearing on Camp Raid is Delayed," *Knoxville News-Sentinel*, June 12, 1963. See also: trial transcript, General Sessions Court for Blount County, Tennessee, and the Juvenile Court for Blount County, Tennessee, and *The State of Tennessee* v. *Robert L. Gustafson* et al. In files of Highlander Research and Education Center, Inc.

30. "Highlander Camp Burns; Grand Jury Probe is Set," *Maryville-Alcoa Daily Times*, June 24, 1963.

31. "Deputy Describes Workcamp Events," *Maryville-Alcoa Daily Times*, June 25, 1963.

32. "Seven Highlander 'Campers' Ruled Guilty," *Knoxville Journal*, June 27, 1963.

33. Edward D. Lynch, attorney, Knoxville, Tennessee, personal interview with author, August, 1971.

34. *Ibid.* See also: William F. Kunstler, *Deep in My Heart* (New York: William Morrow & Company, 1966), pp. 242–43.

CHAPTER 14

1. "An Interview With Myles Horton: It's a Miracle—I Still Don't Believe It," *Phi Delta Kappan.* XXXXVII (May, 1966), pp. 490–97.

2. Horton, "People's Needs Make an Educational Program" (unpublished speech, Bergen Folk High School, Bergen, The Netherlands, June, 1957), Highlander Papers (Social Action Collection, State Historical Society of Wisconsin), Box 31, folder 5.

3. Hart, *Light from the North* (New York: Henry Holt & Co., 1926), p. 149.

4. Cooper, letter to Horton, May 28, 1955, Highlander Papers, Box 38, folder 2.

5. Joe Begley, Blackey, Kentucky, personal interview with author, May, 1970.

6. Horton, "What Adult Education Should Be, How Highlander Works, and the Sea Islands: An Example of Follow-up" (unpublished, undated notes), Highlander Papers, Box 67, folder 6.

7. Philip S. Forner, ed., *The Life and Major Writings of Thomas Paine* (New York: Citadel Press, 1961), p. 612.

8. Begley Interview.

Index